8/6/9

Wisdom and Philosophy

Also available from Bloomsbury

*The Bloomsbury Research Handbook of Chinese Philosophy
and Methodologies*, edited by Sor-hoon Tan
*The Bloomsbury Research Handbook of Indian Aesthetics and
the Philosophy of Art*, edited by Arindam Chakrabarti
*The Bloomsbury Research Handbook of Indian Epistemology
and Metaphysics*, edited by Joerg Tuske
*The Bloomsbury Research Handbook of Indian
Ethics*, edited by Shyam Ranganathan
Comparative Philosophy without Borders, edited by
Arindam Chakrabarti and Ralph Weber
Confucius: A Guide for the Perplexed, Yong Huang
Doing Philosophy Comparatively, Tim Connolly
Landscape and Travelling East and West, edited by
Hans-Georg Moeller and Andrew K. Whitehead
Understanding Asian Philosophy, Alexus McLeod

Wisdom and Philosophy

Contemporary and Comparative Approaches

Edited by
Hans-Georg Moeller and Andrew K. Whitehead

Bloomsbury Academic
An imprint of Bloomsbury Publishing Plc

B L O O M S B U R Y
LONDON · OXFORD · NEW YORK · NEW DELHI · SYDNEY

Bloomsbury Academic

An imprint of Bloomsbury Publishing Plc

50 Bedford Square	1385 Broadway
London	New York
WC1B 3DP	NY 10018
UK	USA

www.bloomsbury.com

BLOOMSBURY and the Diana logo are trademarks of Bloomsbury Publishing Plc

First published 2016

Paperback edition first published 2017

British Library Cataloguing in Publication Data

A catalogue record for this book is available from the British Library.

ISBN: HB: 978-1-4742-4869-3
PB: 978-1-3500-4550-7
ePDF: 978-1-4742-4870-9
ePub: 978-1-4742-4868-6

Library of Congress Cataloging-in-Publication Data

Wisdom and philosophy : contemporary and comparative approaches / edited by Hans-Georg Moeller and Andrew Whitehead.– 1 [edition].
pages cm
Includes index.
ISBN 978-1-4742-4869-3 (hb)-- ISBN 978-1-4742-4868-6 (epub)-- ISBN 978-1-4742-4870-9 (epdf) 1. Philosophy, Comparative. 2. Wisdom. I. Moeller, Hans-Georg, 1964- editor.
B21.W57 2016
109–dc23
2015030969

Typeset by Fakenham Prepress Solutions, Fakenham, Norfolk NR21 8NN

Contents

Introduction

Andrew K. Whitehead and Hans-Georg Moeller

One of the perennial questions philosophers have been asking themselves is what it actually means to do philosophy. According to the ancient Greek term—*philosophia* (φιλοσοφία)—philosophy is the "love of wisdom." The ambiguity of the phrase as rendered in English affords alternative meanings. The philosopher, as the "lover of wisdom," can be understood either as the object of wisdom's love, and therefore as fortunately blessed as wise, or as the subject who strives towards, and desires, wisdom. But if, as the suspicion goes, those in love are not necessarily in the best position to perceive accurately the object of their affection, the question may be raised: has the actual nature of wisdom so far evaded many philosophers? Particularly in the context of contemporary academic philosophy, the association between philosophy and wisdom is, arguably, more problematic than ever.

Already, we find one potential source for the divergences and antagonisms among schools of thought concerning the meaning of philosophy in the Greek conception of *sophia* (σοφία), which carries the alternative senses of "skill," "knowledge of," "acquaintance with," and even "sound judgment." In fact, as is shown throughout this volume, these different senses each serve as cornerstones and guideposts for distinct contemporary philosophies.

Despite significant changes in meaning, over time, the term philosophy has an unbroken history of several millennia and links not only the postmodernists and analytic philosophers of our day with the Presocratics and Platonists of ancient times but also Western with Eastern traditions which have now entered the sphere of world philosophy. In contemporary academia, these links tend to focus on the meaning of *sophia* as judgment or knowledge of: wisdom as epistemology. This should not be surprising, if only in light of how wisdom—and in turn the love of wisdom—is conceived in different languages.

The English term "wisdom" stems from the Old High German *Wistuom*, combining (and thereby conflating) "wise" with the abstract suffix of state—*tuom* (judgment). Philosophy is therefore—and rather appropriately in light of the contemporary academic philosophical landscape—"the love of wise judgments." Curiously, before the term *Philosophie* was taken up, the traditional German term for philosophy during the Enlightenment was *Weltweisheit*, which translates as "wisdom of the world" or "world-wisdom."

Those who nowadays search for a philosophy living up to the name of "love of wisdom" tend to look specifically to "oriental" traditions to reconnect the discipline with its "true" or "original" mandate. Trying to account for this tendency requires caution, however, and a deliberate overlooking of the treatment of "philosophy" in contemporary China and Japan. In the mid-nineteenth century, the Japanese philosopher Nishi Amane coined the neologism *tetsugaku* (哲學) to translate what he had encountered as philosophy in the academic institutions of the West. While the term was originally left untranslated and merely transliterated as *hirosohi* (ヒロソヒ), Nishi's move in 1874 to *tetsugaku* marked a deliberate removal of wisdom (*ken* 賢) from the Japanese conception of philosophy. In its place, Nishi posited "clarity" (*tetsu* 哲).[1] Nishi explicitly chose this formulation in order to emphasize that philosophy was to be understood as an applicable science grounded in the reality of the world. Through Western sources, where it was used to describe the practices of academic philosophers, the term was later given to the Chinese as *zhexue* (哲学). The contemporary academic locution for philosophy in China and Japan is therefore the "science of clarity"—a far cry from the "love of wisdom."

The inclination of Western philosophers to look to the ancient classics of the East, however, is mirrored by the inclination of Eastern philosophers to look to the ancient classics of the West. In other words, there is a driving need to re-engage with wisdom in its classical sense. Philosophers have become dissatisfied with the epistemological emphasis, at least as this emphasis has been construed for the last several centuries.

In its current state, the academic meaning of philosophy might best be expressed in the subtleties of its Flemish rendering as *Wijsbegeerte*, where *begeerte* carries the multiple meanings of "want," "greed," and "covetousness." In this light, it might be said that this volume therefore reflects a broader tendency in the field, finding dissatisfaction in coveting wise judgments, and a resurgent aspiration to return to the "love of wisdom." Both the overwhelming compulsion to treat wisdom as a commodity that one lacks and trades and the intellectual derivatives built on its epistemological exchange value are to be left by the wayside. The consensus that it is high time that we should return to the embrace of wisdom's love in the lived world continues to grow.

The essays collected in this volume question from an intercultural perspective the nature of the relationship between wisdom and philosophy. They discuss similarities and differences between Western and Eastern pursuits of wisdom and reflect on attempts to combine them.

Contributors cover topics such as Confucian ethics, the acquisition of wisdom in pre-Qin literature, and anecdotes of stupidity in the classical Chinese tradition, while also addressing contemporary topics such as global Buddhism and analytic metaphysics. Offering original contributions to comparative philosophy, the authors look at ideas and arguments of thinkers such as Confucius, Zhuangzi, and Zhu Xi, alongside the works of Aristotle, Plato, and Heidegger. They thus provide new ways of understanding how wisdom connects to philosophy, and underline the need to reintroduce it into the practice and meaning of philosophy today.

The essays of the first section of this volume approach the topics of wisdom and philosophy as these are found in the Classical Chinese traditions of Confucianism, Daoism, and Buddhism, with a focus on different practices of wisdom and the recognition of wisdom's ineffability.

In the first chapter, Robin R. Wang offers new perspectives on the practice and pedagogy of charioteering in early China. Wang discusses charioteering, articulated as "syncretic genius," as an exemplification of the state of *zhonghe* (中和), or inner-harmony, that goes not only "beyond the paradoxical existence recognized from Plato to Hegel," but also "direct[ly] to human actions."

Jim Behuniak seeks out a negative definition of wisdom by examining various stories concerning the Man from Song (*Songren* 宋人). He contends that, if wisdom represents anything in the Chinese tradition, "it likely represents the contrary of whatever the *Songren* 宋人 is doing," and notes that such a representation of wisdom is comparable to John Dewey's conception of intelligence, as "involving the coordination of means and ends in effective action."

Karl-Heinz Pohl draws our attention to a number of different, overarching, commonalities to classical Far Eastern teachings, not least a focused orientation towards action. Taking up Pierre Hadot's language of "ways of life," Pohl examines the theoretical force of seeing into the unity of knowledge and action, and the Chinese emphasis on the ineffable, the empty, and non-action. Recognizing the performative self-contradiction lying at the heart of his own enterprise—and, by extension, the performative self-contradiction lying at the heart of the writings of the thinkers with whom he engages—he concedes that his essay, if it were "consistently philosophical, i.e. in the sense of the teachings presented here, … would consist [of] a clean-white sheet of paper."

The second section of essays presents a number of comparisons of different conceptions of wisdom, and the wisdom of comparing. Drawing distinctions between differing conceptions of wisdom and differing accounts of the existential life-world, these essays also uncover striking similarities, suffusing elements, and shared first principles across philosophical traditions.

In Chapter 4, William Franke works through the idea of apophaticism as it relates to the European and the Chinese traditions. Focusing on these different traditions and their respective foci on the philosopher and the sage, and asserting a considerable difference in style between the two cultures, Franke shows how "the differences between the two cultures show themselves to be comprehended finally in their common and even, in some sense, universal possibilities."

Paul Allen Miller, also working through the distinction between wisdom as knowledge and wisdom as action, and borrowing from a wide array of sources, notes how comparative philosophy can be used to destabilize one's own self-understanding and to open up novel forms of discourse. Additionally, Miller contends, careful and attentive comparative analyses can unsettle orthodox conceptions of wisdom commonly used to forge homogenous traditions, showing them to be diverse and divided.

In his article "Anonymous Sages: Wisdom and Fame in Sino-Greco Philosophy," Geir Sigurðsson discusses the role of fame, both in contemporary society and, more paticularly, in the history of philosophy, East and West. He finds that "the quest for glory, the desire that one's reputation reach wide and far, is found in most if not all ancient traditions at all times," and concludes that want of fame is in effect a very human desire, regardless of culture or historical epoch.

May Sim makes a comparison of the attitudes towards wisdom in the works of Aristotle and Zhu Xi. She pays specific attention to the fundamental metaphysics in both these philosophical projects, and notes how, for both Zhu and Aristotle, understanding the myriad things inevitably leads to an underlying One principle. Drawing from Zhu's *taiji* and Aristotle's God as first principles, Sim discovers that both thinkers inevitably reach the same underlying question at the heart of wisdom: "What is being?"

Steven Burik's contribution makes use of a comparison of Martin Heidegger's thought with Daoism, namely with the *Zhuangzi*. Burik contends that both Zhuangzi and Heidegger share a concern that their contemporaries were excessively preoccupied with knowledge and ultimately failed to engage with or address the far more serious issue of wisdom. Noting that they can be understood as contextualists of a sort, Burik argues against broad epistemological misappropriations of Heidegger and Zhuangzi, on the grounds that they "both think that when we think properly, we do in fact realize a world, rather than just correspond to it."

The third section includes essays that bring contemporary concerns with wisdom into mainstream debates encompassing spiritual practices, issues of globalization, climatology, and environmental ethics, and the role of conceptual metaphors in the establishment of philosophical goals.

Sean McGrath frankly assents to the view that "philosophy today is threatened on all sides," and that the culture in which philosophy now discovers itself has never been as "obdurately un-philosophical" as it is today. In addition, drawing on the rift between knowledge and wisdom, and the emergence in the seventeenth century of a new model of philosophy as "knowledge of knowledge," McGrath reminds us that "philosophy was originally a practice of attending to oneself on the assumption that one was not yet wise, not yet knowing, and needed to undergo a transformation before one could even consider oneself capable of knowing." With this in mind, we are invited to heed the call to practical philosophy, and to attend to our psychological, spiritual, ecological, and political first ports of call, our thinking and desiring, our hopes and our fears.

In Chapter 10, Wes DeMarco emphasizes the importance of wise questions in the pursuit of wisdom, and the role such questions play in making one wise. In truly pluralistic fashion, DeMarco contends that today "we need a globe of world philosophies to burn away our personal fixations and socially sedimented presuppositions and expose them."

In his paper "Future-Oriented Philosophy and Wisdom East and West," Martin Schönfeld finds that philosophy, currently reduced to negative reasoning, may have lost its way. He advocates a change of course, prescribing in particular that we should "learn from the type of rationality displayed in the climate sciences." He defines wisdom as "existentially relevant information," with the qualification that such information is information important for existential flourishing. He concludes that wisdom has therefore three characteristics: it is ethical, aesthetic, and holistic.

The final chapter, by Victoria Harrison, details the role of conceptual metaphors in establishing and supporting the goals of philosophy. She reminds us that the goal of early Western philosophy was grounded in ocular metaphor, while the goal of early Chinese philosophy was grounded in locomotive metaphor. Harrison contends that, stemming from these metaphors, there emerge two distinct understandings of wisdom as knowledge. In the West, the ideal state of knowledge is conceived as the God's eye view. In the East, by contrast, knowledge is "predominantly thought of in terms of the ability to find one's way effectively in the natural and social worlds." As Harrison points out, this also means "that the ideal of knowledge so conceived can be characterized as perfected action."

The editors would like to thank all of those who have helped to make this volume possible. In particular, we would like to thank Seth Crownover for his invaluable assistance in preparing the final versions of the text. We would also like to thank the University of Macau for finances in support of editing and Andrew Wardell of Bloomsbury Publishing for his patience and support.

Note

1 It is worth noting that the language Nishi borrows from the classical Chinese canons demonstrates rather clearly that wisdom in that epoch meant the cultivation of personal virtuosity that would allow for optimum coalescence with one's environments. In accordance with this tradition, most contemporary philosophers understand 哲 as a very good choice because, as it is used in the classical language at least, it does mean "wisdom."

Part One

Chinese Wisdom

1

The Wisdom of Charioteering (*Yu* 御): Old Practice, New Perspectives

Robin R. Wang

A scholar of Chinese history once claimed that "Chinese religious and philosophical thinkers are sometimes celebrated for their syncretic genius, for their ability to build bridges between various traditions, as opposed to digging ditches around them" (Henderson 1999: 107). What is this syncretic genius and how can we learn from it? I will first briefly explain that this syncretic genius is coded in Chinese metaphysics and an ontological way of understanding the world. Then I will present a concrete case that demonstrates the cultivation and practice of this genius.

The building blocks of Chinese wisdom

In the Chinese eye, nature and the human world appear to follow a few amazingly simple rules. In other words, the world can be explained in terms of a few basic underlying principles. They provide many accounts for what is observed in terms of the basic principles. The most important of these principles is perhaps the pervasiveness and effectiveness of the *yinyang* concept (Wang 2012). The *yinyang* can be seen as the building block of the Chinese way of thinking.[1] This building block allows us to see the world in a different light and lifts our standpoint to a more balanced scheme. We read from *Daodejing*, Chapter 42: "*Dao* generates one, one generates two, two generates three, three generates the myriad things … Everything embodies *yin* and embraces *yang*, blending these *qi* to achieve the *he* (harmony)." This statement provokes some interesting philosophical questions: Why are myriad things the result of three even though everything consists of *yin* and *yang*?[2] Could one (*yin*) plus one (*yang*) be greater than two? If so, how? The term "*chong* 沖" here is the same as "*zhong* 中" (harmony) in the classic Chinese. This *zhong* is the state of *yinyang* interaction and a cherished value in *Daodejing*.

The *Taipingjing* 太平經 ("Treatise of Great Peace"),[3] an early Daoist text written after Laozi's *Daodejing*, expands on this notion more explicitly. Throughout the text there are many discussions and applications of three terms: *yin*, *yang*, and *zhonghe* 中和 (central harmony) (Jilin 2001: 202):

> Primordial *qi* (vital energy) has three kinds: primordial *yin* (*tai yin*), primordial *yang* (*tai yang*) and *zhonghe*. Form (*xingti* 形体) has three kinds: heaven, earth and human being. Sky has three kinds: sun, moon and star, the North Pole is in the middle; earth has three kinds: mountain, river and plains; human beings have three kinds: father, mother and child; governing has three kinds: minister, subject, and people. In order to have the great peace (*taiping* 太平) in the world these three elements must be united and become one ... The amalgamation of the three *qi* is the great harmony (*taihe* 太和). The great harmony comes from the *qi* of great peace. If these three *qi* are diminished, there will be no one united *qi* and the great harmony will not occur, neither the great peace. The core of *yinyang* is *zhonghe*. Once the *qi* of *zhonghe* is realized, the myriad things will flourish, people will harmonize, and the kingdom will be at peace. (Jilin 2001: 29–31)

Clearly *zhonghe* can be seen in two features: one is the interaction of *yin* and *yang*; the other is the triad of the *yin*, the *yang*, and the *yinyang*. For the *Taipingjing*, this triad is the root of great harmony and peace. "*Yin* and *yang* mutually receive and interact to become *he*. They form a triad. The three *qi* in a joint devotion and interface will nourish all things ... Harvesting these three *qi* will generate heaven and earth and reach the great peace" (Jilin 2001: 128). The *Taipingjing* also shows how these three constituents, as the primal building blocks, rally together in making heaven above, earth below, and human being between. If and only if these three *qi* are in their proper places will the world weave into one harmonious whole. "If there is *yang* without *yin*, there will be no life and peace will vanish; if there is *yin* without *yang*, there will be no life and peace will vanish; if there is *yin* and *yang* but no *he*, there will be no transmission of kinds, and this will also lead to extinction" (Jilin 2001: 128).

The triad or the three has thus captured a special eminence in this classic text. In Chapter 30 of the *Taipingjing*, we read: "Primordial *yin* (*taiyin*), primordial *yang* (*taiyang*), and *zhonghe* are the three *qi* (vital energy) which form the *li* (principle) and its interactions. Human being in a pivotal position must know it deeply" (Jilin 2001: 29). Chapter 48 is devoted to the *zhonghe*. Three is itself a state of being. The *yinyang* itself goes beyond a one and two that is merely reciprocal, complementary, or interdependent. There is a transformative thirdness mediating between these two.

This "thirdness," or *zhonghe*, may be formulated as harmony. Harmony is from the Greek word *"harmonia"* which means "a fitting together." There exist plenty of discussions regarding this in philosophical texts. Cartesian causal harmony is meant to explain the "non-atomistic side of entities: they are intrinsically what they exist as only by virtue of their relation to other things ... their location in a web of causal relationships" (Amaral 1987/88: 514). Harmony as a form of causal explanation "is grounded on the concept of causality adumbrated" (Amaral 1987/88: 514).

In Chinese, *he* (harmony) refers to the bringing of all different elements into a proper proportion. The *he* of *yin* and *yang* entails a proper configuration at a given time and place. This triad is the universe itself as well as the primary explanatory devices of natural kind, qualities, elements, events, and the world. François Jullien formulated a new concept of "logical tendency" to illuminate what the history of Chinese thought suggests about the Chinese view of nature and the world. This "logical tendency":

> [i]ncorporates two ideas that Chinese thought cannot dissociate: first, the notion that in reality everything always comes about immanently as a result of an internal development, with no need to invoke any external causality; second, the idea that this spontaneous process is itself a supremely regulatory force and that the norm it expresses constitutes the basis for transcending reality. (Jullien 1999: 231)

However, Jullien does not offer the reason for this "logical tendency." The explanatory role of the *yinyang* triad can be utilized in this issue. The world is constituted naturally in a way that exhibits the patterns established by the interaction of *yin* and *yang*. The *yinyang* is a property of all existence yet ultimately causes *sheng* 生 things to emerge, exist, and endure. There is no other external source needed to explain the change and movement of things. As the *Yijing* declares, "One *yin* and one *yang* are called Dao." *Yinyang* is the necessary and sufficient condition of the occurrence of things, and it also fits most human explanatory needs. Whenever an occurrence has the property of the *yinyang*, the mode of behavior or phenomenon of movement and change will appear.

The *yinyang* triad plays a pivotal role in the Chinese way of discerning the human body, good health, and a proper way of life. It explains physiological functions and pathological changes in the body and guides diagnoses and treatment. With *yin* flourishing smoothly and *yang* vivifying steadily, they regulate themselves so to maintain equilibrium. *Yin* and *yang* do not exist in isolation but interact in a dynamic state. The world, from celestial orbs to terrestrial plants and animals, exhibits a consensus of parts, a natural harmonious nexus and order. Who is responsible for this harmony then? In many Westerners' minds, God or the soul concurs with this operation and is held accountable for it. However, in the Chinese mind, the *yinyang* triad is liable for the nexus and order. The *yinyang* embraces all things, enters all existence, and governs the course of all changes. The *yinyang* is both the foundation of harmony and the harmony itself. Evolutionary biologists may ask the question: "What are the sources of the overwhelming and beautiful order which graces the living world?" (Kauffman 1993: xiii). They see the spontaneous emergence of order and the occurrence of self-organization. This is the complexity of an organism. Contemporary biology, mathematics, chemistry, and physics all reveal the power of self-organization and spontaneous order in complex systems. These show that natural selection, formulated by Darwin, is not the sole source of order in organism. There are self-ordered properties in complex living systems. "The unexpected spontaneous order is this: Vast interlinked networks of elements behave in three broad regimes:—ordered, chaotic, and a complex regime on the frontier between order and chaos" (Kauffman 1993: xvi).

The *yinyang* is also a structure of being. It is said that Nietzsche once articulated being as "an invention of weary men who cannot endure a world of ceaseless change and eternal becoming" (Vaught 2004: 108). Nietzsche is right to see the history of ontology as the history of nihilism, for there is a tension between being and time. His insight influenced Heidegger to question whether, and how, Being (with a capital "*B*") is rendered frozen and static when understood in contrast to time. However, the *yinyang* triad perceives being as a continual process of reconfiguration within time and space. The *yinyang* transcends time to posit a spatial vision of reality as a unity of time and space. It thus reveals a pattern, or, in Jullien's words, a "logical tendency." For example, *yang* is *dong* 動 (active), moving in time; *yin* is *jing* 靜 (passive), stillness in space. In one case, as *yang* fills in *yin* it will receive the form, grounded in space, or spatialization. This will be the case of *yang* getting *yin*; in another case, when *yin* receives *yang*, it will get time, moving in space, or temporalization. Time-*yang* is integrated into the space-*yin* or space-*yin* is integrated into the time-*yang*. Thus novelty emerges in the transition from possibility to actuality. The *yinyang* becomes forces embedded in nature and guiding, shaping, or directing natural processes from within. It is the internal guiding factor for human actions.

The *yinyang* triad reflects the diversity and variations of the differential patterns of *yin* and *yang*. Take other important philosophical concepts, for example, *ti* 体 (structure) and *yong* 用 (function). In Chinese medicine, *yin* is identified with the structure (*ti*), and *yang* with the function (*yong*). This provides an interesting way to grasp human biological systems and to model good health. For example, if one builds the structure in a certain way, such as by weight lifting, then one's function will perform well at certain sporting activities, such as being a football player. On the other hand, if one builds the structure differently, possibly by doing aerobic exercises focused on improving endurance, then one's function is more likely to be exercised well if one then becomes a runner. This reveals the expected pattern that differing compositions of *yin* and *yang* will bring about various effects.

Riding horse: The way of cultivating wisdom

The *yinyang* paradigm is a perpetual living mirror of the world that demonstrates the ternary structure of reality. Characterizing this state as *zhonghe* goes not only beyond the paradoxical existence recognized from Plato to Hegel but also directly to human actions. Let us take a specific case, namely riding horses, from early Chinese history. Horses played important roles in early Chinese people's lives. Managing horses effectively was a necessary condition for success, and horse-driven chariots were crucial for early military battles. The horse was a symbol of military culture, and could be the sign of victory as well as the image of a king. The *sima* 司馬, the officers of the Cavalry (literally officers of the horse, *ma*), were also the officers for military affairs during the Zhou Dynasty, and the term "horse" was used to refer to military leaders in the Shang Dynasty.

The horse was also a very significant image in many early Chinese texts. It was even a common exemplar for debates about language and logic: the most famous argument of Gongsun Long 公孫龍 (320–250 BCE) was that "a white horse is not a horse." The *Zhuangzi* goes so far as to say that "the myriad thing are one horse" (萬物，一馬). There is a special relationship between human beings and horses. We read from newly excavated bamboo strips that the way of riding horses has the same significance as managing water or planting crops:

> Yu the Great's moving of the waters was by following the *Dao* of water. Zao Fu's riding of horses was by following the *Dao* of horses. Hou Ji's planting the earth was by following the *Dao* of the earth. There is nothing that does not have its

Dao, but the *Dao* of human beings is nearest. Thus, gentlemen first select the *Dao* of human beings. (Liu 2003: 122)

The way of riding horses is in Chinese called the *yu* 御—the skill of steering a chariot. The *Huainanzi* 准南子 takes charioteering as the application of *yinyang*:

> Therefore, the Great Man calmly has no worries and placidly has no anxieties. He takes Heaven as his canopy; Earth as his carriage; the four seasons as his steeds, and yin and yang as his charioteers. He rides the clouds and soars through the sky to become a companion of the power that fashions and trans-forms us. Letting his imagination soar and relaxing his grip, he gallops through the vast vault [of heavens] … Thus, with Heaven as your canopy, nothing will be uncovered; With Earth as your carriage, nothing will be unsupported; With the four seasons as your steeds, nothing will be unemployed. With yin and yang as your charioteers, nothing will be incomplete. (Roth 2010: 52)

The four seasons are the horses, and *yinyang* is the driver. In this way, the Great Man can ride through the clouds and beyond the sky. He will go with transfor-mation and change, doing as he pleases and unfolding with rhythm. He gallops an infinitely vast land.

The *Huainanzi* here compares *yinyang* to *yu* 御, the skill of steering a chariot. *Yu* is one of six ancient arts in the *Zhouli* (*Rituals of Zhou*).[4] The character for *yu* consists of three parts: walking (*xing* 行), a rope (*sheng* 繩), and human being (*ren* 人). Putting them together, a human being holds the reins while riding a horse; thus, it is the art of navigating a path for a horse-drawn chariot. Of course, this can extend to navigating any path, from one's personal life to political organizations. We can speculate—why would horse riding be one of the six arts? It is about training someone to become a superb horse-rider through the cultivation of a *yinyang* intelligence by which one can easily and artfully locate oneself in relation to one's milieu.

Zhouli lists five ways for evaluating excellence in horse riding (Wang 1980: 193). The first (*ming he luan* 鳴和鸞) is synchronizing the sound of two bells on the carriage. If the horse and carriage move smoothly, the bells will make rhythmic sounds that can measure the skill of the driver. The second (*zhu shui qu* 逐水曲) is passing through dangerous and complicated winding roads along a river without falling down into the water. The third (*guo jun biao* 過君表) is demonstrating good temperament by staying calm and showing sincerity and respect while passing important sites. The fourth (*wu jiao qu* 舞交衢) is crossing busy traffic intersections smoothly. The fifth (*zhu qin zuo* 逐禽左)

is herding animals onto the left in order to put them in the best position for hunting. As we can see, the elements of horse riding go beyond winning races.

In the *Hanfeizi's* 韓非子 commentary on the *Daodejing*, there is a classic story concerning King Zhao of Jin's learning the art (*shu* 术) of charioteering. After learning the art, King Zhao was eager to defeat his master. He requested three races with three different horses but he lost all three times. He was angry at the master and thought that he had not taught him a complete skill. The master told him:

> I have given you all the techniques you need to ride a horse. However, there is a deficiency in your usage of these skills. The most important thing for the art of charioteering is to have the horse peacefully reside with the chariot and to have the rider's heart/mind come together with horse. However, you only care about who is in front and who is behind. If you were behind, you worried about catching me; but if you were ahead, you worried about being caught by me. There is always a rider either ahead or behind. If all of your attention focuses on me, how can you come together with the horse? This is the reason why you lost the race. (Chen 2000: 93)

Clearly, a good horse rider must be able to work peacefully with a controlled flow that responds to unrestrained forces and variations, and not focus on one single specific external fact such as who will win the race. Skill at charioteering is not a case of courage (*yong* 勇), but is rather a demonstration of a kind of intelligence (*zhi* 智), a strategy for becoming an embodied navigator.

The five standards above define a good charioteer. Based on the *Huainanzi's* metaphor, we can see them as demonstrations of a kind of *yinyang* intelligence. This technique or *shu* can be analysed from two distinct points of view.

First, *yinyang* intelligence is rooted in a view of the universe as an organic self-generating system. Self-organization and self-stabilization presuppose inter-action between system and environment. In the case of the *shu* of horse riding, effective interaction occurs through movement. The immediate interfaces of navigating a horse-drawn carriage include the horses and their power, the terrain, the weather, and one's purpose. The rider is linked to the many external factors that may disturb his or her inner state and elicit different kinds of response. It is a kind of open system that within itself deals with environmental disturbances and processes. The *Huainanzi* tells us that you feel with your hand yet respond through your heart/mind. This is a common saying, *dexin yingshou* (得心應手), "getting it through your heart/mind and responding with your hands." In this aspect, the world to a rider is not observed but felt. The whole nexus of senses (including vision) is a felt response. Like the sting of the sunlight or rush of the wind, the act of seeing has a similar feeling. It involves the mind and body working together. The *Liezi* presents another description of the art of charioteering:

> Internally, one focuses the centre of the heart/mind; externally, one unites with the will of the horse. One is able to go forward and backward but there is a centre and one goes around it as if with a compass. One can take the road on a long journey yet still have strength to spare. (Graham 1990: 183)

Riding horses, one can distinguish the internal (focusing the heart) from the external (the horse itself), but the crucial point is being able to reach the center. *Liezi* clarifies further that one receives (*de* 得) the bit and responds with the bridle; one receives in the bridle and responds in the hand; one receives in the hand and responds with the heart/mind. This way one sees without eyes, and urges without a goad; relaxed in the heart/mind and straight in posture, holding six bridles and pacing twenty-four hooves to advance, withdraw, and swing around with perfect precision. The heart/mind plays a key role in adjusting the situation. One's heart/mind is synchronized with, and functions with, the natural flow of the horse and chariot. Here the rider is in a condition lacking deliberateness or discursive thought, but has a great awareness that allows overall optimal performance. The rider also reaches at a stage of *he* (harmony) as the way of heaven and earth. One feels here and now, yet can respond there and then.

Zhu Xi, the influential Song Dynasty Confucian, uses the analogy of horse and rider to discuss the movement and stillness of *taiji* ("Great Ultimate") and *qi*:

> The movement of *Taiji* generates yang, stillness generates yin. *Taiji* is *li* (pattern); *qi* is movement and stillness. When *qi* moves, *li* moves, too. They are interdependent and cannot be separated. *Taiji* is like the horse rider and movement and stillness are like the horses. Horses hold the horse rider and the rider rides the horses. (Li 1999: 2376)

We see a conception of *yinyang* strategy as attunement and embodiment in the *Zhuangzi*. In chapter 24, a disciple is eager to learn and get the *Dao*. He thinks that getting *Dao* will enable him to get a cauldron of water to boil in the winter and to make ice in the summer. This appears to be good method: winter is cold, so one needs boiling water; and summer is hot, so one needs the coldness of ice. Yet, the master answers that this is only using *yang* to evoke *yang* and using *yin* to evoke *yin*. The getting of *Dao* is different. He begins by placing two zithers in different rooms, and when he plucks a note on one, the corresponding note on the other resonates. He then changes the tuning of one string so that it matches no proper notes, but, as soon as he plucks it, twenty-five strings on the zither resonate with it. This one sound is like the master of all the others, simply by stimulating them to resonate with it (Ziporyn 2009: 103).

Liezi tells the story about making music. The spring hints at the notes of the fall; the winter hints at the notes of summer (Graham 1990: 108). Music not only shows the root scale that is associated with the four seasons, but, more importantly, it reveals a pattern of hidden forces. In this sense, *yinyang* is not about matching one thing to another, but rather about resonating with the hidden forces at work in any given situation, using such resonances in order to bring about results skilfully.

The second aspect of *yinyang* intelligence is found in adaptivity. Horse riding works with external forces and internal constraints that together lead to adaptive self-organization. In this facet, adaptation is not synonymous with stability or harmony (*he*), but is closer to functional efficiency in coping with actual environmental disturbances. It is more about efficacy than about harmony. For example, what if the horse goes slowly but the rider needs to travel faster? The rider is required to initiate a way to make the horse go as fast as it can. The rider must engage in yielding and pulling movements, a dynamic *yinyang* play: giving and taking, pushing and pulling, with the powers of the horse. The *Liezi* explains: "equalizing the give and the pull is the ultimate principle of dealing with the world" (Graham 1990: 104). What is the "equalizing" (*jun* 均)? It is the center of the wheel that can turn to face any direction. The rider can reach his or her goal only by working with it, negotiating all variables to attain the desired result. The rider incorporates his surroundings into his perception–response loops in order to maintain efficacy.

Horse riding also requires human adaptation, affecting the reorganization of inherited behavior patterns to fit the existing environmental situations. This *yinyang* intelligence as an adaptation is an indispensable instrument for the interaction between oneself and the world. *Yinyang* is a configuration of forces: fundamental forces that can be exerted only by certain types of configuration and the qualities that emerge from such configurations. This is the rhythm of human life, earth's changes, and heaven's power. This configurative force *shen yu* 神喻 or the state of *xuanmiao* 玄妙 (recondite transcendence) represents the continual *yin* and *yang* reconfigurations that lead to *Dao*. Only sages know how to use or obtain *Dao*. *Dao* is not just getting things but knowing how to use power: navigating a boat in moving water, or using the wind to sail at sea. This can extend to navigating any path, from one's personal life to political organizations. Hence, we can say that wisdom is based upon knowledge, but a part of wisdom is shaped by uncertainty and activities. The art of the rider not only provides us with a conceptual understanding of wisdom, but, more importantly, it offers a way to be wise, or to become wise, for a flourishing life.

Notes

1   According to John H. Holland, "Building blocks are the pervasive, critical foundation of an ability to act with insight in a complex world. Human perception, for example, consists primarily in combining well-known, simple components to describe familiar phenomena ... A little thought shows that we approach all objects, familiar and unfamiliar, via combinations of familiar building blocks" (2002: 26).

2   The *yinyang* concept plays important conceptual roles in sustaining the Chinese culture. Its diversified functions can be easily recognized in history, religion, art, medicine, philosophy, and all aspects of life.

3   There have been a few hotly debated issues surrounding this text. One is its date. It has been said that there were three texts that bore this name during the Han dynasty. But the current text was believed to come from the end of Eastern Han and was collected in *Original Daoist Text* Ming dynasty.
    The other issue concerns the text's authorship. The consensus is that this is not a single author's work, but that of a few authors through a period of time.

4   The other five arts are: rites 禮, music 樂, archery 射, calligraphy 禦, and math 書.

Works cited

Amaral, P. (1987/88), "Harmony in Descartes and the Medical Philosophers," *Philosophy Research Archives*, vol. 13.

Chen, Q. 陳奇猷 (2000), *Hanfeizi* 韓非子新校注, Shanghai: Shanghai Guji Press.

Graham, A. C. (trans.) (1990), *The Book of Lieh-Tzu: A Classic of Tao*, New York: Columbia University Press.

Henderson, J. B. (1999), "Strategies in New-Confucian Heresiography," in K. W. Chow, O. C. Ng, and J. B. Henderson (eds), *Imaging Boundaries: Changing Confucian Doctries, Texts, and Hermeneutics*, New York: SUNY Press.

Holland, J. H. (2002), "Complex Adaptive System and Spontaneous Emergence," in A. Q. Curzio and M. Fortis (eds), *Complexity and Industrial Clusters*, Heidelberg: Physica-Verlag.

Jilin, Y. 杨寄林 (ed.) (2001), *Taipingjing* 太平經: *Classic of Great Peace*, Shijiazhuan: Hebei People's Press 河北人民出版社.

Jullien, F. (1999), *The Propensity of Things: Toward A History of Efficacy in China*, J. Lloyd (trans.), New York: Zone Books.

Kauffman, S. A. (1993), *The Origins of Order: Self-Organization and Selection in Evolution*, Oxford: Oxford University Press.

Li, L. (ed.) (1999), *Sayings of Zhuzi* 朱子語類, vol. 94, Beijing: Chinese Press 中華書局.

Roth, H. D. (trans.) (2010), *The Huainanzi, A Guide to The Theory and Practice of Government in Early China*, New York: Columbia University Press.

Vaught, C. G. (2004), *Metaphor, Analogy, and the Place of Places: Where Religion and Philosophy Meet*, Waco: Baylor University Press.

Wang, B. (commentary) (1980), *Zhouyi Lueli* 周易略例, Youlie Lou (ed.), Beijing: Chinese Press, 中華書局.

Wang, R. R. (2012), *Yinyang: The Way of Heaven and Earth in Chinese Thought and Culture*, Cambridge: Cambridge University Press.

Zhao, L. (ed.) (2003), *Guodian Chujian Jiaoyi* 郭店楚簡校釋, Fuzhou: Fujian People's Press.

Ziporyn, B. (trans.) (2009), *Zhuangzi: The Essential Writings with Selections from Traditional Commentaries*, Indianapolis and Cambridge: Hackett Publishing Company, Inc.

2

Lessons from Stupidity: Wisdom and the Man from Song

Jim Behuniak

It is unclear just how the "Man from Song" (*Songren* 宋人) acquired his reputation, but classical literature is replete with stories of his stupidity. These stories were commonly used in early China, as they appear in more than one text and serve more than one purpose. For instance, the story of the Man from Song who spent three years fashioning a mulberry leaf out of precious material (some say ivory, some say jade) appears in the *Liezi*, *Hanfeizi*, and *Huainanzi*. The story relates that the end product was so delicate and life-like that it could not be distinguished from actual mulberry leaves. The Ruler of Song was so taken with this work that he granted the Man from Song royal patronage and a generous salary at public expense, allowing him to continue making his precious leaves. For *Liezi*, this story illustrates how foolish it is for humans to waste time trying to replicate *dao* 道 through their own efforts (Graham 1960: 161). For *Hanfeizi*, the story illustrates the foolishness of a single person trying to produce a result unilaterally when such results emerge from a conglomerate of forces (Liao 1959: i, 220–1). For *Huainanzi*, the story illustrates how oblivious humans can be to the relations of scale in the transformations of *tian* 天 (Major, Queen, and Meyer 2010: 798). For a Mohist, the story would probably illustrate the foolishness of government waste.

Any single *Songren* story can be used to make a variety of philosophical points. The same can be said for other literary allusions in early Chinese texts, such as those drawn from the *Shijing* 詩經 or the *Shujing* 書經. What is noteworthy about the Man from Song stories, however, is that everyone who uses them, regardless of philosophical perspective, agrees that the Man from Song is *stupid*. His stupidity is generic in kind, something that transcends or precedes different philosophical schools and their agendas. As a universal emblem of poor thinking, the Man from Song represents habits of thought that are *generally* frowned upon in early China. In this respect, he provides an avenue through which to think about "wisdom" in the tradition. Rather than pursue a positive account of "wisdom" through terms like *zhi* 智 or *ming* 明, each of which has a range of meanings in different texts, one might begin with the Man from Song's shortcomings and then look for "wisdom" in the opposite direction. If "wisdom" represents anything in this tradition, it likely represents the contrary of whatever the *Songren* is doing.

Upon examination, I find that the Man from Song stories suggest that early Chinese "wisdom" is similar to what John Dewey called "intelligence." For Dewey, intelligence involves the coordination of means and ends in effective action, and this is what the *Songren* consistently lacks. Aristotle's notion of "wisdom" (*sophia*), that is, the static contemplation of fixed ends, is not particularly helpful in understanding the shortcomings of the *Songren*. In fact, such "wisdom" might only perpetuate his failings. Aristotle's notion of "prudence" (*phronesis*) is more helpful, but it offers no real advantage over what Dewey calls "intelligence," or so I will argue.

On a practical level, to spend years fashioning an object out of ivory or jade only to have it become virtually identical to something that one can pick up off the ground is simply foolish. It is a purposeless waste of time. The Man from Song is known for his engagement in such fruitless pursuits. Sometimes these take the form of failed business plans. In the *Zhuangzi*, we learn that the Man from Song invested all his money in caps to sell to the inhabitants of Yue, only to learn that people in Yue don't wear caps (Watson 1968: 34). The inverse of such bad thinking is also his. We learn in *Zhuangzi* of members of the Song clan who sell their family hand lotion recipe to an anonymous itinerant for a hundred pieces of gold. The itinerant, in turn, presents the formula to the king and is rewarded with a fortune many times greater (Watson 1968: 34–5). Zhuangzi uses this story to illustrate what it means to be oblivious to "using the big" (*yongda* 用大), only intending to show that two parties can use the same thing in different ways. The actual stupidity of the *Songren* is not used didactically in this case. If it were, it might illustrate the foolishness of fixating on short-term ends, not realizing opportunities to their full potential, or losing sight of the big picture.

The Man from Song is generally seen as oblivious to key features of his situation. Hanfei tells the story of the Man from Song who struggles with a wine selling business. He has an excellent product, fair prices, conspicuous signage, and courteous service. Still, no one buys his wine. Having no clue what the problem is, he asks a village elder why his business fails to attract customers.

The elder tells him that the problem is his dog. "He's too fierce," the elder tells him. He reveals that the dog bites children when they are sent to pick up wine for their parents (Liao 1959: ii, 105). The Man from Song had no idea that this was happening right outside his shop door.

Generally speaking, the Man from Song is someone who lacks the ability to act in ways that are effective and productive. His failure, however, takes two forms. In carving jade leaves and selling his family recipe, he fails to convert his energies into a means to some worthy end. By ignoring his vicious dog and overlooking the aversion of certain people to wearing caps, he fails to achieve his ends by ignoring some inadequacy in their means. Instrumentally speaking, the Man from Song is a disaster case, in terms of both ends and means. He might rashly take hold of some goal as an end-in-itself and force the issue, only to destroy any means to achieving that goal. In the *Lüshiqunqiu* for instance, we find the Man from Song wishing for his carriage to be pulled by a horse. When his horse does not pull the carriage, he beheads it and casts the head into a river. He proceeds to get another horse. When that horse does not pull his carriage, he cuts *its* head off. He gets a third horse, and does the same thing (Knoblock and Riegal 2001: 49–2). He also makes the inverse mistake. The Man from Song will take up some means and boldly propose a fantastic end that cannot possibly be realized through their use. In *Hanfeizi* we find him promising a king that he will engrave a female ape on the edge of a thorn. The king supports him in this undertaking, but the product never materializes. A retainer finally reminds the King that, "as a rule, the instruments of engravers must always be smaller than their objects." In other words, there is no way that the means at his disposal can achieve such ends. This time, rather than a horse's losing its head, the Man from Song is on the receiving end. The king executes him for not carving the ape (Liao 1959: ii, 35–6).

Structurally, the Man from Song stories point out types of stupidity that result when a working relationship between means and ends breaks down. On this basis, we can consult these stories to understand what "wisdom" might mean in the Chinese tradition. At least since Aristotle, "wisdom" (*sophia*) has been associated with the proper choice of ends. Aristotle teaches that wisdom involves the use of reason to apprehend universal truths about what the world is and what we should aim for. This faculty, for Aristotle, is separable in principle from the particulars of human activity. In fact, it is best enjoyed *as* disconnected from the means of productive activity, since "this activity alone would seem to be loved for its own sake; for nothing arises from it apart from the contemplating, while from practical activities we gain more or less apart from the action" (McKeon 2001: 1104). "Prudence" (*phronesis*), on the other hand, has to do with proper deliberation with respect to human activity and its results. This being so, it concerns itself not only with ends but also with the particular means through which ends are realized. For Aristotle, prudence is not "concerned with universals only—it must also recognize the particulars; for it is practical, and practice is concerned with particulars" (McKeon 2001: 1028). Ideally, prudence maintains continuity between its ends and its means—or, as Aristotle sees it, its "universal" and "particular" aspects. In contrast to "wisdom" (*sophia*), prudence focuses on "the latter [particulars] in preference to the former [universals]" (McKeon 2001: 1029).

Aristotle has a lot to say about the proper relationship between means and ends in activity, but his bifurcation of *sophia* and *phronesis* renders him a less than ideal pathway into Chinese thinking. Generally speaking, Chinese thinkers are not found reasoning about universal truths in isolation from practical activity. Mozi represents one exception, as his notion that "heavenly intention" (*tianzhi* 天志) furnishes an unvarying "standard of appropriateness" (*yizhifa* 義之法) invites us to look outside human experience for that standard (Johnston 2010: 159–61). Aristotle's notion of "wisdom" (*sophia*) may be of some use in understanding what Mozi was driving at. The fact that Mozi is regarded as unorthodox in both Confucian and Daoist quarters, however, only underscores his eccentricity.

This is where John Dewey becomes helpful, because, unlike Aristotle, he initiates no separation between "wisdom" and practical activity. Following convention, Dewey also identifies "wisdom" with the proper formulation of ends. "Wisdom," he writes, "is the ability to foresee consequences in such a way that we form ends which grow into one another and reinforce one another" (Dewey 2008a: vii, 210). Unlike Aristotle, however, Dewey does not mean by "ends" objects that are fixed and finished in the nature of things, separable in principle from activity. Ends for Dewey are not apprehended through *sophia* or *theoria*, but rather arrived at through activity and experience. Ends change and grow as experience changes and grows. As Larry Hickman explains, "'goals' for Dewey are what he calls 'ends-in-view'—ends that are alive and active only as they exhibit continuous interplay with the means that are devised and tested in order to secure them" (Hickman 1992: 12). The instrumentalism that results is not, Hickman observes, a "straight-line instrumentalism" (1992: 13). It stresses reciprocity and continuity between means and ends in activities that are fulfilling, and that succeed in securing what we want. Any bifurcation between means and ends signals a problem for Dewey, a glitch in smoothly running activity—something that needs to be addressed and fixed. Dewey does not appeal to "wisdom" in such cases. He uses that term very rarely, in fact. He appeals instead to "intelligence."

It probably would not matter to the Man from Song if we charged him with a lack of "wisdom" or a lack of "intelligence." His stupidity, however, is more suggestive of a lack of "intelligence" than a lack of "wisdom" (*sophia*). As I have argued, means and ends are always coming apart for the Man from Song, and this signals behavior lacking in intelligence. As Dewey says, "The cases in which ends and means fall apart are the abnormal ones, the ones which deviate from activity which is *intelligently* conducted" (Dewey 2008a: xiii, 235, my italics). As the Man from Song stories illustrate, the opposite of intelligence manifests itself in many ways. Generally, however, these failures takes two forms: means separated from ends, resulting in aimless and pointless behavior; and ends separated from means, resulting in heedless and abrupt behavior. Dewey recognized both. The Man from Song exemplifies each.

Consider the famous story of the rabbit and the stump. In Hanfei's telling, the Man from Song once found a rabbit in his field that had run into a stump. It broke its neck and died. "Free dinner," the Man from Song thought. He then put all endeavors aside and passed his days watching the stump, waiting to obtain another rabbit by the same means (Liao 1959: ii, 276). In this case, the stupidity lies in fixating on those means without recognizing how disconnected they are from the desired end. "Stump watching" (*shou zhu dai tu* 守株待兔) now stands as an idiom for idle and pointless behavior: the type that results from laziness of mind and unthinking routine. Meanwhile, at the other polarity, we have the famous story in the *Mencius* of the Man from Song who wishes for his crops to grow. He is so eager to reach this goal that he starts pulling on the shoots to help them grow more quickly. When his son learns of this practice, he rushes out to find that all his father's crops have died (Van Norden 2008: 40). "Shoot pulling" (*ba miao zhu zhang* 拔苗助長) now stands as an idiom for heedless and abrupt behavior: the type that results when ends are considered supreme and any means will do. Each type of behavior regards itself as intelligent—but wrongly—because each exhibits a fatal separation between means and ends. One half of what ought to be a continuum is taken up, and the other half is neglected.

As Dewey sees it, "A man is stupid or blind or unintelligent" in activities in which "he does not know what he is about, namely, the probable consequences of his acts." Such intelligence relies on a form of bi-directional thinking: both the relation of "present conditions to future results" (means to ends) and the "future consequences to present conditions" (ends to means) must be involved.

By Dewey's measure, one is "imperfectly intelligent" when one of two conditions obtain. One is either content with "looser guesses about the outcome than is needful, just taking a chance with [one's] luck"—a good description of the stump watcher; or, one is "[forming] plans apart from study of the actual conditions, including [one's] own capacities"—a good description of the shoot puller (Dewey 2008b: ix, 110). In either case, Dewey would advise the Man from Song that:

> You have to find out what your resources are, what conditions are at command, and what the difficulties and obstacles are. This foresight and this survey with reference to what is foreseen constitute mind. Action that does not involve such a forecast of results and such an examination of means and hindrances is either a matter of habit or else it is blind. In neither case is it intelligent. To be vague and uncertain as to what is intended and careless in observation of conditions of its realization is to be, in that degree, stupid or partially intelligent. (Dewey 2008b: ix, 138)

There is no room here for "wisdom" (*sophia*) as the detached contemplation of fixed ends that do not grow out of particular circumstances. Again, the nearest one comes in the Chinese tradition to such other-worldly "wisdom" is Mozi's claim to know "heaven's intention" (*tianzhi* 天志), that which he regards as the "clearest standard in the world" (*tianxia zhi mingfa* 天下之明法). Mozi claims that such knowledge enables him to clearly evaluate and classify the actions of others (Johnston 2010: 243). The Confucian and Daoist traditions each distance themselves from Mozi and his methods, however, insisting on a more practical approach with respect to both means and ends. The more mainstream adversaries to Mozi would agree with Dewey that "an intelligence which defines, describes, and classifies merely for the sake of knowledge is a principle of stupidity and catastrophe" (Dewey 2008b: iv, 29).[1]

In this connection, it is worth dwelling a little more on the "shoot pulling" episode. Exploring its context, it is possible to tease out an important issue: namely, the relationship between enjoyment, the status of ends, and the contingencies of experience. Mencius uses the "shoot pulling" story in connection with his observation that Gaozi does not understand the virtue of "appropriateness" (*yi* 義) because he makes it "external" (*wai* 外).[2] This foreshadows the first "Gaozi" chapter in the *Mencius*, where Gaozi claims that "respecting the elderly" is appropriate (*yi*), and appropriateness is external (*wai*). Mencius refutes this claim by suggesting that if "respecting the elderly" is appropriate, and "appropriateness" is external, then before long we will be respecting old horses. So it goes, if "respecting the elderly" is a universal end-value to be realized by *every* possible means. Resisted here is the postulation of "respecting the elderly" as a fixed, universal standard, "external" to any practical considerations that might pertain to its realization. Gaozi responds by doubling down, claiming that he treats elderly people from the state of Chu exactly as he treats elderly people in his own family. Thus, he concludes, "Appropriateness is external." Mencius responds famously, and curiously: "Enjoying the roast meat of a person from Qin is no different from enjoying my own roast meat ... is enjoying roast meat, then, also external (*wai*)" ? (Van Norden 2008: 145–7).

As Mencius elsewhere observes, the enjoyment of roast meat is a common pleasure for humans (Van Norden 2008: 193). The question that he poses is whether or not this fact, and the fact that he would enjoy a roast from his own kitchen in the same way as from any another, means that "enjoying roast meat" (like "respecting the elderly") is an end-value that stands "external" to whatever circumstances are implicated in our desire for it. Mencius is suggesting here that it is not, and we are left to wonder what his analogy means. As further evidence that Dewey had something to say about everything, this is what he had to say about enjoying roast meat:

> The first time roast pork was enjoyed, it was *not* an end-value, since by description it was not the result of desire, foresight, and intent. Upon subsequent occasions it was, by description, the outcome of prior foresight, desire, and effort, and hence occupied the position of an end-in-view. (Dewey 2008a: xiii, 227)

These words are from Dewey's 1939 work, *Theory of Valuation*. They are written in response to Charles Lamb's 1888 essay, "A Dissertation Upon Roast Pig." This short work, an exquisite example of Victorian-era Orientalism, attributes to Chinese culinary history an episode that sounds as if it could have featured the Man from Song. Lamb relates a story (taken, he says, from "a Chinese manuscript") of one Ho-ti and his foolish son, Bo-bo, born vegetarians, peaceably cohabiting with pigs. Playing with fire one day, Bo-bo carelessly burns down their house, incinerating the pigs in the process. Dewey will summarize the rest:

> While searching in the ruins, the owners touched the pigs that had been roasted in the fire and scorched their fingers. Impulsively bringing their fingers to their mouths to cool them, they experienced a new taste. Enjoying the taste, they henceforth set themselves to building houses, inclosing pigs in them, and then burning the houses down. (Dewey 2008a: xiii, 277)

Dewey relishes the humor of Lamb's story in the same way that he would have relished the Man from Song stories. Both are parables of stupidity born of a mismatch between means and ends.

The lesson that Dewey draws from the Ho-ti and Bo-bo story is a serious one, and I am inclined to think that there is also something serious to draw from the Man from Song stories, *and* from Mencius' suggestion that our desire for roast meat is not "external." The challenge is to pull it all together. The lesson that Dewey draws from "A Dissertation Upon Roast Pig" is that the *value* of any given end is not an intrinsic, universal property. Sure, roast pork tastes great, but it is not worth our burning down house after house in order to procure it. If it were, then the story of Ho-ti and Bo-bo would not strike us as ridiculous. The *worth* of roast pork as an end-value is continuous with that of the *means* through which it is procured. Or, as Dewey explains: "The *value* of enjoyment of an object *as* an attained end is a value of something which in being an end, an outcome, stands in relation to the means of which it is a consequence" (Dewey 2008a: xiii, 277). This is an elaborate way of saying what Mencius also means to say in suggesting that the enjoyment of roast meat is not "external." What this means in the context of his debate with Gaozi is that, for Mencius, "appropriateness" (*yi*) is not a universal value or property that transcends our desires, our histories, the means at our disposal, or the consequences of their use—it is not a property that simply *attaches* itself to ends (such as "respecting the elderly"), remaining fixed and universal, always and forever. If it did, then before long we would be respecting old horses, as Mencius suggests.

For Dewey, an end-in-view does not wait upon faculties like "wisdom" (*sophia*) or "contemplation" (*theoria*) to apprehend it as an invariant, unwavering goal "external" to activity and its evolving means. Similarly for Mencius, "appropriateness" (*yi*) does not wait upon what Aristotle calls "wisdom," but rather upon what Dewey calls "intelligence," a quality that remains situated in the dynamic interplay between means and ends *in* activity. In terms of Dewey's logic, the knowledge of what is "appropriate" (*yi*) is acquired through the process of inquiry—it is not simply *had* in a moment of contemplation. "Contemplation proper," for Aristotle, "is the enjoyment, not the acquisition, of knowledge" (Urmson 1988: 121). The disconnected, "external" (*wai*) nature of such an enjoyment is what Mencius means to call into question in his debate with Gaozi. One who exercises intelligence is cognizant of the fact that means and ends are *not* disconnected: means entail ends, and ends entail means. They inform one another. Overlooking this is what makes the *Songren* so hopelessly stupid. He expects to achieve the best results, but his actions are always frustrated by his fixation on only one *half* of what ought to be considered a *whole* situation.

This characteristic shortcoming is nicely summarized in one final episode, drawn from the *Leizi*. Strolling along one day, the *Songren* stumbled upon half of a split tally that someone had lost in the street. He took it home and stored it away, taking it out occasionally to admire it and to count the indentations on its broken edge. "I'll be rich any day now," he said to his neighbors. "I'll be rich any day now"! (Graham 1960: 179).

Notes

1   Parentheses removed.
2   Gaozi is likely a Mohist, although his philosophical pedigree is unclear.

Works cited

Dewey, J. (2008a), *The Later Works of John Dewey, 1925–1953*, Jo Ann Boydston and Kathleen Poulos (eds), 17 vols, Carbondale: Southern Illinois University Press.

Dewey, J. (2008b), *The Middle Works of John Dewey, 1899–1924*, Jo Ann Boydston and Kathleen Poulos (eds), 15 vols, Carbondale: Southern Illinois University Press.

Graham, A. C. (1960), *The Book of Lieh-Tzu: A Classic of Dao*, New York: Columbia University Press.

Hickman, L. (1992), *John Dewey's Pragmatic Technology*, Bloomington: Indiana University Press.

Johnston, I. (2010), *The Mozi: A Complete Translation*, Hong Kong: The Chinese University of Hong Kong Press.

Knoblock, J. and Riegal, J. (2001), *The Annals of Lü Buwei*, Palo Alto: Stanford University Press.

Liao, W. K. (1959), *The Complete Works of Han Fei Tzu: A Classic of Chinese Political Science*, vols 1 and 2, London: Arthur Probsthain Publishers.

Major, J. S., Queen, S., and Meyer, A. (2010), *The Huainanzi: A Guide to the Theory and the Practice of Government in Early Han China*, New York: Columbia University Press.

McKeon, R. (2001), *The Basic Works of Aristotle*, New York: The Modern Library.

Urmson, J. (1988), *Aristotle's Ethics*, Oxford: Blackwell Publishers.

Van Norden, B. (2008), *Mengzi: With Selections from Traditional Commentaries*, Indianapolis, IN. Hackett Publishing Company.

Watson, B. (1968), *The Complete Works of Chuang Tzu*, New York: Columbia University Press.

3

The Wisdom of the Unsayable in the Chinese Tradition

Karl-Heinz Pohl

Concerning Eastern teachings such as Daoism, Buddhism, and Confucianism, there is often widespread confusion about how these are to be classified—as religion or as philosophy. This problem, however, is culturally homemade: the distinction between religion and philosophy based on European cultural traditions often does not apply when we leave our culture behind. Thus, the Eastern teachings, which are often referred to as "wisdom religions" (e.g. by Hans Küng), are either religion *and* philosophy or *neither* religion *nor* philosophy; whichever way you prefer ideologically.

As is well known, there is a certain "family resemblance" (as Wittgenstein would put it) between Daoism and Buddhism. There is, however, very little that connects these Asian philosophies and religions with the European tradition emanating from Greco-Roman and Christian thought. This does not mean that their philosophemes would be fundamentally alien to the Europeans: at most they do not belong to the European mainstream. So the family resemblance could certainly be extended to certain European philosophers and schools: There is in Europe a tradition—from the pre-Socratics through the apophatic theology and mysticism of the Middle Ages to existentialism and philosophy of language of modernity—that has very much in common with Daoism and Buddhism. Hence, a blend of selected passages from Heraclitus (cf. Wohlfart 1998: 24–39), Neo-Pythagoreanism, Sextus Empiricus, Gnosticism, Pseudo-Dionysius the Areopagite, Nicholas of Cusa, Meister Eckhart, Jacob Boehme, Montaigne, Hegel (cf. Wohlfart 1998: 24–39), Heidegger, Wittgenstein, Derrida, et al. could result in a little book that, in the essence of its central texts, would differ very little from the Far Eastern tradition.

The concepts of God in Eastern teachings, however, are hardly comparable with those of the Abrahamic religions; that is, speaking about God is not an issue. In Confucianism, which forms a tradition oriented towards secular and social ethics in China, a metaphysical connection to a transcendent "Heaven" (*tian* 天), responsible for the ethical functioning of the universe, does play a role. But Confucius explicitly refrained from discoursing on this topic;[1] hence we find little in Confucian literature that discusses the nature of Heaven. In recent, neo-Confucian, discourse, the topic "immanent transcendence" (*neizai chaoyue* 內在超越) appears to have become an issue (cf. Xin and Ren 1992), but this should be understood quite differently from its treatment in modern Western philosophy, for example, from that of Jaspers (Sarin 2009: 208). Rather, the idea behind it is this: although there is a supreme good in Confucianism (attributed to a transcendent Heaven as the metaphysical origin of a fundamentally ethically good human nature), this highest good is not considered to lie outside the ways of man, but is instead believed to be immanent. That is, it manifests itself in the fulfilment of interpersonal obligations or in the practice of the virtue of "humanity" (*ren* 仁).

Daoism and Buddhism in some ways form complementary teachings of wisdom to the Confucian tradition. In contrast to Confucianism, of which it is often said that its teachings lead "into the world" (*ru shi* 入世), Daoism and Buddhism follow entirely different interests, and thus it is said of both that they are leading "out of the world" (*chu shi* 出世). In addition, Daoism holds the view—in stark contrast to Confucianism—that the "Way" (*dao* 道) of the universe ("Heaven and Earth") is not an ethical one. As the author (or authors) known as Laozi puts it (Chan 1969: §5): "Heaven and earth are not humane. They regard all things as straw dogs."[2]

Whereas Confucianism as a philosophy is concerned with worldly wisdom in the moral and ethical sense, Daoism is much more an art of life—as living in harmony with nature—or even an art of survival. Buddhism, however, which has—by an adaptation of Confucian structures and Daoist thought—found a specific character in China, is marked by a combination of knowledge and wisdom. Some schools of Buddhism, especially popular in China, take the so-called "Wisdom Sutras" (*Prajnaparamita Sutras*) as their base; they show, among other things, that all phenomena (*dharmas*) arise in dependence upon multiple causes and conditions ("dependent co-arising"). Thus, in a logically coherent argument, they point out their relativity and hence their ultimate "emptiness".

If one were to look for an overarching commonality of these Far Eastern teachings, it would be, in the first place, their orientation on action. They are, to echo the well-known title of a book by Pierre Hadot called *Philosophy as a Way of Life*, "ways of life" or exercises in worldly wisdom. In other words, they are less concerned with knowledge and more with action or, in the words of the famous Chinese Neo-Confucian Wang Yangming (1472–1529 CE), with the "unity of knowledge and action" (*zhi xing he yi* 知行合一). This unity had once existed also in ancient European philosophy, but in the Western philosophical tradition it was lost, as Hadot has convincingly shown, when the Christian religion in the Middle Ages carried over from ancient philosophy the practice of spiritual exercise.

Where the focus is on doing, it means less talking, because—as is well known—people have always been measured not by their words but by their actions. And thus there is the popular saying that the true philosopher, namely the wise, excels less by talking than by action, or even by silence: As the proverb says, speech is silver but silence is golden. Confucius is known, moreover, for not wanting to talk too much: "The Master [Confucius] said, 'I would prefer not speaking.' Zi Gong said, 'If you, Master, do not speak, what shall we, your disciples, have to record?' The Master said, 'Does Heaven speak? The four seasons pursue their courses, and all things are continually being produced, but does Heaven say anything?'" (Legge 2006: *An.* 17:19).[3]

Or think of the snappy response that Boethius (c 475–525 CE) gave once to the question of a would-be philosopher, who asked him, "Do you now recognize that I am a philosopher?": "I would have known it if you had kept silent" (*Intellexeram, si tacuisses*). This has led to the saying, still used to confront a foolish person who disqualifies himself by speaking: "If you had been silent, you would have remained a philosopher" (*Si tacuisses, philosophus mansisses*). And, concerning the significance of knowledge in philosophy, Socrates, the greatest sage of the Western tradition, with his dictum "I know that I know nothing" has set standards which even today—remember the flood of writings of our philosophers—are still being missed by miles. At best, only the sceptics, Pyrrho of Elis, Sextus Empiricus, or—in modern times—Wittgenstein have come to comparable realizations. Thus, Wittgenstein says towards the end of his *Tractatus Logico-Philosophicus*: "We feel that even when all possible scientific questions have been answered, the problems of life remain completely untouched. Of course there are then no questions left, and this itself is the answer" (1922: §6.52). And he concludes the treatise with the sentence: "Whereof one cannot speak, thereof one must be silent" (1922: §7).

Socrates' dictum, at the end of the Middle Ages, resonates with Nicholas of Cusa's "learned ignorance" (*docta ignorantia*), which is in the tradition of apophatic theology, that is, the medieval Christian School, which assumes that God cannot be spoken of in a positive way. As we will see, there are "family resemblances" between this teaching of non-speaking to the one found in the Chinese tradition of wisdom.

Below, some basic principles of Daoism and Buddhism will be presented, notably concerning the title of this essay: the saying of the unsayable. Subjects for discussion include emptiness, relativity, paradoxes, namelessness or knowledge of ignorance. Buddhism will be discussed mainly in the form of one particular school, known as Madhyamaka, which leads back to the Indian philosopher Nagarjuna in the second century CE. As there is already a well-known study by Karl Jaspers which compares Daoism (via Laozi) with Nagarjuna (Jaspers 1978), here, related texts will be discussed, for example the Buddhist "Wisdom Sutras" (*Prajnaparamita*) (referred to above), which were highly influential in China and are attributed also to the school of Nagarjuna. The author's approach is less that of a philosopher so much as that of a philologically inclined historian of culture. If it were to be consistently philosophical, in the sense of the teachings presented here, the essay would consist of a blank sheet of paper.

Daoism

The following remarks will deal first, in detail, with the philosophy of Daoism (not the Daoist religion): its basic features will be presented, such as negative action, that is, non-doing (*wu wei* 無爲), as well as the knowledge of not-knowing. There is discussion also of related topics, such as emptiness, paradox, and relativity.

The central classical texts of Daoism, which will be referred to below, are, first, the *Daodejing*,[4] attributed to the legendary Laozi (composed possibly between the sixth and fourth centuries BCE). This consists of sayings, divided into eighty-one chapters (which, however, offer no coherence of system or argument). It is considered, worldwide, to be the most important of the philosophical books of Daoism, and, after the Bible, the work translated into the greatest number of languages. Second, at some point between the fourth and third centuries BCE, we have the book, *Zhuangzi*, which is attributed (at least in certain parts) to its eponymous author. The two texts differ less in their content than in their manner of speaking. Whereas the *Daodejing* is a highly condensed and poetically suggestive text, the *Zhuangzi* is a compendium of stories, parables, and dialogues, which, in their imagery, are as entertaining as they are profound and cryptic.

Laozi

One of the central (and initial) statements of the book, *Daodejing*, (and of Daoism in general) is that the *Dao*—the underlying reason of being, which is called the Way—in its unfathomable totality of realizations is not accessible to cognition. We may get an inkling of its working in the world, but it remains hidden from access by language, understanding and knowledge. The beginning of the *Daodejing* reads, accordingly: "The *Dao* that can be told is not the eternal *Dao* (*Dao ke dao, fei chang dao* 道可道 非常道)."

   In the original Chinese, this sentence offers interesting facets of understanding that are not present in translation. The character *dao* not only means "Way" but carries the additional meaning "to speak." It thus occurs in this sentence not twice (as in the translation), but three times. In addition, there is no discernible distinction between nouns and verbs in classical Chinese; in other words, a word/character can usually be used as either a verb or a noun. (This linguistic non-distinction between things and actions can, incidentally, offer deeper conceptualization in philosophy of language, inasmuch as objects become events, suggesting a non-material interpretation, that is, a process understanding, of the world.) The character *dao* can thus also be read in a verbal sense, that is, not only as "to speak" (its second meaning) but also from its basic meaning as "way." So the initial sentence of this classic can be understood thus: "The *Way* that can be trodden as the *Way* is not the eternal *Way*." Or: "The *Dao* that can be taken to be the *Dao* is not the eternal *Dao*." Seen from this linguistic perspective, the first sentence gives the book an opening with manifold meaning and indeterminacy that could correspond to a basic intention. One has to add, however, that seen from a historical perspective, this terse sentence may originally have had quite another intention, as a criticism of other philosophical schools, such as Confucians or Mohists, who also spoke of the *Dao* as of their Way, and who knew how to explicate this eloquently. Hence, it would be wise (remaining with our topic) to keep to historical grounds, even with the revered classics, and not to use inappropriate mystification.

   When the *Way* cannot be fixed as the *Dao*, either with words or in any other manner, what remains are only circumlocutions, approximations, or paradoxes (such as in the "learned ignorance"—*docta ignorantia*—of Nicolas of Cusa). Thus, it is said of the wise man who has managed to approach the Way:

> A wise man has no extensive knowledge; He who has extensive knowledge is not a wise man. (Chan 1969: §81)

He who knows does not speak. He who speaks does not know. (Chan 1969: §56)

Therefore the sage desires to have no desire, he does not value rare treasures. He learns to be unlearned. (Chan 1969: §64)

To know and yet (think) we do not know is the highest (attainment); not to know (and yet think) we do know is a disease.

To know that you do not know is the best. To pretend to know when you do not know is a disease. Only when one recognizes this disease as a disease can one be free from the disease.

The sage is free from the disease. Because he recognizes this disease to be disease, he is free from it. (Chan 1969: §71)

Whereas in normal life knowledge lies in higher esteem than ignorance, in the passage above this hierarchy is turned upside down: The wise man knows that he knows nothing. If ignorance, however, is considered to be the ultimate state, then this evaluation can be verbalized only in paradoxes—that is, not according to common-sense reason—or in approximations.

One of the, few, approximations characterizes the "Way" as "being by itself so" (*ziran* 自然) as it is; it functions—like the course of nature—by itself. Thus, in a central chapter of the *Daodejing* we read:

There was something undifferentiated and yet complete, which existed before heaven and earth. Soundless and formless, it depends on nothing and does not change. It operates everywhere and is free from danger. It may be considered the mother of the universe. I do not know its name; I call it *Dao*. If forced to give it a name, I shall call it Great. Now being great means functioning every-where. Functioning everywhere means far-reaching. Being far-reaching means returning to the original point.

Therefore *Dao* is great. Heaven is great. Earth is great. And the king is also great. Man models himself after Earth. Earth models itself after Heaven. Heaven models itself after *Dao*. And *Dao* models itself after Nature (*ziran*). (Chan 1969: §25)

Here, first of all, we have again the consideration that the *Dao* cannot be told or pinpointed. The crucial statement, however, is at the end of the passage: whereas man, earth, and Heaven are ruled, or modeled, by a higher instance, the model/ rule (*fa* 法) of the *Dao* is nature, that is, "being by itself so" (*ziran*). What does this mean? The *Dao* reveals itself in spontaneous, natural action. It happens by itself just like the changing of the four seasons, the growing of plants, the blowing of the wind and the drifting of the clouds. The consequence for human beings, who achieve insight into this "by itself so" functioning of the *Dao*, is: "no action" (*wu wei*). This means not complete passivity but avoiding any attempt to stir the course of things too deliberately with self-interest. Instead, one should let things go, living in accordance with the spontaneous and unfathomable workings of nature and adapting to its constant changes. Hence, the book recommends—with paradox formulations—a strategy of diminishment in leading one's life:

> The pursuit of learning is to increase day after day. The pursuit of *Dao* is to decrease day after day.

> It is to decrease and further decrease until one reaches the point of taking no action. No action is undertaken, and yet nothing is left undone. (Chan 1969 §48)

There is a further approximation to the *Dao*, which is called "reversion" (*fan* 反). Reversion can be observed in the tendency of the Way to turn around the course of things—at least in the long run—and to achieve, in this way, a balance between extreme possibilities. Hence, it is said in the *Daodejing*: "Reversion is the action of the *Dao*. Weakness is the function of the *Dao*" (Chan 1969: §40).

A reversion usually takes place when things have reached an extreme point— be it in the course of the sun after it has reached its zenith, or in the course of the four seasons after summer or winter. As one orients oneself along this principle of nature, the unbalanced parts in one's life will be straightened out naturally.

A further insight into the working of the *Dao* can be achieved by realizing the basic relativity of all being—another important topic in the *Daodejing*. The phenomena of the world are manifested in binary structures. Hence, we perceive things always within the framework of their basic relativity—just as light and dark, sound and silence condition one another:

When all the people of the world know beauty as beauty, there arises the recognition of ugliness.

> When they all know the good as good, there arises the recognition of evil. Therefore: Being and non-being produce each other; difficult and easy complete each other; long and short contrast each other; high and low distinguish each other; sound and voice harmonize each other; front and behind accompany each other.

> Therefore the sage manages affairs without action and spreads doctrines without words.

All things arise, and he does not turn away from them. He produces them but does not take possession of them. He acts but does not rely on his own ability. He accomplishes his task but does not claim credit for it. It is precisely because he does not claim credit that his accomplishment remains with him. (Chan 1969: §2)

Since opposites condition one another, it would be wrong to demand only one of them, because, whether we want it or not, we will get the other as part of the binary structure. A *Daoist* wise view on reality would therefore be: to understand this basic duality and relativity of things as manifestations of the *Dao* and to transcend this relativity by abiding in a realm beyond the opposites.

A final central topic in the *Daodejing* is "emptiness," or "void." One could say that emptiness is more essential than fullness as it has an infinite potential; and it dwells beyond any categorization. (Emptiness is also an important concept in Buddhism, there, however, more in the form of a tactical or logical concept. See below.) In the book, *Laozi*, emptiness is illustrated metaphorically: for example, the essence of a pot of clay is the empty space with which it can contain things; in a wheel it is the emptiness of the hub:

Thirty spokes are united around the hub to make a wheel, but it is on its non-being that the utility of the carriage depends.

Clay is moulded to form a utensil, but it is on its non-being that the utility of the utensil depends.

Doors and windows are cut out to make a room, but it is on its non-being that the utility of the room depends.

Therefore turn being into advantage, and turn non-being into utility. (Chan 1969: §11)

Summarizing, one could characterize the *Daodejing* as attempting to circumvent the unsayable in its workings, that is, in approximations such as "being itself so" or "reversion." Apart from this, we encounter a largely negative strategy, as common-sense theses will be turned around. When there is no room for any positive proposition about the *Dao*, there will be in the end—if one would not rather remain silent—only paradoxes or images.

Zhuangzi

The inability to talk about the *Dao* is a central theme, also, in the second Daoist classic, the *Zhuangzi*. The book is popular because of its many parables and witty dialogues, including the following two:

Knowledge wandered north to the banks of the Black Waters, climbed the Knoll of Hidden Heights, and there by chance came upon Do-Nothing-Say-Nothing. Knowledge said to Do-Nothing-Say-Nothing, "There are some things I'd like to ask you. What sort of pondering, what sort of cogitation does it take to know the Way? What sort of surroundings, what sort of practices does it take to find rest in the Way? What sort of path, what sort of procedure will get me to the Way?"

Three questions he asked, but Do-Nothing-Say-Nothing didn't answer. It wasn't that he just didn't answer—he didn't know how to answer!

Knowledge, failing to get any answer, returned to the White Waters of the south, climbed the summit of Dubiety Dismissed, and there caught sight of Wild-and-Witless. Knowledge put the same questions to Wild-and-Witless. "Ah—I know!" said Wild-and-Witless. "And I'm going to tell you." But just as he was about to say something, he forgot what it was he was about to say.

Knowledge, failing to get any answer, returned to the imperial palace, where he was received in audience by the Yellow Emperor, and posed his questions. The Yellow Emperor said, "Only when there is no pondering and no cogitation will you get to know the Way. Only when you have no surroundings and follow no practices will you find rest in the Way. Only when there is no path and no procedure can you get to the Way."

Knowledge said to the Yellow Emperor, "You and I know, but those other two that I asked didn't know. Which of us is right, I wonder?"

The Yellow Emperor said, "Do-Nothing-Say-Nothing—he's the one who is truly right. Wild-and-Witless appears to be so. But you and I in the end are nowhere near it. Those who know do not speak; those who speak do not know. Therefore the sage practices the teaching that has no words. The Way (*Dao*) cannot be brought to light; its virtue cannot be forced to come. [...] So it is said, He who practices the Way does less every day, does less and goes on doing less, until he reaches the point where he does nothing, does nothing and yet there is nothing that is not done." [...]

Knowledge said to the Yellow Emperor, "I asked Do-Nothing-Say-Nothing and he didn't reply to me. It wasn't that he merely didn't reply to me—he didn't know how to reply to me. I asked Wild-and-Witless and he was about to explain to me, though he didn't explain anything. It wasn't that he wouldn't explain to me—but when he was about to explain, he forgot what it was. Now I have asked you and you know the answer. Why then do you say that you are nowhere near being right?"

The Yellow Emperor said, "Do-Nothing-Say-Nothing is the one who is truly right—because he doesn't know. Wild-and-Witless appears to be so—because he forgets. But you and I in the end are nowhere near it—because we know."

Wild-and-Witless heard of the incident and concluded that the Yellow Emperor knew what he was talking about. (Watson 1968: §22)

Here, again, it is significant that the normal order of things is turned upside down. As to questions that apply to the nature of the *Dao*, ignorance and forgetfulness appear more appropriate answers than alleged knowledge. That is, in the words of the *Daodejing*, the speaker turns out to be not knowing and the knower as not speaking. The second dialogue addresses a similar theme:

Master Dongguo asked Zhuangzi, "This thing called the Way—where does it exist?"

Zhuangzi said, "There's no place it doesn't exist."

"Come," said Master Dongguo, "you must be more specific!"

"It is in the ant."

"As low a thing as that?"

"It is in the panic grass."

"But that's lower still!"

"It is in the tiles and shards."

"How can it be so low?"

"It is in the piss and shit!"

Master Dongguo made no reply.

Zhuangzi said, "Sir, your questions simply don't get at the substance of the matter. When Inspector Huo asked the superintendent of the market how to test the fatness of a pig by pressing it with the foot, he was told that the lower down on the pig you press, the nearer you come to the truth. But you must not expect to find the Way in any particular place—there is no thing that escapes its presence! Such is the Perfect Way, and so too are the truly great words. 'Complete,' 'universal,' 'all-inclusive'—these three are different words with the same meaning. All point to a single reality." [...]

"That which treats things as things is not limited by things. Things have their limits—the so-called limits of things. The unlimited moves to the realm of limits; the limited moves to the unlimited realm. We speak of the filling and emptying, the withering and decay of things. [The Way] makes them full and empty without itself filling or emptying; it makes them wither and decay without itself withering or decaying. It establishes root and branch but knows no root and branch itself; it determines when to store up or scatter but knows no storing or scattering itself." (Watson 1968: §22)

Between the *Dao* as the ground of reality and the manifest things of the world no line can be drawn; consequently, in its workings, there is no difference between high and low, between ants and excrement. This seems to be simply pantheism, but Zhuangzi would probably respond to it as above; namely that it misses the point of the matter: If you try to narrow the "Way" with the drawing of any line—for example with terms such as pantheism—there is no escape from things.

Zhuangzi's aim, like that of the *Daodejing*, is to show the unity of opposites. The following parable illuminates the consequences of not recognizing this unity. People who do not understand this principle live like the monkeys in the story called "Three in the Morning":

To wear out your brain trying to make things into one without realizing that they are all the same—this is called "three in the morning." What do I mean by "three in the morning"? When the monkey trainer was handing out acorns, he said, "You get three in the morning and four at night." This made all the monkeys furious. "Well, then," he said, "you get four in the morning and three at night." The monkeys were all delighted. There was no change in the reality behind the words, and yet the monkeys responded with joy and anger. Let them, if they want to. So the sage harmonizes with both right and wrong and rests in Heaven the Equalizer. This is called walking two roads. (Watson 1968: §2)

A quintessence of this thinking is to accept both positions (walking two roads), that is, even seemingly incompatible positions. This means recognizing the relativity of all things—even life and death—and to achieve a freedom beyond the thinking in opposites. So, Zhuangzi says about life and death:

The True Man of ancient times knew nothing of loving life, knew nothing of hating death. He emerged without delight; he went back in without a fuss. He came briskly, he went briskly, and that was all. (Watson 1968: §6)[5]

To know the conditional nature of all things and concepts in view of their respective opposites includes insight into the relativity of one's own standpoint, that is, to see things *sub specie aeternitatis*:

Everything has its "that," everything has its "this." From the point of view of "that" you cannot see it, but through understanding you can know it. So I say, "that" comes out of "this" and "this" depends on "that"—which is to say that "this" and "that" give birth to each other. [...] Therefore the sage does not proceed in such a way, but illuminates all in the light of Heaven. He too recognizes a "this," but a "this" which is also "that," a "that" which is also "this." His "that" has both a right and a wrong in it; his "this" too has both a right and a wrong in it. So, in fact, does he still have a "this" and "that"? Or does he in fact no longer have a "this" and "that"? A state in which "this" and "that" no longer find their opposites is called the hinge of the Way. (Watson 1968: §2)

It is the subjective relativity of all knowledge that leads to different perspectives, and thus also to misperceptions and misunderstandings. Given this condition—and since everyone insists on his perspective and his mistakes—Zhuangzi arrives at sceptical positions concerning language in general:

Therefore I say, we must have no-words! With words that are no-words, you may speak all your life long and you will never have said anything. Or you may go through your whole life without speaking them, in which case you will never have stopped speaking. (Watson 1968: §27)

Since the essence is unsayable, it is his goal "to get along without words," and hence Zhuangzi says, again with one of his paradoxical formulations: "Where can I find a man who has forgotten words so I can have a word with him?" (Watson 1968: §26).

The transcending of relative positions is also the theme of the following story. After first exemplifying with a gnarled tree how to prolong one's life by uselessness, namely to escape the ax of a carpenter, Zhuangzi indicates that this again is relative, because uselessness can also sometimes cost one one's head. Hence, the best position is beyond the usual polarities such as usefulness and uselessness:

Zhuangzi was walking in the mountains when he saw a huge tree, its branches and leaves thick and lush. A woodcutter paused by its side but made no move to cut it down. When Zhuangzi asked the reason, he replied, "There's nothing it could be used for!" Zhuangzi said, "Because of its worthlessness, this tree is able to live out the years Heaven gave it."

Down from the mountain, the Master stopped for a night at the house of an old friend. The friend, delighted, ordered his son to kill a goose and prepare it. "One of the geese can cackle and the other can't," said the son. "May I ask, please, which I should kill?"

"Kill the one that can't cackle," said the host.

The next day Zhuangzi's disciples questioned him. "Yesterday there was a tree on the mountain that gets to live out the years Heaven gave it because of its worthlessness. Now there's our host's goose that gets killed because of its worthlessness. What position would you take in such a case, Master?"

Zhuangzi laughed and said, "I'd probably take a position halfway between worth and worthlessness. But halfway between worth and worthlessness, though it might seem to be a good place, really isn't—you'll never get away from trouble there. It would be very different, though, if you were to climb up on the Way and its Virtue and go drifting and wandering, neither praised nor damned, now a dragon, now a snake, shifting with the times, never willing to hold to one course only. Now up, now down, taking harmony for your measure, drifting and wandering with the ancestor of the ten thousand things, treating things as things but not letting them treat you as a thing—then how could you get into any trouble?" (Watson 1968: §20)

Central, here, is the idea of holding the mean between extremes, that is, to rise above thinking in opposites and to look at things as from the perspective of eternity (we will encounter a similar strategy later in this essay, when discussing Nagarjuna and his doctrine of the Middle Way). Also central to the above story is the passage "treating things as things but not letting them treat you as a thing". The "self-cultivation" of the Daoist sage aims precisely at the nurturing of this inner freedom and detachment, namely, as above, he "rests in Heaven the Equalizer" (Watson 1968: §2).

Summarizing, we find in Daoism patterns of reasoning and figures of thought exemplifying the following content: (1) The unity behind the diversity of the objective world; (2) the relativity of all existence, as well as the relativity of points of view; and (3) the impossibility of having knowledge of the fundamental reality (the "Way") and therefore the impossibility of speaking about it. The ultimate truth is thus, in the end, a non-truth; and the method of achieving the goals of Daoism, that is, to recognize this non-truth, is a non-method: on the one hand, non-action (*wu wei*), letting things go with non-intervention; on the other hand, speaking in absurdities, paradoxes, and in images and parables, in order to convey an inkling of the unsayable for the non-wise. Since the essence cannot be expressed in words, Zhuangzi's attempts to say the unsayable are—and his book is full of it—nothing but parables, allegories, and images (*yuyan* 寓言, translated below as "imputed words"). In his own writing:

These imputed words which make up nine tenths of it (i.e. my words) are like persons brought in from outside for the purpose of exposition. [...] It is the fault of other men, not mine [that I must resort to such a device, for if I were to speak in my own words], then men would respond only to what agrees with their own views and reject what does not, would pronounce "right" what agrees with their own views and "wrong" what does not. (Watson 1968: §27)

However, speaking in images is popular not only among the Daoists: one can easily find this preference in other instances in the Chinese history of ideas. So it is said in the "Great Commentary" (I.12) to the *Book of Changes* (*Yijing* 易經), one of the most revered classics of the Confucian tradition (which, however, also contains a lot of Daoist thought and is the source of *Yin-Yang*-thought):

> The Master said: "Writing does not exhaust words, and words do not exhaust ideas. If this is so, does this mean that the ideas of the sages cannot be discerned?" The Master said: "The sages established images in order to express their ideas exhaustively." (Lynn 1994: *Xici Zhuan* I.12)

Although the term images here refers to the relatively abstract "images" (hexagrams) of the *Book of Changes*, the above passage with its core content of language scepticism has nevertheless made a great impact on Chinese philosophy, and aesthetics in general, because it emphasizes that images are stronger and more meaningful than writing or purely discursive words.

Buddhism

In Buddhism, there are patterns of thought and reasoning that in many ways resemble those of Daoism. This applies to all schools of Buddhism, schools true to their Indian origin as well as those that emerged in China through a fusion with Daoism, especially Chan (Japanese: Zen) Buddhism.

Virtually all religions try to answer the question of how good and bad deeds are repaid during or after life. The explanation given by Buddhism is that man, through good and evil deeds, creates "*karma*" (deed, work) that determines his further existence in a perpetual cycle of rebirth (*samsara*). Good *karma* leads to new life, on a higher level, bad *karma*, correspondingly, to life on a lower level. This cycle can be broken only by the realization of "four noble truths": (1) Life is suffering; (2) this suffering is due to ignorance and the "thirst" for life with all its sensual pleasures; (3) there is a way out of this vale of tears; (4) the resort is located in the "eightfold path," offered by Buddhism as a way of practice. The "eightfold path" represents a mixture of ethical life, right knowledge, and spiritual contemplation.

Fundamental to the success of Buddhism in China was a development originating in India during the two centuries before the Christian era: the transition from Hinayana (Small Vehicle) to Mahayana Buddhism (Great Vehicle). This change had significant consequences: whereas Hinayana offered salvation from *samsara* only to those who were willing to "tread" the eightfold path through an ascetic monastic life, Mahayana Buddhism (as a great vehicle) offered salvation to all human beings—including the laity—through the knowledge that all are already enlightened, and possess Buddhahood, although they do not recognize it. The ideal figure was now no longer the ascetic and austere *Arhat* (Chinese: *luohan* 羅漢), but the Bodhisattva, an aspirant to Buddhahood who renounces admission into *nirvana* (the extinction of the walks through all existences of *samsara*) in order to devote himself to the salvation of all suffering beings.

Madhyamaka—the "Middle Way"

For the development of Buddhism in China, a special direction of Mahayana Buddhism was important: the school of the "Middle Way," which originated in India around Nagarjuna in the second century CE. The school's aim was to reach—through a logical chain of refutations of any position and its counter-position—a view of reality by which nothing can be attributed a substance in the world. Nagarjuna's systematic "empty logic" (cf. Cheng 1984) is based on two assumptions that are fundamental to the spirit of original Buddhism: (1) the relativity of all phenomena (*dharma*) in the world; and (2) dependent co-arising. The former means (similarly to the discussion in the context of Daoism above) that all *dharmas* can be defined only in relation to others (life is not death, joy is not pain, and so on); the latter means that all things arise in dependence upon various causes and conditions and that, consequently, none of the countless manifestations of the world possesses a definitive or absolute reality: they are empty (*shunyata*) of inherent existence. It also includes a concept that can be found already in Hinayana, namely the illusory nature of the "self": What we call our "self," according to the Buddhist point of view, is just a convention or, more precisely, a random composition of different physical and mental factors of existence (*skandhas*). Hence, while we can observe in the European tradition a historical trend toward development of the self to self-expression and self-realization (as it surely culminates in the modern era), we find in the context of Buddhism (with all due caution against such generalizations) something of an inclination toward emptying the self, or to self-transcendence and self-forgetfulness. In Mahayana, and especially in Nagarjuna, we find this view of the insubstantiality of the self extended to all forms of existence. This is the topic of the so-called "Wisdom Sutras" (*Prajnaparamita*), from which Nagarjuna has emerged as commentator and systematizer.

As the perception of the world is bound to conventions—definitions based on opposites—and as all conceptual thinking is relative, Nagarjuna is pulling the rug out from under our way of conceptual thinking, and attempting, in a manner of speaking, "to stop the world." His method is a so-called tetralemma of "Fourfold Negation" (*catuskoti*, or in Chinese, *siju* 四句—"four set"), that is, negating: (1) being, (2) non-being, (3) both being and non-being, and (4) neither being nor non-being (Cheng 1984: 67).[6] As to the question of substance or non-substance of any phenomenon, according to Nagarjuna none of the four positions applies. So it seems that at the end of this logic the "emptiness" (*sunyata*, Chin.: *kong* 空) of the world appears. "Empty" does not mean, however, that the world does not exist, but that nothing exists by itself, that all existence is attributable only to the fickle interaction and mutual causality between factors of existence. In other words, nothing has permanence by itself, and there is nothing "substantial" that we can rely on. Thus, in the end, this doctrine holds a hovering position between affirmation and negation of the world; that is, a "middle way" (Chinese: *zhongdao* 中道) between these binary positions.

The logic of relativity is, however, also true to *nirvana*: it can be spoken of only in contrast to *samsara*. To this extent, *nirvana* is not only not something "substantial," which one could rely on, but, ultimately, also, "empty." Thus, Madhyamika Buddhism comes to the conclusion that one cannot distinguish between *samsara* (the world of forms) and *nirvana* (the void): rather, that both are identical. To put it in the words of the influential "Heart Sutra" (*Prajnaparamita-Hridaya Sutra)*, the shortest (the "heart" in the title stands for the core of the wisdom teachings) but the most famous of the Wisdom Sutras:

> Form is not different from emptiness, and emptiness is not different from form. Form itself is emptiness, and emptiness itself is form. (cf. Suzuki 1985: 222–38)

This position has become known in Chinese Buddhism as that of "non-duality" (*bu er* 不二). It is a point of view which—similar to the views in Daoism— eludes further elaboration.

The "Vimalkirti Sutra"—entering the gate of non-duality

Next to the Heart Sutra, the Vimalakirti Sutra contains the best-known illustration of the idea of "non-duality" (interestingly, the topic is not "unity").

This sutra, highly popular in Tang China (from the seventh to tenth centuries CE), describes a dispute between Buddhist saints and the layman Vimalakirti, in which the layman proves to be better versed in the Buddhist "doctrine of emptiness" than the Bhuddist representatives. The highlight of the sutras is a dialogue between Vimalakirti and Manjusri (a disciple of the Buddha and Bodhisattva of wisdom) on entry into the "gate of non-duality." After the other Bodhisattvas have given their opinion on the subject, they turn to Manjusri as the most honorable among them, and ask him for his opinion. Initially, he criticizes the contributions of the previous speakers as insufficient; then he elaborates eloquently on the subject:

> After the various bodhisattvas had thus each made their explanations, [Vimalakirti] asked Manjusri, "How does the bodhisattva enter the Dharma gate of non-duality?" Manjusri said, "As I understand it, it is to be without words and without explanation with regard to all the *dharmas*—without manifestation, without consciousness, and transcending all questions and answers. This is to enter the Dharma gate of non-duality."
>
> Manjusri then asked Vimalakirti, "We have each made our own explanations. Sir, you should explain how the bodhisattva enters the Dharma gate of non-duality."
>
> At this point Vimalakirti was silent, saying nothing.
>
> Manjusri exclaimed, "Excellent, excellent! Not to even have words or speech is the true entrance into the Dharma gate of non-duality." (McRae 2004: IX 148)

While Manjusri is still wordy, trying to say the unsayable, Vimalakirti reacts in the only possible way: in the cultural history of China, it has become known as the "thundering silence of Vimalakirti". The episode can be found on numerous murals of Buddhist caves, and the legendary wisdom of the layman Vimalakirti—and the popularity of the Sutra with the same name—has certainly contributed to promoting a kind of Buddhism not only in the province of monks (and nuns), who were supposed to leave their families, but compatible with Chinese (Confucian) family values.

Jizang and his strategy of double truths

A tactical means of achieving a non-dual view of reality was already laid out by Nagarjuna, that is to speak of "double truths." By this, Nagarjuna means to say that one may talk in a generally intelligible way about mundane things in everyday contexts: he calls this "worldly truth" (Chinese: *sudi* 俗諦). But while people on the whole tend to have an approving attitude to the world, the Buddhist tendency is initially rather the reverse. In this respect, the "real/absolute truth" (Chinese: *zhendi* 真諦) is the view from the standpoint of "emptiness." In the so-called Chinese Sanlun School ("Three Treatises"),[7] the Chinese Buddhist Jizang further elaborated this idea—already laid out in the "Fourfold Negation." Following Nagarjuna's structure of double truths, he developed a system of repeated denials with which he finally arrives at emptiness or the insubstantiality of all things and beings. He treats these two categories of truth to the question of substance or emptiness on three levels, as follows:

Worldly:	*Absolute*:
1. Substance	1. Emptiness
2. Duality (Substance *and* Emptiness)	2. Non-Duality (neither Substance nor Emptiness)
3. Duality and Non-Duality	3. Neither Duality nor Non-Duality

That is to say: While looking at the world from the viewpoint of worldly truth, one commonly speaks on the first level of substance, whereas the Buddhist point of view, as an absolute truth, sees only emptiness as the ultimate reality. However, if we hold fast to an absolute truth of "emptiness," as a contrast to "substance," it will, on the second level, turn again into a worldly truth, namely that of a duality between two extremes: substance and emptiness. Thus, the absolute truth, seen on this second level, is non-duality (neither substance nor emptiness). On the third level, however, adherence to these two alternatives would lead again to a worldly point of view, that is, the affirmation of a new "duality": the distinction between (the extremes) duality and non-duality. The absolute and final truth on the third level, accordingly, is the negation of this new "duality": neither to affirm nor to deny this antithesis of duality and non-duality. Lastly, therefore, the position of "non-duality" also has to be dismissed as relative only; in other words, one can confront it, as Vimalakirti impressively demonstrated, only by remaining silent. And so Jizang, in the end, holds a middle way between affirmation and negation of the world (cf. Fung 1983: vol. ii, 296).[8] In the wake of Nagarjuna, he wants to show that, seen from a Buddhist perspective, things or reality are insubstantial or "empty"—they have no existence, and if we ascribe to them a being, it is so only on a worldly level.

That which is true regarding the notions of *nirvana* and "non-duality" (that they are only relative) applies also to the basic concept of "emptiness." Although for the Buddhist the world is empty, he, also, must, in the end, depart from the concept of "emptiness," because it exists only in the context of and in opposition to "substance" or "fullness" (cf. Fung 1983: vol. ii, 295–7). To keep clinging to the notion of emptiness would mean not only to remain attached to thinking in dual or opposite terms but even to attribute a (metaphysical) "substance" to emptiness. Moreover, according to this dialectic, a seemingly "correct" view of things, if you try to hold on to it, will turn into a one-sided and therefore "wrong" view; hence, one must give up this view, also, in order to reach an enlightened state of consciousness: that of non-attachment.

Without regard being given to this background, the Madhyamaka school is often accused of nihilism; however, this would indeed mean not only to attribute a "substance" to the concept of "emptiness" but even to raise it to an absolute level. Instead, it should be emphasized that the "empty logic" is seen as being merely a tactical tool used ultimately to disclose attachment to unrealities (delusion, greed, etc.) as the cause of all suffering and, therefore, to liberate man from this attachment. True to its analogy of Buddhist teaching's being a raft that you can leave safely when the river is crossed (see below), both the concept of "emptiness" and the Buddhist doctrine have to be left behind once the state of non-attachment is reached. Thus, we find in the Mahayana tradition a tendency to relate to the unsayable, or the conceptually elusive reality that transcends all relativity—Buddha nature—as "suchness" (*tathata*, Chinese: *zhenru* 真如), and to denote the Buddha, accordingly, as the "One-who-has-thus-come," or "Thus-gone" (*tathagata*, Chinese: *rulai* 如來). Especially in the notion of "suchness," there is a parallel to Daoism, namely the approximation to the ineffable *Dao* as that which is "from-itself-so" (*ziran*).

The Diamond Sutra

Next to the short "Heart Sutra" (from which the key sentence on non-duality is quoted above) the "Diamond Sutra"—*Vajracchedika Prajnaparamita Sutra*, literally "The diamond that cuts through the illusion"—is one of the most influential Wisdom Sutras dealing with the topic of saying the unsayable. Although "emptiness" is never explicitly mentioned in the text, it is implicit at the center of this sutra (Lehnert 1999: 91). Here, we also regularly find paradoxical formulations whose aim is to break intellectual habits and common-sense logic.

A theme of this sutra is the question of what we observe in reality: the things themselves, or only their outward signs, which can be deceptive. For example, which signs characterize a true Buddha? (Traditionally, a Buddha possessed thirty-two signs by which he could be recognized.) To this question of his disciple, Subhūti, the Buddha replies:

> The mortal possession of signs is in every case vacant and delusive. If one sees that the signs are not signs, then one sees the Tathagata (i.e. Buddha). (Patton n.d.: §5)

In this context, the "sign" stands for all manifestations (*dharmas*) which have no independent substantial presence but refer only to something else, in an endless chain. The signs or names of manifestations are thus, like language in general, nothing but conventions of relativity—one has to see through this relativity and recognize its "signlessness" (emptiness). In pursuit of this recognition, a paradoxical reasoning pattern is used consistently in the "Diamond Sutra" which says: *A* is not *A*, and therefore it is called *A*. So, also, in the following example:

> The Buddha addressed Subhuti: "This sermon's name is the Diamond Perfection of Wisdom (*Vajra Prajnaparamita*). By way of the words of this title, you should receive and uphold it. For what reason? Subhuti, the Buddha says that it is the perfection of wisdom, so it is not the perfection of wisdom." (Patton n.d.: §13)

Perfect wisdom is, as you might say, its dissolution as non-wisdom. Thus, there is no doctrine of emptiness to hold onto or to be conveyed. In an afterthought to the sentence just quoted, the Buddha says, therefore: "The Tathagata has nothing to teach." Elsewhere, this idea is elaborated further by the analogy referred to above, that the teaching of the Buddha is like a raft, which serves to get people to the other side but must then be discarded:

> You monks! Know that my expounded Dharma is like the bamboo raft. The honoured Dharma must be relinquished, how much more so what is not the Dharma? (Patton n.d.: §6)

However, this statement is also meant to be understood only on a "worldly" level. So the Buddha says later:

> Subhuti, what do you think? Do you say that the Tathagata composes this thought: "I shall save the sentient beings"? Subhuti, do not compose that thought. What is the reason? Really, there are no sentient beings the Tathagata saves. If there were beings the Tathagata saved, the Tathagata then would have a self, a personage, beings, and a soul. Subhuti, the Tathagata has explained that an existent self is then not a self. Mortal men regard their persons as being a self. Subhuti, mortal men, the Tathagata has explained, then, are not mortal men. They are called "mortal men." (Patton n.d.: §25)

Here the Buddha confirms the above-mentioned (section 2.a) view of the illusory nature of the self in Buddhism. Significantly, he finishes his teaching with a verse (*gatha*) that captures its essence as non-teaching:

All of the existent, conditioned *dharmas*
Are like dreams, illusions, bubbles, shadows;
Like dew and also like lightning:
Thus should they be contemplated. (Patton n.d.: §32)

Thus, the best means to speak about the unsayable and the doctrine of emptiness—as before with Laozi and Zhuangzi—is the poetic mode, that is, to speak of it through similes and parables.

The meaning of the sutra, then, is to "cut through the illusion of our thinking," namely to develop a consciousness that is attached to nothing and which does not take its perceptions and experiences as an indication of the actual existence of the signs and forms (and this includes all *dharmas*, including *nirvana*, etc.). Emptiness as an issue manifests itself in the structure of reasoning by which it is shown that each argument is relative and thus empty. In more general terms, the philosophical *and* religious aim of the Wisdom Sutras is therefore—similar to Zhuangzi—to understand the subjective conditioning of all knowledge. It is this conditioning which leads to misconceptions of reality, which in turn causes the suffering of existence. Hence, the cessation of suffering as the ultimate goal of Buddhism happens by "cutting through the illusions of our thoughts."

Chan (Zen) Buddhism

The development that took place in China through the reception of Madhyamaka Buddhism (such as the *Sanlun* School of Jizang), the "thundering silence" of Vimalakirti and the prevalence of the Wisdom Sutras, culminated to a certain extent in the emergence of the most typical school of Buddhism in China: Chan Buddhism. It flourished in China during the period from the eighth century through to the thirteenth century. Now known as the "Zen" school in Japan, this form of Buddhism goes back, in practice and methodology (as in meditation), to those basics that developed in China; it took, however, a significantly different path of development in Japan. The original Chan is characterized by its converting into practice the most radical of the insights presented above, so consistently remaining silent on the issues raised. This feature is already present in its founding legend. The Chan-tradition is said to have begun when the Gautama Buddha, in a sermon, once held up a flower in his fingers without saying a word. All disciples looked blank; allegedly only Kasyapa responded, with an understanding smile (cf. Suzuki 1933: 87); for this reason, he is regarded as the first patriarch of Chan. While this story is likely to be a legend, it was certainly invented for a specific purpose (and has exerted a considerable significance throughout its history of being heard), namely, to illustrate the essence of conveying a message beyond verbal or doctrinal mediation.

Seen from this background, for a Chan Buddhist it would be illusory to seek *nirvana* or Buddhahood; in fact, searching for it (as blind attachment) would actually impede the endeavor. An enlightened view of reality, thus, cannot be gained by means of special exercises, for example meditation, but through pure mindfulness in the present moment, that is, in the living here and now (including all its ordinariness). For this purpose, Chan Buddhism again developed special methods, such as seeking answers to questions that cannot be solved intellectually (Chinese: *gongan* 公案, Japanese: *koan*; for example, "What is the sound of one hand clapping?" [cf. Watts 1957: 174f]).⁹ In this way, the adepts are led by their masters, not only spiritually but also existentially, into a crisis from which, then, a "sudden enlightenment" can arise.

Enlightenment, however, can also be described as a negative experience, like the emptying of a bucket containing virtually all collected knowledge and effort when suddenly its bottom is broken through. And so, again, on the one hand, the experience of emptiness cannot be understood conceptually, but at best through images; on the other hand, the strategy of a Chan Buddhist master is similar to that of the book, *Zhuangzi*, that is, to respond to questions about the nature of Buddhism (in the so-called anecdotes known in Chinese as *wenda* 問答, or "Question and Answer," and in Japanese as *mondo*) with absurdities, irrationalities and ultimately silence—or with caning. Such is also a well-known answer to the question of the essence of the Buddha: that he is like a pail of water from which the bottom is broken through (Suzuki 1985: 236).

Entirely foreign to Chan Buddhism is the idea of a divinity of the Buddha.¹⁰ While the Buddha was worshiped in both the Hinayana and Mahayana traditions, Chan is characterized by a complete lack of respect for him. As the legend goes, the historical Gautama Buddha is said to have declared after his birth: "Above me the sky, and below me the sky. I alone am the Venerable One." This story was commented on as follows by the Chan master Yunmen (d. 966): "If I had been with him at the moment as he said this, I would have killed him with one stroke and would have thrown his body into the mouth of a hungry dog" (Suzuki 1985: 60). Another example is: "If you meet the Buddha, kill him." But these are only guidelines to ward off being dazzled by conceptualizations of the world or empty words.

Thus, one could say that nothing is sacred for the Chan Buddhists, but this, also, would miss the point, because, in Chan, just as in Confucianism and Daoism, the everyday occurrences represent the holy and transcendent: "Carrying water and chopping firewood—all this is none other than the wonderful 'Path'" (Fung 1983: vol. ii, 402ff.). One might therefore describe Chan Buddhism as the "Path" (*dao*) of "transcendent everyday life." In any case, the way to Buddhahood leads no longer to the long road of self-sacrifice or a life behind monastery walls. To be a Buddha means: just not to try to become a Buddha. Instead, it is important to keep an attentive non-attached mind in daily life, which is not the same as leading a normal everyday life. From these basics, one can see the close relationship to Daoism. In fact, much Chinese Chan Buddhism is nothing but Daoist philosophy in Buddhist guise.

Conclusion

Let us, finally, highlight again the differences between Laozi/Zhuangzi and Nagarjuna (and the Madhyamaka School as presented with the corresponding sutras). In Nagarjuna we have not only a theory of knowledge but also a strict logic, which, however, is not easy to follow, in all its implications, with an everyday mind. Here we may see a parallel with European thinking, and this is certainly no coincidence, since language, grammar, and thought patterns in India have more in common with their counterparts in Europe than they do in China. Thus Nagarjuna's concept of "emptiness" (*sunyata*) is a logical concept that requires explanation. It bears witness to thinking in conditional, instead of substantial, terms (Yuan 1998: 37). Moreover, Nagarjuna's logic is tied to a premise that must be accepted in the first instance: conditioned co-arising. Like Derrida,[11] who arrives at logical *aporias* since he does not, ultimately, deconstruct his own system of deconstruction, Nagarjuna, operating his system consistently, would find himself in similar problem areas, since "conditioned co-arising" is also a convention of relative naming (namely, to "un-conditioned co-arising").[12] However, Nagarjuna is certainly able to lead those who want to follow him into dizzying heights of thought, only to let them then fall into an abyss, which, however, in his paradoxical language, is seen as enlightenment.[13]

By contrast, the thought of Laozi and Zhuangzi is more playful, and their ways of expression are more poetic. They speak in metaphors and parables or cavort consciously in absurdities. Additionally, their philosophy is neither epistemology nor ontology nor logic; rather it represents a philosophy of life, or, better, an art of living that delights in the contradictions of life, rather than trying to squeeze a logical durable sense out of the world. If, for example, Laozi speaks of emptiness, he does not do this, as would Nagarjuna, in a logical way, but instead with an image (a hub of a wheel, a window in the wall, etc.), where the images are not without a brightening effect. And, finally, questioning the reasonableness of it all, the answer would be: silence—and possibly speaking in paradoxes, or, better yet, in striking poetic images. In Chan Buddhism, as a specific synthesis of Chinese Buddhism and Daoism, the playfully anarchic Daoist train of thought continues to live on in a number of ways.

Thus, in China and Japan it remained essentially reserved to the realms of poetry and art (for example, Zen paintings) to raise sensitivities for the unsayable. For this reason, the chapter concludes with a poem by the poet-hermit Tao Yuanming (365–427 CE)—one of the most famous poets in Chinese literary history. In a few simple, but famous, lines, Tao Yuanming shows how one can succeed from the first to preserve a non-attached and Daoist serene attitude to life, that is, a spiritual freedom everywhere (specifically, by keeping a distance from the world in the heart/mind). This is the previously mentioned art of life of Daoism. In addition, the poem ends, like Wittgenstein, with a philosophical silence, and thus on a very Daoist note—the knowledge of the inexpressibility and inscrutability of the nature of things, that is, with an allusion to the above-mentioned opening sentence of the *Daodejing*: We can get an inkling of the true sense of the world, but we cannot put it into words.

I built my hut beside a travelled road
Yet hear no noise of passing carts and horses.
You would like to know how it is done?
With the mind detached, one's place becomes remote.
Picking chrysanthemums by the eastern hedge
I catch sight of the distant southern hills:
The mountain air is lovely as the sun sets
And flocks of flying birds return together.
In these things is a fundamental truth
I would like to tell, but lack the words.

("Twenty Poems After Drinking Wine" in Hightower 1970: 130)

Notes

1   "Zi Gong said, 'The Master's personal displays of his principles and ordinary descriptions of them may be heard. His discourses about man's nature, and the way of Heaven, cannot be heard'" (Legge 2006: 5.13).

2   All translations from the *Daodejing* are taken from Chan 1969. John Gray uses Laozi's image of "straw dogs" for a general critique of Western style civilization: Gray, 2002.

3   Throughout the text I abbreviate *Analects* as "*An.*" so as to distinguish it from the other Confucian texts included in Legge's book.

4   Richard John Lynn has translated the title into English as "The Classic of the Way and Virtue."

5   See also Pohl 2004.

6   For Nagarjuna see also Ramanan 1966 and Streng 1967.

7   These are Nagarjuna's "Fundamental Verses on the Middle Way" (*Zhonglun*), Nagarjuna's "Treatise on the Twelve Gates" (*Shièrmenlun*) as well as Aryadeva's (Nagarjuna's student) "Hundred-Verse Treatise" (*Bailun*).

8   Regarding Jizang, see also Cheng 1984: 50ff.

9   A Chinese version of the Diamond Sutra is the oldest printed book (868 AD). It was found in Dunhuang and is now in the British Museum in London.

10   A well-known collection of *gongan* is Huikai n.d.: *Wumenguan* (Gateless Gate).

11   Nagarjuna also treats the question about God as meaningless and futile (unanswerable). Hence, by dismissing both positions as correlative, he holds a middle between theism and atheism. Cheng, 1984: 89, 94f.

12   The similarities in the strategies of post-structuralism (deconstruction) and the Madhyamaka School are striking. One could mark the difference between the two (at least in their effects or intentions) in that post-structuralism has opened a new philosophical discourse in its attack on essentialist thinking. It led to an extensive critique of political, social, and aesthetic ideas (also to questioning all hierarchies), revealing or liberating what was previously obscured or subordinated. Intentionally or unintentionally, the results of this endeavor have become not only liberation and plurality, but also mannerism and arbitrariness. The concern of the Madhyamaka School, on the other hand, is fundamentally religious: liberating man from the attachments and entanglements of life as the cause of all suffering. The purpose of its strategy of denial, when consistently carried out, should lead to a state of spiritual non-attachment. For a comparison between Derrida and Madhyamaka see Cai 1993a: 183–95 (this article also explicates Jizang's "double truths"); Cai 1993b: 389–404. A comparison between Zhuangzi and Deconstruction can be found in Allison 2003: 487–500.

13   As to a critique of Nagarjuna by the Yogacara school see Cheng 1984: 25.

Works cited

Allison, R. A. (2003), "On Chuang Tzu as a Deconstructionist with a Difference," *Journal of Chinese Philosophy,* 30/3–4 (September/December), 487–500.

Cai, Z. Q. (1993a), "Derrida and Madhyamika Buddhism: From Linguistic Deconstruction to Criticism of Onto-theologies," *International Philosophical Quarterly,* 33/2: 183–95.

Cai, Z. Q. (1993b), "Derrida and Seng-zhao: Linguistic and Philosophical Deconstructions," *Philosophy East and West,* 43/3: 389–404.

Chan, W. T. (1969), *A Source Book in Chinese Philosophy,* Princeton: Princeton University Press. http://www.bu.edu/religion/files/pdf/Tao_Teh_Ching_Translations.pdf (accessed 10 March 2015).

Cheng, H. L. (1984), *Empty Logic: Madhyamika Buddhism from Chinese Sources,* New York: Philosophical Library.

Fung, Y. L. (1983), *A History of Chinese Philosophy,* 2 vols, D. Bodde (trans.), Princeton: Princeton University Press.

Gray, J. (2002), *Straw Dogs: Thoughts on Humans and Other Animals,* London: Farrar, Straus and Giroux.

Hadot, P. (1995), *Philosophy as a Way of Life,* Oxford: Blackwell.

Hightower, J. R. (1970), *The Poetry of T'ao Ch'ien,* Oxford: Oxford University Press.

Jaspers, K. (1978), *Lao-tse, Nagarjuna: Zwei asiatische Metaphysiker,* Münich: Piper.

Legge, J. (2006), *The Chinese Classics, Vol. I: Confucian Analects, the Great Learning, and the Doctrine of the Mean,* Oxford: Cosimo Classics. Available from http://ctext.org/analects (accessed 10 March 2015).

Lehnert, M. (1999), *Die Strategie des Kommentars zum Diamant-Sutra,* Wiesbaden: Otto Harrassowitz.

Lynn, R. J. (1994), *The Classic of Changes: A New Translation of the I Ching as Interpreted by Wang Bi,* New York: Columbia University Press.

McRae, J. R. (trans.) (2004), *The Vimalakirti Sutra,* (Taishō 14/475), Numata Center for Buddhist Translation and Research, Berkeley, CA.

Patton, C. (trans.) (n.d.), *The Diamond Sutra.* Available from http://reluctant-messenger.com/diamond_sutra.htm (accessed 10 March 2015).

Pohl, K. H. (2004), "'... that to philosophize is to learn to die'—East and West: Montaigne's Views on Death Compared to Attitudes Found in the Chinese Tradition," in H. G. Möller and G. Wohlfart (eds), *Philosophieren über den Tod,* Edition Chora, Köln: 39–50.

Ramanan, K. V. (1966), *Nagarjuna's Philosophy,* Rutland VT and Tokyo: Charles E. Tuttle & Co.

Sarin, I. (2009), *The Global Vision: Karl Jaspers,* Bern: Peter Lang AG, Internationaler Verlag der Wissenschaften.

Streng, F. J. (1967), *Emptiness: A Study in Religious Meaning,* Nashville: Abingdon Press.

Suzuki, D. T. (1933), *Essays in Zen Buddhism (Second Series)*, London: Luzac.

Suzuki, D. T. (1985), *Essays in Zen Buddhism (Third Series)*, London: Luzac.

Unknown (n.d.), *Heart-Sutra*. Available from http://lapislazulitexts.com/shorter_prajnaparamita_hrdaya_sutra.html (accessed 10 March 2015).

Watson, B. (trans.) (1968), *The Complete Works of Chuang Tzu*, New York: Columbia University Press. Available from http://terebess.hu/english/chuangtzu.html (accessed 10 March 2015).

Watts, A. W. (1957), *The Way of Zen*, Harmondsworth: Penguin.

Wittgenstein, L. (1922), *Tractatus Logico-Philosophicus*, C. K. Ogden (trans.), London: Cosimo Classics. Available from http://www.gutenberg.org/ebooks/5740 (accessed 24 May 2015).

Wohlfart, G. (1998), "Sagen ohne zu sagen. Lao Zi und Heraklit—eine vergleichende Studie," *Minima sinica* 1: 24–39.

Wumen Huikai 無門慧開 (n.d.), 無門關 (Gateless Gate): Katsuki Sekida (trans.). Available from http://www.sacred-texts.com/bud/zen/mumonkan.htm (accessed 10 March 2015).

Xin, H. and Ren, J. (eds) (1992), *Neizai chaoyue zhi lu—Yu Yingshi xin ruxue lunzhu jiyao* (On the Road towards Immanent Transcendence: A Collection of Writings on Neo-Confucianism by Yu Yingshi), Peking: *Zhongguo guangbo dianshi chubanshe* (Chinese Broadcast and Television Publishing Company).

Yuan, Y. C. (1998), *Die Behandlung des Gegensatzes—über strukturelle Verwandtschaft zwischen Hegels "Logik" und Nagarjunas "Madhyamaka-Karika,"* Ph.D. Thesis, Universität des Saarlandes, Saarbrücken.

Part Two

Wisdom Compared

4

The Philosopher or the Sage? Apophaticism in Europe and China[1]

William Franke

François Jullien has expressed strong reservations on multiple occasions with regard to philosophies that appeal to the unsayable or, more exactly, "the ineffable," and to anything that has an odor of mysticism about it. I aspire to draw attention to other possibilities of thinking the unsayable, possibilities that he has perhaps not glimpsed or has not, in any case, seized upon, possibilities that nevertheless are comprehended under this word and its synonyms. I wish, however, to underscore that, in pursuing a thinking of the unsayable as I understand it, I find myself remarkably close to the thought of François Jullien, and in profound resonance with the overall motivating intentions of classical Chinese thinking as he presents it. My thinking resonates specifically with a thinking that opens itself to what precedes and exceeds the articulated and systematic thought of philosophy. Certainly, there are some disputes that would still separate François Jullien, at least at first, from a philosophy of the unsayable as I construe and advocate it. These disputes concern particularly the status and function of "transcendence," and what each of us refers to as the "theological." For François Jullien, it is a grave misunderstanding to want to find something theological in classical Chinese thought. His work undertakes to show the contrary in detail and sometimes with vehemence. Nevertheless, if one understands the theological by starting from negative theology, things are different, indeed radically different, and even the opposite of what they otherwise appear to be. A certain apophaticism is in its essence a rigorous and sometimes aggressive critique of every concept, especially of every theological concept. It is then not so surprising, after all, that apophatic theology should suggest important analogies with the fundamental tendencies of classical Chinese thought such as those that François Jullien has helped us to rediscover in provocatively new ways.

In fact, as an apophatic thinker, I am deeply indebted and grateful to François Jullien for having opened up to me a whole series of paths leading from Europe to China. My apophatic project advocating the *universality* uniquely of *that which is not* relies on the work of François Jullien as its indispensable path-breaker (*défricheur de chemin*) in entering the territory of intercultural philosophy. Jullien's work has enabled me to individuate aspects of Chinese thought that I understand as aspiring likewise to a type of universality that must necessarily remain implicit and which, so remaining, can in principle be only negative in any of its expressions.

I engage in this dialogue with François Jullien, furthermore, on the basis of a program of research, or, more exactly, of thought, that pivots on theology, or, more precisely, on negative theology taken as a critical resource and finally as a means of infinite self-criticism of every possible philosophical formulation.[2] This program parallels that of François Jullien, who utilizes Chinese culture as an astonishingly rich resource for a comprehensive and radical critique—in reality a self-critique—of Western philosophical thought, starting from the exterior vantage point provided by China. My critique is more internal in the sense that it issues from within Western tradition and even from its deepest and most buried roots, those that are least known and most misunderstood. I evoke the *interior* Other, that of Western apophaticism, which functions to a great extent in parallel with the *exterior* Other, that of China, which is insistently evoked throughout by François Jullien in his philosophical reflection, as remaining exogenous to, and having practically no contact with, European culture up to modern times.

In proposing a thinking that is turned always towards the other, I consider myself to come close in my approach to the method of François Jullien, as well as to be in line with a characteristic orientation within Chinese thought itself, one that he champions. And yet I entertain a relation to an Other that reveals itself to be other than his. The genre of thought in question fights shy of philosophy in the strict (and surely also reductive) sense—that is, of the proposition rigorously demonstrated; of logically argued and systematically developed discourse, or even of articulated language. This other-thinking is deployed rather in the margins and between the lines of strictly rational discourse. Thus, the point of such pronouncements is to be found, rather, in what they do not say, or not directly, anyway. It is what they, none the less, enable to be understood that allows us to open up a breach and create points of entry for what François Jullien designates as *wisdom* (*la sagesse*) in its distinction from philosophy (programmatically in *Un sage est sans idée*).

The apophatic can be found in the West, even before the Greeks, in divination and magic, and then in Greece, with its mysteries, notably the Eleusinian, and their rites executed in the form of pantomime, as well as in the cult of silence among diverse types of shamans and other sages and proto-philosophers up to Pythagoras, Empedocles, and Heraclitus. In such forms, the apophatic precedes and in a way anticipates the logos, even before accompanying it along the course of its historical journey. The apophatic, in effect, rewrites and redesigns the history of philosophy and even the pre-history of the logos in negative—undermining and subverting it from within, and from before its entry upon the scene. In forms barely discerned in negative by cultural anthropology, which sound out the night of time, furthermore, the vestiges of the apophatic remain, and mark a whole ensemble of traditions that are propounded in contestation of the logos and its hegemony across the entire trajectory of Western thought.

Neoplatonism begins, with Plotinus, to disconcert and confound the logical propositions of classical philosophy by an experience beyond the sayable. It eventually brings about the total collapse of the logos in the extreme and unsurpassable aporetics of Damascius (480–550 CE) at a historical point of closure for ancient philosophy—emblematically, with the dissolution in 529 of the Academy at Athens, of which Damascius was the last *diadochos* or "successor." Apophatic thought or wisdom is passed on from these thinkers to certain mystic philosophers of the Middle Ages, including Christian mystics such as Dionysius the Areopagite and John Scott Eriugena, as well as Sufis (Ibn Arabi) and Kabbalists (Moses de León). It is formulated then in a more critical-rationalist speculative vein by Maimonides and Meister Eckhart, by certain Scholastics, and by Nicolas Cusanus, but it also emerges eventually in the experiential mode of the Carmelite mystics and Silesius Angelus in the baroque era. It can be traced up to Romanticism, to this movement's revolts and excesses aiming at the infinite. And it emerges irrepressibly again in the calamitous erosion of confidence in rational discourse in the *fin de siècle* Vienna of Wittgenstein, Hugo von Hofmannsthal, and Fritz Mauthner. Gustav Klimt and Arnold Schoenberg, in their respective aesthetic media of painting and music, also pursue the expressiveness of silence. Finally, among myriad postmodern writers and thinkers, from Jacques Derrida and Maurice Blanchot to Samuel Beckett, there is a radical reflection on the inevitable failure of all narrowly rationalizing discourse. This reflection harbors a protest that murmurs all through the course of Western thought, but it resounds most intensely and insistently at pivotal epochs such as those highlighted in this historical synopsis.

It is in this alternative history, alternative even to history itself, that I propose to find the equivalents, or at least the analogues, of this perennial anti-philosophy for which François Jullien refers us to China, especially to its founding and most classic texts. At the same time, I wish to stress that François Jullien is himself a connoisseur of this other non-history of the non-logos in Western philosophy. Especially worthy of note are his subtle discussions, in *Le détour et l'accès*, chapter XII, paragraph 4, of Damascius at the culmination of ancient Greek apophatism.

Nevertheless, I do not want to give the impression that I am going to take up the advocacy of Western tradition, against the intentions of François Jullien to find at the source of Chinese wisdom that which seems to be lacking from the resources of Western thought in its most canonical forms. It is not by *refusing* the displacement to China but by *complementing* it through reflections bearing on this *other* Occident, that of the unsayable, that I propose to enter into dialogue with François Jullien. The unsayable is that which was never said or thought, except indirectly, throughout the (Western) history of thinking of the logos. Through comparison with Chinese thought it can be made to emerge finally as what this thought was really about, even while, for the most part, the unsayable went unidentified and unrecognized because of its inaccessibility to direct, methodical treatment by the logos. In this manner, I intend to integrate the indispensable insight that Jullien has gained through displacement to his Chinese heterotope, that is, by his disciplined exercise of taking up distance, voluntarily, from that which is most his own, in order to be able better to appropriate it, with more critical objectivity. In effect, the passage by way of the intercultural has shown itself to be equally inescapable for my own work. An apophatic philosophy, and in any case my own, cannot avoid becoming intercultural. It was already engaged upon the intercultural even before I knew that it was, and I follow François Jullien with enthusiasm along this path. I recognize in him an incomparable guide and leader in bringing to consciousness the intercultural turn of philosophy that has made such an indelible mark on our own epoch.

Thus, far be it from me to wish to abide within the West under the fallacious pretext that there is no need to go to the other end of the world in order to discover what we already have here in our midst, if we only wish to open our eyes. My idea is not to economize on the Chinese excursion. On the contrary, the spirit of apophaticism requires adventure abroad, even in the most foreign parts possible, including that which is foreign to the human altogether—by which I mean, for instance, the divine. Divinity is perhaps the most radical self-estrangement that human imagination can undertake to explore because it claims power and precedence over the human, depriving the latter of its sovereignty. Furthermore, and inseparably, this incitation to a vertical self-transcendence is expressed and realized concretely in the exigency of exposing oneself also, without exclusions, to all possible foreign encounters that present themselves along the horizontal axis of our encounter with other human cultures.

It is not, however, François Jullien's intention, in the end, to play different civilizations, particularly Europe and China, off against each other. His discourse aims rather at the globality which comprehends the two in a face-to-face encounter: this is a globality that *com*-prehends the two on the basis of the gap between them. I believe that, at root, I am working with the same intent as he is, or at least not against him, in attempting to individuate a type of wisdom that in the West, too, specifically in its apophaticism, gives the lie to the sovereign and magisterial pretensions of philosophy. Furthermore, we are united in the attempt to discover in the bosom of philosophy itself an alternative wisdom as dynamically alive in the work of self-critique.

In my view, then, it is not by categorically excluding the West from the genre of wisdom that China has developed so ingeniously that one will be able to better implement the critique of the logos and of its domination over virtually all modes of philosophical reflection. The differences between the two cultures show themselves to be comprehended finally in their common and even, in some sense, universal possibilities. I am convinced, especially through reading *De l'universel, de l'uniforme, du commun et du dialogue entre les cultures*, that it should be possible to reach a certain understanding with François Jullien on this head. I suspect that the major difference, the veritable and tenacious bone of contention between us in this dialogue, concerns rather our evaluation and, even more fundamentally, our underlying conceptions of theology.

Theology, in the discourse of François Jullien, has a tendency to assume the role of that which must be surpassed in order to liberate thought from the confining bonds that have too often held it captive in its most canonical expressions in the Occident. It is by means of a contrast with all theologizing thought that François Jullien is able to give a more precise (although admittedly only a negative) sense to the other possible (*l'autre possible*) of thinking which is dear to him—this other possibility of thinking which he assiduously works to bring to light and to valorize. Theology is deemed in his discourse, in common agreement with a good part of contemporary philosophical discourse in France and in the modern, secular West generally, to restrain and to vitiate the "possibles" of thought, to restrict their full range. According to this widely shared prejudice, the weight of theology and the imprint of the theological on

Western thought have been capable of arresting the progress of the authentic wisdom which, by contrast, the sages of China knew how to follow all the way to the end. Theology finds itself accused effectively of leading Western thought into a cul-de-sac.

Starting from this realization, Jullien seems to suggest, we ought to be able the better to discern the true possibles of thought here in Europe and China alike, and indeed universally. Thought, finally emancipated from theology, would, according to this scenario, be free from extraneous trammels and in a position to deploy itself infinitely. Thought would have failed to do so in the West up to the present because of the sway of the theological incumbent upon the ways and means followed by our thinking, for the most part unconsciously, ever since its Greek and Hebrew origins.

Is it really necessary, however, to inculpate and ostracize theology in this way, as a scapegoat in order to produce sense, and, particularly, in order to bring our thought to its most vital and fecund possibilities? The objective of the thinking that François Jullien develops through his reception of classical Chinese wisdom is to break with the practice that consists in making sense always a function of exclusion, thus relying on a binary logic of oppositions. It is rather through an orientation to globality that we seek sense or rather the *senses* that necessarily succeed one other and undo each other and—in any event—escape from every supposedly definitive formulation of sense. François Jullien performs such an openly inclusive movement of thought, by taking cues from Chinese models, and I do the same, basing myself on Occidental apophaticism.

A question that arises, at this point, is that of whether the possibles of thinking individuated by François Jullien in Chinese wisdom may not be available also to the West, specifically in its apophatic thinking. Or better, is it not the *im*possibles of thought (those seen and focused especially by what I call apophatic thought) which remain at the bottom of the two traditions as establishing the basis of the *universal* (im)possibles of thought? The possibles of thought exist always already (*immer schon*) as specifically determined by the languages and cultures within which they are thought, and thus as separate from one another. It is rather in colliding against that which it is *im*possible to think that all forms and varieties of thought meet together in a common impotence, one which can subsequently become infinitely productive. This impasse works productively in differentiated ways across innumerable cultures and their typological variations throughout geographical space and historical time.

Theology, thought negatively, has no thinkable or sayable content. It is not identified with any concept or with any thing at all but consists rather in the denial of the sufficiency of every concept and of every possible enunciation in the appeal and challenge to think them still further and still more deeply. St. Anselm's celebrated definition of God as "that than which nothing greater can be thought" is already perfectly apophatic. This formula prescribes only the imperative to press always further in pursuing the infinite potential to think always more.[3] This extension of the infinite, just as it excludes no possible from the being of God, likewise excludes none of the inexhaustible connections between all things, which also belong to the Creation and thus make up part of the infinite glory of the Creator. In effect, it is only through them and their immanent being that this glory of the transcendent being (*esse*), or God, can express itself, be it ever so little and inadequately. Thomas Aquinas makes this argument explicitly in *Summa theologiae* Ia, *Questio* 12 on how God is known by us ("Quomodo Deus a nobis conoscitur"), and it subtends his entire theological outlook.

A note of caution, however, is in order here. The "always more" that is in question signifies always more abnegation and always more radical critique of all that which seems to be established: thus it is not to be confounded with the ideology of heroism or of undertaking to do what is always more or even most difficult. Such idealisms are effectively critiqued by François Jullien, following his Chinese sources, for example, in his *Traité de l'efficacité*. In pages on "doing nothing" (*ne rien faire*), Jullien shows, in an apophatic spirit, that very often less *effort* produces more *effect*, and that remaining in retreat, holding back, not acting, can often prove more efficacious than charging ahead with all the force and impetuousness of overt, swashbuckling action (chapter VI). The focused nature of deliberate, willful action might be detrimental to keeping in step with and remaining receptive to the overall course of the universe in which all things are accomplished. As chapter 37 of the *Daodejing* observes: "Dao does nothing, yet nothing is left undone." We have to be able to look beyond our own projects so as to be able to see what is really done or left undone in the order of things that matters more than we can know or understand. What apophatic thought recommends, finally, is going always further only in the *dissolution* of all of the positive structures that shackle thought. This precisely is what the kenotic spirit of Christianity also does, and this self-critical practice is what apophatic theology raises to a level of conscious philosophical reflection.

In translating itself onto an existential and ethical terrain, theology valorizes itself as the most radical critical negation of self, because it implies a renunciation and abandonment of the very faculty of self-judgment. My own critical power subjects me to a Judge who is other than and more just than I. The radicality of unlimited self-critique and the radicality of the recognition of the other meet a certain limit in theology. For God is other with respect to all my thoughts and with respect to my very world itself, other to the point of being able to dispose of my being and of having a certain authority to command even my freedom, which can no longer take itself for absolutely sovereign. Theology aims towards a sphere beyond every concept, even beyond every supposedly theological concept. One can and certainly must mistrust any instance that, in the guise of a superior Subject, claims to authoritatively command one's own freedom. But one must remember that every *representation* of such an authority finds itself also immediately undermined by the uncompromising critique that is carried out by negative theology. What is aimed at in this recognition is reality itself, beyond every particular representation, reality as manifest rather in the course of things met with in the world as a whole. God is the God of all and is therefore revealed in all and everywhere rather than being confined to any one place or culture or language. This "All" may even include how things ought to be, beyond how they simply are already, since such a comprehensive reality cannot be opposed to idealities or to anything else.

The first absolute exigency of a negative theology is thus to take into account the globality of all. Of God, as ultimate reality beyond our capacity to know and even simply to conceive, nothing can be predicated, but nothing can be denied of or excluded from such a God either, as Pseudo-Dionysius clearly recognizes in *De caelesti hierarchia*, chapter 2, 141B. Everything is theophany and all things together constitute God's self-revelation, as Ibn al Arabi, likewise, affirms in *The Bezels of Wisdom*. At least at the level of the effective verdict, the course of things in the world is somehow the final judge (even if the world is never completely final either, not *this* world anyway). Classical Chinese thought, according to François Jullien, tends to refer to this process as the unique effective regulation of the world, and as without appeal. It is not that this "natural course of things" can be grasped in a realized form or as a fixed concatenation of causes, nor that it can be made immediately evident. It should certainly not be identified with empirical reality. On the contrary, it, too, is invisible and even, I would add, inconceivable as such, yet at the same time omni-conceivable: all possible conceptions grasp and reveal an aspect—or aspects—of it. The unlimited potential to remain in contact with all these possibles distinguishes the better part of wisdom.

One will surely object, but what need of the word "God" to say this? In effect, there is no logical necessity. But the fact is that the conceptions of God, as well as of the divine and the sacred, belong to the landscape, so to speak, or to the historical record of the nature-and-culture of humanity, which does not exclude certainly the dimension of *being a person* from the whole of things. It is not by eliminating the personal from our conception of either the divine or the sacred, or even simply of nature, that we discover the truth in its nakedness. It is rather by inclusion of all that which belongs to history as well as to nature (the two being inconceivable, at least for us, except in their mutual reciprocity) that we are able to attune ourselves to the natural course of things, which includes our own evolution as well. Not to presume to guide this process, but rather to give or surrender oneself to it by realizing one's own potentials without limit, taking into consideration that in any case one cannot escape from this larger, all-encompassing context, is the theological gesture par excellence when it is stripped down to its epitome. That this whole be personalized or not is not the essential thing, given the fact that the concept of the person, like every concept, serves only to open thought to that which surpasses every concept—in this case, specifically, every concept of the person.

In trusting oneself to the whole to which one belongs, the theologically believing "person" recognizes that which is "God" or "transcendence" or "the unconditioned" or "the absolute" or … In fact, all these terms are employed only in order to be subsequently emptied of sense, in order to be broken open to the inconceivability of the infinite relations that traverse us and that constitute us, even as they constitute the world. Neither is the essential thing the manner in which one conceives of the theological or figures it at the outset, considering that every conception, like every figuration, is irremediably inadequate and only serves to be surpassed. It is in accepting the "apophatic" conditioning of our historically evolved being that we are best able, starting from our own different situation as Occidentals, to reach the wisdom promulgated by Chinese classics in for us their most authentic and potentially valuable possibilities. If I persist in qualifying this procedure as "theological," I do so out of respect for the history of this discourse and its preeminence as a matrix of some of the most radical, searching, and sophisticated reflection on the limits of language and its necessary failure vis-à-vis reality. In theological tradition, discourse is rendered particularly *fertile* in its relation to the reality of ultimate, extreme possibles, but also in relation to those possibles that are the most banal and omni-present.

The theological, conceived thus, is not a theme or a content or a concept. It is of the order of the imaginary and of the practical as well—of the practice of infinite critique for the purpose of opening oneself to the inconceivable totality of the world that can only be imagined (or be thought metaphorically). This does not amount to representing the world definitively as any representable thing or as circumscribed by any notion, or by no matter what concept. The world intended here is nothing delimited but is rather in the process of transcending *itself* by means of becoming always other. I submit that allowing this self-transcending to take place and to be realized by means of dismantling all our restrictive conceptualities is the effective operation of the theological such as it is carried out by apophatic critique throughout Occidental history, but equally, even if in other words and terms, by Chinese wisdom such as we are led to discover it in its remarkable apophatic subtlety by the studies of François Jullien.

Theology would seem to be on the side of the foundational, the assured, the ideal. However, thought negatively, it is in fact just the opposite: theology opens thought to its own abyss. Moreover, apophatic theology thinks not only on the basis of abstractions, but more essentially on the basis of the incarnate, of the flesh and the sensory, which are always inexhaustible and thus ungraspable in their concreteness. In France, protagonists of the famous "theological turn" of phenomenology have been particularly insightful in demonstrating and in underscoring this indefinable, infinitely interpretable and fertile valence of names such as "God." This is verified by the metaphors deriving from the super-latively rich archives of theology concerning the phenomenologically "given" in the works of Michel Henry, Jean-Luc Marion, Jean-Louis Chrétien, and others. Thomas-Olivier Venard, Jean-Ives Lacoste, and Jean-Luc Nancy also deserve citation as authors who, in our time, are leading the way in renewing theological language in its apophatic registers.

Of course, there is a certain dogmatic theology that is stagnant in its refusal to think anything new, a kind of theology that could and perhaps should be delivered up for ritual banishment and sacrifice, if only these were able to preserve or restore to health the community of thinkers. But should that "theology" alone be allowed to represent what is understood under this name by contemporary thought striving to become genuinely open to all possible senses and challenges? This sclerotic theology, which repeats its fixed formulas without (re)thinking them, exists, but that does not give us a right (and much less a good reason) to ignore the incomparable resources for the most original thinking also conveyed by theology in its astonishing creativity in virtually any epoch of culture. Neither should we neglect its unlimited potential as a form of thinking that reaches beyond the limits of the logos and capable, consequently, of defying and unsettling, and thereby renewing thought still today. In effect, we stumble here upon exactly the same objectives as those expressly advanced by François Jullien.

One can treat negative theology as a variant or deviant form of theology, an attempt to recuperate it and so to save it from succumbing to otherwise devastating critiques; or else, inversely, one can understand negative theology as the first matrix of theological thought and, more broadly, of critical thinking per se, recognizing the fundamentally negative status of thought as such. François Jullien knows negative theology and expounds some of its source texts, particularly texts in Plotinus and Damascius, but he seems to consider it most often as derivative rather than as standing at the origin of theology and of the logos as such. One ought, however, as he well knows, to consider things in their first arising and full potential (*essor*) rather than only in the limited actualizations that derive from them. It is not the pious repetitions of the platitudinous *discourse* of theology that one must view primarily, but rather the seminal insights and creative inspiration from which it arises. Every meaningful discourse is preceded, or is at least potentially exceeded, by an event of thought, of illumination in darkness. This is emphatically underscored by apophatic thought, which in this respect corresponds to Chinese wisdom as it is revealed to us by François Jullien.

This leads us to confront the delicate question: is there not, after all, something that is quasi-theological in China, something held in common between Chinese wisdom and theological wisdom, specifically in its apophatic form, which is to say in its being *un*formed or without form, according to the slogan "the great image has no form" that is taken by François Jullien from the *Book of Dao*? Something of this order is what I am attempting to place into evidence. And yet negative theology is nothing definable. It escapes from every attempt at characterization. It intimates truth only in giving the lie to every effort to lend substance and an assured status to the real in its foundations (figured as divine). Therefore, a philosophical approach can proceed only by indirect and specifically critical routes. Indeed, in the end, negative theology does not even "exist," as Jacques Derrida already suspected in his efforts to take on this "impossible" subject (see esp. Derrida 1992).

In an analogous manner, "the evidence of things" evoked by Jullien insistently and confidently cannot be grasped directly but rather only by way of the negation that it implies. Therefore, given that negative theology does not have any consistency that would permit it to be grasped as such, and that it is perceived only by its effects, exactly like Chinese wisdom in Jullien's exegesis of it, and that it does not perhaps even exist, it cannot be made manifest except negatively, through demonstration of the vanity of the attempts to refuse, or even to undermine and deny, it.

I will just note in passing that it is possible to glimpse here the great question of a truly fundamental difference between a thinking axised on reflexivity, such as that of the West all through its philosophical tradition, including negative theology, and an approach that ignores reflexivity, one of thought that simply opens itself to the other naturally, as if by instinct. And yet we could also say: "by its reflexes." The word is significant! Thought can and perhaps must be understood as reflection from its earliest beginnings. In the end, Jullien does not maintain that Chinese culture is not just as reflective as Western culture is. And, conversely, neither does the *via negativa* exclude the movement "upstream" (*en amont*), to a stage preceding reflection, in order to find a completely "instinctive" response that no longer retains anything negative. The *negatio negationis*, too, might eventually take away all negativity—"take all away" (*aphele panta* ἄφελε πάντα) as Plotinus urges—and teach us to reflect no longer. This has indeed been the approach typical of numerous mystics in their quest for utter simplicity. As thought negatively, reflection endeavors to reflect itself out of the circle of reflection itself.

Apart from these possibilities, which exceed the limits of philosophy, the justification for evoking negative theology consists in the insufficiency of any philosophy based on a description of the world that excludes such possibles. Hence the insufficiency of pure "immanence" understood as the exclusion of transcendence. We know very well that the theological question can play itself out also in terms of transcendence versus immanence. Employing one of the most common modes of rejecting the theological, Jullien often insists on immanence as the key to Chinese thought. He emphasizes how Greek thought, by contrast, from Plato onwards took the way of transcendence, with his theory of ideas, which are also ideals. Jullien emphasizes, furthermore, how, even before Plato, notably in his teacher Pythagoras, the bias towards transcendence was already inscribed in the penchant for mathematical formalization that exits the world of the sensible and concrete in favor of abstractions. The same goes for the laws, and even for law as *eros*, whether as object or as engenderer of desire: all of these foundations of Western civilization display a sharp tendency to turn elsewhere and to look beyond the evidence of lived reality, as it is given to the senses, for the principles that found, justify, and motivate the course of the world. They postulate a base separate from this reality in its concrete and immediate manifestation.[4]

However, François Jullien knows that it is not enough to make himself the advocate of immanence without taking account also of the transcendence that it seems only nominally to exclude. His choice, like that of opting for China, cannot be a choice simply for immanence, to the exclusion of transcendence—if, indeed, it were even a matter of a choice, since human choices, in this view, are always secondary to the propensities of things themselves. This genre of discourse always runs the risk of falling into binary dichotomies from which, in fact, Jullien wishes to liberate us. Accordingly, it is necessary to recognize the weight and operativity of a certain species of transcendence even in classical Chinese culture.

Jullien affirms, for example, in the concluding chapter of *Dialogue sur la morale* that Chinese wisdom, in the form of moral consciousness, gives access to the unconditioned, but he denies that the unconditioned can be represented in a stable or adequate manner. In other words, "Heaven" is an expression for that which constantly escapes from every finite representation but which nevertheless must be pursued infinitely by a chain of metaphorical indications and incitements that is never terminated nor even terminable.

My approach begins from the observation that we cannot think of immanence as a separate thing or as an objective fact. At most, we can speak of *representations* of immanence and equally of *representations* of transcendence, and at this level of representation it is perfectly clear that the one, immanence, is the negation or the opposite of the other, transcendence, and for this reason is implicated in it—of course, as denied, but nevertheless as at least *implicitly* thought, conceived, said. Therefore it is not a question of choosing one, rather than, or without, the other. Transcendence *is* immanence, and vice versa, whenever one withdraws from, and despairs of, the very possibility of its representation. The whole is there in immanence, in the *between* (Jullien's *entre*): the beginning and the end are only representations projected from this between. Yet the "between" itself remains unsoundable and inexhaustible. The mystery and the unconditionedness of transcendence are already there, fully present and potent in the "between." All that is real and lived in transcendence is effective prior to its representation: the representation can and must be dispensed with. It is the same procedure as in negative theology, which likewise dispenses with representations of God, the transcendent par excellence. Presumably liberation in the name of immanence would mean that one had no need of transcendence, but it was only by negating the *representations* of transcendence that one conceived of immanence in the first place. It is, finally, only the outside and the beyond of representation that is cogently aimed at in this term "transcendence," and the same holds for "immanence." Thought radically, either term means, and reminds us, that the world of representations is not sufficient unto itself but is compelled instead to explode into an infinite series of representations.

Apophatic consciousness constrains us always to pay attention to this difference that the fact of representing or of saying something makes. Jullien finely analyses this predicament in his book, *Si parler va sans dire: Du logos et d'autres ressources* (1988), on whether "speaking" goes without "saying" and on the resources of the logos. Things and reality in their globality are not accessible for us, except as so many negations of our sayings. Things as such are always that which cannot be said. They are in this sense *impossibles* of thought—and *impossibles* of saying. Thought and its possibles thus meet a certain unsurpassable limit, one that is impossible for it to think. But it is starting precisely from here that we must think—thus without being able first to establish a foundation that is justified and capable of accounting for itself and susceptible of systematic elaboration. I believe that, despite their hailing from two culturally and historically different worlds, Chinese wisdom and Western apophatic discourse are comparable in the face of the radical failure of saying in its inability to grasp the real in the way envisaged by the logical proposition. The two cultures have no common measure, but they share one and the same problem, to which they respond in their respective styles, and these are as different as can be.

I would wager to say, finally, that the predisposition of Chinese wisdom to rely on the natural inclination of the heart (*xin*), and thus to follow the incessant natural course of change inherent in things themselves, rather than to impose formal models of thought on the basis of theoretical considerations, amounts to a manner of incarnating the *dis-position* that is infinitely open and which I call "theological"—in a negative sense, of course. It is only in distrusting the artifice of thought that is not guided by the natural evolution of things, and consequently in negating our own constructions superimposed on reality, that we let things be what they are and permit them to manifest their *thus* (*ainsi*, in Jullien's vocabulary) in the spirit of *Gelassenheit* or "letting be" as described, for example, by Meister Eckhart.

The authentic theological mode of thinking does not consist essentially in positing a concept of the Supreme Being or of anything else, whatever it may be, but in the fact of giving over every concept to a higher understanding and a more all-encompassing consciousness than one's own. God is for us the inconceivable par excellence. To recognize God or the divine is nothing else but trusting oneself in practice and in life to the order of things as they might be "upstream" from every intervention concocted by human thought and institutions, with their models and ideals, their differentiations and definitions. I say "God" because things are infinitely variable and in this sense ungraspable and therefore susceptible to being expressed in the richest and most fertile vocabulary we possess for indicating the infinite, the interminable, and the unfathomable. I have no illusions that it will be easy for us to be in agreement about this. Only our lives themselves can persuade us of one or another vocabulary as being more conformable to, or more revealing of, the depth of our experience—and of its fecundity. Philosophically speaking, it is only critique that enables us to exchange points of view, permitting us no longer to keep to our own particular perspectives but, instead, to allow them to evolve without fetters. Such critique requires that we hold our "convictions" in suspense, at least rhetorically, however indispensable they may prove to be in practice.

Of course, such a reflective posture of suspicion, even vis-à-vis oneself, is an attitude characteristic of the Occident: it is Cartesian par excellence in its prizing philosophical doubt as a self-evident value. Jullien denies that such a predisposition to doubt is prevalent in classical Chinese thought. Nevertheless, I propose self-suspension as a particular approach to a common, or even a universal possibility—one which would be neither an affirmation nor a position but rather the abandoning of all fixed determinations, and this *is* quintessentially characteristic of classic Chinese thought as Jullien construes it. For this purpose, it is necessary to look beyond language and its fixed forms and categorical norms. It is only the dynamism of language, or poetic language in its creative emergence, which can indicate this "beyond" of language itself, where the word strives toward its destination through a constant suspension or transcendence of itself. François Jullien himself observes how in China "this commonality which is the condition of possibility of discussion never arises in the discussed" (*"ce commun qui est la condition de possibilité de la discussion n'affleurant jamais dans le discuté"*), and thus "the veritable stake of the word finds itself always outside the word and the true conversation is tacit" (*"l'enjeu véritable de la parole se trouve toujours hors parole et le véritable entretien est tacite"* [2006: 106]). I think that this is valid not only for China but universally.

The common for the Daoist is found not in that which is articulated in a discourse, or more exactly in a dia-logue, but rather in the retraction of words, or in the retreat from linguistic formulations in the face of the unconstrued course of things. This is necessary in order to remove the partial, biased, and exclusive viewpoints inherent in words, as François Jullien says, in specifying that the common intelligence aimed at by the Daoist thinker realizes itself "by reabsorption of words accompanying the dissolution of points of view" (*"par résorption des paroles accompagnant la dissolution des points de vue,"* [2006: 109]). That means reabsorption into the total receptivity that reigned at the stage before all enunciations and before the inevitably exclusive choices made by any discourse. All this converges completely with the modalities of apophatic discourse. Accordingly, I find that Jullien develops from his Chinese sources, in exemplary fashion, exactly what I understand to be apophatic philosophy.

If I might, nevertheless, be allowed to avow what I find, all the same, to be a limit to the opening in principle without limits discovered in the works of my partner in this "dialogue," I would observe that there are some factors in contemporary lay French culture which militate powerfully against a com-prehension of theology, and that commonly conspire in devaluing, delegitimizing, and deriding it, or even, much worse, in rendering it obscure. These factors are anticlericalism and certain triumphalistic versions of the philosophy of the Enlightenment. François Jullien, like his public, is sensitive to both, and to such an extent that they are practically preconditions of the very intelligibility of discourse, or at least of its persuasiveness, in the highly laicized France of today. This is, after all, the intellectual milieu or community of interpretation which François Jullien most directly addresses through his ideas and writings.

As much as political correctness in France hardly allows laicism to be questioned, nevertheless history furnishes much evidence that, wherever religion and civil society are cut off and isolated from each other, both turn out as a result to be denatured and become, in certain respects, incomprehensible to one another. The authentic religiosity of the human being is not something other than its social tie, not therefore something to exclude, and neither does society hold together without taking into account this dimension, among all the others, including the infinity of the relations with others that constitute us as human. The true or the best comprehension of human affairs is found "upstream" (*en amont*) from divisions and separations such as those constituted by the dictates of laicism—this holds even for the purpose of understanding the advantages and perhaps the practical necessity of a compromise arrangement such as that of laicism itself. Laicism, I submit, needs to rediscover its own religious roots, in a negatively theological sense, in an unavowable, unconfessable, but none the less indispensable, community (Blanchot 1983).[5]

I believe that the thought of François Jullien, in its continuing evolution, is on the way to placing into question these prejudices typical of his intellectual world. His work itself may begin to suggest how these fixed positions, these biases, as well as their opposites, are at risk of becoming cultural blindnesses or atavisms. Most recently, Jullien's *De l'intime* develops a reflection giving to transcendence its full phenomenological value within the experience in question. Here he taps sources such as the Fathers of the Church (Gregory of Nyssa and Augustine in particular) for their valuable illuminations.

Nevertheless, reflex and sometimes scornful or contemptuous rejections of all imagination of an other world or of a life after death still appear in the texts of Jullien. These rejections serve as fixed points and ready references for an assured common sense, a reliable basis of consensus for the philosophy that François Jullien is in the process of elaborating. Yet the definitive exclusion of the sense that such imaginations of the otherworldly might have for the cultures and communities that invented them, that made them evolve, that believed in them, and that lived in and through them, does not seem to me to accord with the exigency of hospitable reception for all possibles of thought. This reception, of course, must be highly differentiated and must take account of our own context and positioning. However, it is necessary to find the means of recognizing their part of possibility in each of these beliefs or ideologies or visions of the world, whatever they may be, without any exclusions in principle, on the sole condition that they be authentically held and lived out by human beings.

I do not expect that my own *parti pris* for theology will be shared, but I can none the less advance a critique against the exclusion of a form of thought that participates essentially in human culture and its evolution. Some would maintain, taking up one aspect alone of Hegel, that the historical role of theology is obsolete. Yet such teleologies always have in them something paradoxically ideological and practically theological in a very positivistic sense. That this purported historical advance is illusory is difficult for we "postmoderns" to ignore, for we have become hyper-conscious of the insidious traps of belief in ideologies of progress.

The possibility that there is something beyond the process of the world, namely, transcendence, or God, is for thought a question of how to represent the world—as either with or without gaps, that is, as opening up or not to its own exterior. The two positions are possible and perhaps even necessary (as in Kant's antinomy of the world as finite and as infinite—both necessary and yet mutually exclusive hypotheses). It is not a question of choosing between the two but of inhabiting the divine milieu from which the two possibles—and all con-possibles—emerge. God, or transcendence, cannot be represented except as the condition and at the same time the *negation* of all possible representations, that is, as the unrepresentable, as the unconditioned, which is nevertheless indirectly or virtually manifest in all representations. Such is the theology that I draw from the sources of apophatic wisdom. I believe that François Jullien envisages something not terribly different, at root, when he interprets the *Dao* as follows:

> By the virtuality that it owes to its constant arising, upstream from the concrete, it refuses to let itself be confined within any particular actualization making it

manifest within the visible. But it is also from this inexhaustible effectiveness at work and too subtle and diffuse not to remain invisible, that every manifestation of existence proceeds (Jullien 2006: 86).[6]

This conception of the origin of the phenomenon as bottomless excludes only a simplistic and realistic conception of God as a thing, the greatest and most powerful Thing of all. And such a reifying conception should likewise resolutely be excluded, or rather relativized, by negative theology. I would specify, however, that an agreement on this may be valid for us in our habitual context among modern, self-reflective intellectuals, but not necessarily in all other contexts. In any case, it is not valid in the same way and according to the same mechanisms. Historically, the least reflective beliefs in God might be expressive of the most authentic experience on the part of a certain people in its course of evolution. The exclusion of belief sanctioned by this argument is only an exclusion relative to our situation and its exigencies and priorities. And philosophy itself certainly belongs among these culturally relative modes of life and relation.

In the end, philosophy itself, as articulate, categorizing, divisive discourse, is perhaps a species of vanity. Philosophical discourse as it is revealed in the light of Chinese wisdom according to François Jullien might be destined to annihilate itself, to draw back before a wisdom that exists only in order to withdraw from its own word. In this, François Jullien would join, *malgré lui*,[7] not only the sages of ancient China but also the apophatic thinkers of Europe and of all times and places: the universal would reveal itself, before all, as that which cannot be said.

Coda

This "dia-logue" has unfolded by necessity in and through words. The question I am left with is this: does it pass through (*dia*) words (*logoi*) in order to go beyond them? Otherwise expressed, is there something else here to savor besides the words? One could ask, in an analogous fashion, is there something else to be lived besides life itself? Death, for example? These are questions that remain open and that intrigue me, all the more so since I sense that the (disavowed) wisdom of François Jullien would be likely to tend in a completely different direction, one opposed to my own *parti pris*. I conclude, therefore, that I still have more to learn from this remarkable thinker.

Notes

1   This chapter is elaborated from an exposition delivered, in its original French redaction, in the presence of François Jullien and addressed to scholars of his work at the colloquium "Des possible de la pensée: Autour des travaux de François Jullien" in Cerisy-la-Salle, France, September 15, 2013, and published as (2015) "Le dia-logue et son au-delà apophatique: avec François Jullien," in Françoise Gaillard and Philippe Ratte (eds), *Des possibles de la pensée: L'itinéraire philosophique de François Jullien*, Paris: Éditions Hermann, 277–98.

2   We might recall that Jean Trouillard, in "Valeur critique de la mystique Plotinienne," pertinently defined negative theology as "infinite critique" (440). He is followed by Hilary Armstrong in "The Escape of the One: An Investigation of Some Possibilities of Apophatic Theology Imperfectly Realised in the West," in *Plotinian and Christian Studies*, XXIIII, who on page 87 defines negative theology as "limitless criticism."

3   It is so read, for example, by Karl Barth in his *Fides quaerens intellectum: Anselms Beweis der Existenz Gottes im Zusammenhang seines theologischen Programms*.

4   This is Jullien's theme especially in *L'invention de l'idéal et le destin de l'Europe*.

5   This has, after all, been the view of that most outstanding representative in our time of the philosophy of the Enlightenment, Jürgen Habermas, especially in *Glauben und Wissen: Friedenspreis des deutschen Buchhandels 2001*. It is also implicit and sometimes explicit in the far-reaching projects of Giorgio Agamben, beginning with *Homo sacer* and notably in *Il regno e la gloria. Per una genealogia teologica dell'economia e del governo. Homo sacer II, 2*.

6   In the original: "*Par la virtualité qu'il doit à son constant essor, en amont du concret, il ne se laissera cantonner dans aucune actualisation particulière le manifestant au sein du visible. Mais c'est aussi de cette effectivité inépuisablement à l'œuvre, et trop subtile et diffuse pour ne pas demeurer invisible, que procède toute manifestation d'existence.*"

7   Jullien dissociates himself from the figure of the sage, especially in part II of *Un sage est sans idée*.

Works cited

Agamben, G. (1995), *Homo Sacer: Il potere soverano e la vita nuda*, vol. 1, Turin: Einaudi.

Agamben, G. (2007), *Il regno e la gloria. Per una genealogia teologica dell'economia e del governo. Homo sacer II, 2*. Vicenza: Neri Pozza.

Armstrong, H. (1979), *Plotinian and Christian Studies*, London: Variorum Reprints.

Barth, K. (1981 [1931]), *Fides quaerens intellectum: Anselms Beweis der Existenz Gottes im Zusammenhang seines theologischen Programms*, Zürich: Theologischer Verlag. The English translation is (1975) *Fides quaerens intellectum: Anselm's Proof of the Existence of God in the Context of his Theological Scheme*, I. W. Robertson (trans.), Pittsburgh: Pickwick Press.

Blanchot, M. (1983), *La communauté inavouable*. Paris: Minuit.

Derrida, J. (1992), "How to Avoid Speaking: Denials," in H. Coward and T. Foshay (eds), *Derrida and Negative Theology*, Albany: State University of New York Press, 73–142; originally (1987) "Comment ne pas parler: Dénégations," in *Psyché: Inventions de l'autre*, Paris: Galilée, 435–95.

Franke, W. (2007), *On What Cannot Be Said: Apophatic Discourses in Philosophy, Religion, Literature, and the Arts*, W. Franke (ed.), 2 vols, Notre Dame: University of Notre Dame Press.

Franke, W. (2014), *A Philosophy of the Unsayable*, Notre Dame: University of Notre Dame Press.

Habermas, J. (2001), *Glauben und Wissen: Friedenspreis des deutschen Buchhandels 2001*, Frankfurt a. M.: Suhrkamp.

Jullien, F. (1988), *Un sage est sans idée, ou l'autre de la philosophie*, Paris: Seuil.

Jullien, F. (1995), *Le détour et l'accès: Stratégies du sens en Chine, en Grèce*. Paris: Grasset.

Jullien, F. (1996), *Traité de l'efficacité*, Paris: Grasset.

Jullien, F. (2006), *Si parler va sans dire*, Paris: Seuil.

Jullien, F. (2009), *L'invention de l'idéal et le destin de l'Europe*, Paris: Seuil.

Jullien, F. (2013), *De l'intime: Loin du bruyant amour*, Paris: Grasset.

Trouillard, J. (1961), "Valeur critique de la mystique Plotinienne," *Revue philosophique de Louvain* 59.

5

Wisdom as Knowledge and Wisdom as Action: Plato, Heidegger, Cicero, and Confucius

Paul Allen Miller

One of the most salient points of comparative work and particularly of work between what can at least at first appear to be the incommensurable traditions of discourse in Europe and Asia is the uncovering of different conceptions and practices of wisdom. If we compare the earliest texts of Chinese philosophy with the founding moments of Western philosophy, particularly in Plato, we quickly discover, most especially if we are working within dominant traditional self-understandings of each tradition, that their precomprehension of what it means to make a true statement, of what it means to be wise, of what it means to hold a meaningful discourse, seems to be very different. From an all too typically arrogant position of Western philosophy, we are told that the Confucian texts, the early Buddhist scriptures, the *Dao*, are, if not simply confused, then mere repositories of a certain practical wisdom, but certainly not philosophy, not discourses of truth. Yet what is revealed by the exercise of translation across the centuries and across cultures—translation both as a linguistic and a hermeneutic practice—is how problematic all these categories are, and how ultimately they are not adequate to their own traditions, covering over as much as they reveal. In short, what I want to argue is, first, that an attentive reading of the Confucian texts or, I would submit, of early Buddhist texts, and I am sure of others as well, with which I am less familiar, can be used to destabilize our own self-understanding and open our discourse, and, perhaps more importantly, our students' discourse, to new practices, new languages, and new arts of wisdom and truth. The second thing I want to argue is that reading from within this comparative perspective, that is, both across space and across time, reveals these traditions themselves to be more heterogeneous, more divided against themselves, than previously thought.

In what follows, I shall first briefly outline Heidegger's concept of Western metaphysics and its relation to truth and Plato's myth of the cave. I shall then look at Foucault's concept of spiritual practice as an alternative concept of truth, not as something seen or stated but as something done, as the love of wisdom. This counterhegemonic position will be shown to exist already within the Platonic corpus itself in texts such as the "Seventh Letter" and the *Laws*, but even in such metaphysical classics as the parable of the divided line. I will argue that it can also be seen within the rhetorical tradition, particularly within the works of Cicero, wherein the distinction between knowledge and action is consistently undermined, and hence that between subject and object, knower and known. I will then turn to certain representative Confucian texts to demonstrate the presence of analogous conceptions of wisdom in the foundational texts of the East Asian tradition. In so doing, I will show that what appears at first to be a discourse of resistance in the West—although one that upon reflection turns out to be the common currency of poetry, rhetoric, and the spiritual—functions instead as the dominant in the wisdom traditions of the East, even as each discourse retains its own particular characteristics.

We begin then with Heidegger, the thinker whose conceptualization of Western metaphysics has proven formative for the last eighty years of European philosophical thought, even as his political legacy has become increasingly troubling. It was Heidegger's contention that the regime of truth under which the West operates was installed most visibly with Plato's myth of the cave (Oudemans and Lardinois 1987: 229; Heidegger 1998: 155). In Heidegger's formulation, *aletheia* ἀλήθεια, the Greek word for "truth," or literally the "unhidden," becomes with Plato a property not of Being's self-revelation but of the relation between already constituted subjects and objects (Heidegger 1998: 167–8, 178; Jones 2011: 189). Truth after Plato's myth of the cave is not located in the realm of Being, the ground of existence, but in that of the "ontic" or the world of entities and objects that we, as subjects, relate to the concepts we possess of their nature, concepts which are either more or less correct (*orthos*, cf. Heidegger 1962: 31). Thus, the humans chained in Plato's cave relate the images projected on the wall before them to the understandings they have formulated of their nature, while the enlightened philosopher on a higher plane relates the phenomenal world of things to their ideal essences (Plato 1997: *Republic* 515b4–c2 and 517b4–6).

Truth, in this world, is a property of the thoughts of the subject, not of the world that enfolds both consciousness and its other (Heidegger 1998: 177, 182; Mortensen 1994: 180–1). This shift in the nature and concept of truth, Heidegger claims, is the beginning of metaphysics (Heidegger 1998: 181). What Heidegger means by "metaphysics" is representational thinking: in the post-Platonic tradition, the world exists for us as a series of "pictures," which are judged and evaluated through the concepts possessed by the subject (Heidegger 1982). Philosophy is the critique, refinement, and manipulation of those concepts. Metaphysics for Heidegger takes the world as a closed unity whose objects exist for use: a finite set of means to a pre-existing set of ends. Life becomes a problem for technology to solve (Irigaray 1984: 123; Mortensen 1994: 80).

Now, I do not want to take Heidegger's reading as absolute, and indeed I am going to problematize it a little later, below, but I do think it does a good job of describing one vision of truth and philosophy that has been dominant in the West and that still dominates most Western social, scientific, and educational thinking, and in our globalized community has become increasingly hegemonic. It assumes at its core a free-standing subject who makes more or less accurate statements about a world of objects that stand in simple opposition to that subject: this is the world of the countable, of technology, and of outcomes assessment. It is the world of classical Newtonian science and of the Cartesian subject. Philosophy, the love of wisdom, on this view becomes the art of insuring that our statements portray an accurate relationship between our mental representations and their external objects (logic), of refining those representations in conformity with their objects (epistemology), and of properly delimiting the nature of the objects to be represented (metaphysics). It becomes the cop on the beat of knowledge, a kind of consumer protection bureau in the market place of ideas.

But as Michel Foucault has argued, within Western philosophy, beginning with Plato himself, there exists an alternative tradition that he labels "spiritual practice":

> The research, the practice, the experience, by which the subject operates on himself the transformations necessary in order to have access to the truth. We will call "spirituality", then the body of researches, practices, and experiences, which can be purifications, practices, renunciations, turning of the gaze [as in the cave], and modifications of existence that constitute, not for knowledge, but for the subject, for the very being of the subject, the price to pay for access of the truth. (Foucault 2001: 16–17)

The primary example might well be the passage from Plato's "Seventh Letter" in which authentic knowledge is described as coming not from written summaries of things known—and hence from the mere truth or falsity of the statements contained therein—but from the continual interaction between master and student (*tribē*) that produces the spark of enlightenment (Plato 1997: 341b–e). This interaction, I would contend, can be seen also in various ironic practices in the dialogues themselves, in which what seem to be statements of truth or falsity are called into question, undermined, or reinterpreted from a radically different perspective.

Thus, while Plato is exhibit *A* in Heidegger's thesis on the dawn of metaphysics in the West, he is also in many ways its strongest, because initial, point of resistance. Heidegger would not disagree, per se. Plato is for him the hinge on which the pivot toward the metaphysical first occurs, but, as such, Plato represents a movement between two understandings of truth and wisdom or, better, of truth versus wisdom. The myth of the cave is not the culmination of that movement, but its beginning.

In fact, as Foucault and others have understood, the Platonic text provides some of the strongest moments of resistance to metaphysical Platonism (Derrida 1993: 81–3; Jones 2011: 43; Sallis 1999: 48–9; Wolff 1992: 241–2; Zuckert 1996: 72, 235). Even such metaphysical classics as the parable of the divided line (in which is described the move from representation to the noetic realm of the ideal, on which all representation is said to depend, and which can therefore be said to be philosophy's true object) turns out always to have an inassimilable remainder, always to have a moment of excess that undermines the separation of subject, object, and representation on which philosophy as the pursuit of wisdom is said to depend. In short, while the parable of the divided line appears to posit a moment beyond representation on which representation itself (and hence all the divisions of the ontic world that flow therefrom) is predicated, in point of fact the parable itself reveals the impossibility of that purely transcendental moment's ever arriving. Indeed, if we read carefully the final description of the noetic in the critical passage, we quickly see that rather than qualifying it as the exclusion of the world of semblance (*doxa*) and of likeness (*eikōn*), it asserts the impossibility of completely escaping that world, even as it posits a different use and different relationship to the *doxic* or to "the way things seem." What follows is a very literal translation that strives to make apparent the complex semantic and imagistic play in Plato's Greek:

> This then is the *eidos* of the intelligible (*noēton*) of which I was speaking with the soul compelled to use the assumptions it has put under itself (*hupothesesi*)[1] concerning the pursuit of this *eidos*, not going to the first principle (*archēn*), since it is not able to step out from (*ekbainein*) and above its assumptions,

but using as likenesses (*eikosi*) the things from which likenesses are made (*apeiskatheisin*) below and those things which in relation to those others have been judged manifest in accordance with their appearance (*enargesi dedoxasmenois*) and are honoured. (cf. Plato 1997: *Republic* 511a4–9)

The noetic, then, is not a realm of pure intellection. Even at the top of the divided line, the soul's intellection is dependent on the hypotheses that it has placed under itself as assumptions like steps or scaffolding: it is an action dependent on a base. The noetic does not escape representation (*eikosi*). It does not escape inscription. But its relation to representation is different from either immediate experience or *dianoia*, thought, "thinking-through." Rather than taking its assumptions as axioms to be used to create deductions in the manner of a geometric proof, the noetic soul uses those assumptions themselves as likenesses. These mental images are opined/judged/believed in (*doxazō*) on the basis of the way they seem to be clear or visible (*enargēs*) in relation to the more common category of images; that is to say, on the basis of the way they appear. These likenesses are not used to create self-identical chains of deduction but to explore their own premises and that which lies beyond them. In this way the philosopher is not trapped in a purely self-referential dream as in the cave (*onar*), but is the one who has a vision that points beyond itself (*hupar*) by refusing to leave its own assumptions unquestioned (Plato 1997: *Republic* 533b–c3). The Platonic philosopher, then, is precisely the thinker who does not mistake the similar for the self-identical, but, rather, always uses the realm of semblance as a way to go beyond not only its seeming self-evidence but also our own definitions of other and same. Thus, at the end of the myth of the cave itself, we are told that the enlightened philosopher, who has been freed from the shackles of the cave and dragged into the light of the sun, and becomes accustomed to the light, even he, is scarcely able to see (*horasthai*) the idea (*idea*) of the Good. He does not intuit it, he does not know it, he literally almost, with difficulty (*mogis*), catches a glimpse (Plato 1997: *Republic* 517b7–c4). Philosophy, on this view, desires what it lacks not so that it can confirm its own self-identity, and not so that it can prescribe that to others, but so that it can transform itself, so that it can become other (Foucault 1984: 15). It is an action. Wisdom is not something you know in a disembodied way, it is something you do.

This distance, then, between knower and known is less than it might appear. On one level, knowledge clearly resides in the possibility of correct representation, in the correspondence between our intuitions, their objects and the propositions and judgments we formulate therefrom. But on another the ability to receive those intuitions, to delimit those objects, and to form those propositions is in Plato and the entire spiritual tradition described by Foucault dependent on a series of repeated actions, regular practices and recognized forms of behavior that make these seemingly disembodied actions possible. This is perhaps nowhere so clear as in forms of traditional education and ritual that also serve as technologies of self-formation in a given cultural context.

Once this aspect of Platonic philosophy is recognized not as an accidental excrescence or a mere rhetorical ornament but as an essential moment in the Platonic love of wisdom, then certain passages that previously puzzled interpreters become explicable. One of these is the extensive discussion of the Athenian institution of the symposium or "drinking party" that stretches across Books One and Two of the *Laws*. We begin with the Athenian stranger discussing with Clinias from Crete and Megillius from Sparta their respective laws and traditions. Drinking parties, we discover, are forbidden in the austere military cultures of the Cretans and the Spartans but are considered an essential part of Athenian civilization; whereas within their martial cultures communal meals are considered to be an essential part of their political civilization, in Athens they are strange and forbidding customs (Plato 1997: *Laws* 626c). The decision to spend so much time discussing what on many levels seems to be a frivolous activity that has very little to do with the noetic world of philosophy has struck more than one commentator as odd. And yet the discussion of the proper role of the drinking party in community life serves as the preamble for Plato's final work of political philosophy. Indeed our friend the Athenian stranger seems to have spent a great deal of time, in both attending them and reflecting on them:

> I have come across a great many, in different places, and I have investigated nearly all of them. However I have never seen or heard of one that was properly conducted throughout; one would approve of a few insignificant details, but most of them were mismanaged virtually all the time. (Plato 1997: 639d–e)

Indeed, the search for the perfect drinking party has led many of us far afield. Yet the Athenian stranger's search, and indeed that of all of us, is not purely a search for immediate pleasure, it is in fact also a search for knowledge and wisdom through practice, for a way of being in the world, even if that is not always, or even often, the result.

The well-regulated drinking party, the Athenian stranger tells us, is a mini society with its own rules and leadership. It builds bonds of social solidarity through mutual enjoyment. It becomes the centerpiece for an entire theory of culture:

I don't want to make you feel that I am saying an awful lot about a triviality, if I deal exhaustively and at length with such a limited topic as drinking. In fact, the genuinely correct way to regulate drinking can hardly be explained adequately and clearly except in the context of a correct theory of culture; and it is impossible to explain this without considering the whole subject of education. (Plato 1997: *Laws* 642a)

Through drinking we test the character of our companions in a controlled setting and learn the limits of our selves. Our courage becomes exaggerated, our inhibitions lower, and in the bosom of an esteemed social institution we are able to have experiences that if undertaken sober or in isolation from others would be considered socially unacceptable or even pathological: "I want to think back over our definition of correct education, and to hazard the suggestion now that drinking parties are actually its safeguard, provided they are properly conducted on the right lines" (Plato 1997: *Laws* 653a). The well-regulated drinking party— and the regulations are key if chaos is not to ensue—becomes a laboratory of experience and a direct means of education that has very little to do with the detached autonomous subject of metaphysics we find in Heidegger's reading of the cave. Rather, education is a process of training the body and the mind in limited experiences that in turn accustom the soul to the appropriate pleasure and create disgust at the inappropriate:

Education has proved to be a process of attraction, of leading children to accept right principles as enunciated by the law and endorsed as genuinely correct by men who have high moral standards and are full of years of experience. The soul of the child has to be prevented from getting into the habit of feeling pleasure and pain in ways not sanctioned by the law and those who have been persuaded to obey it; he should follow in their footsteps and find pleasure and pain in the same things as the old. That is why we have songs, which are really "charms" for the soul. These are in fact deadly serious devices for producing the concord we are talking about; but the souls of the young cannot bear to be serious, so we use the terms "recreation" and "song" for the charms. (Plato 1997: *Laws* 659d–e)

Drinking parties, poetry, song, specific types of food, various bodily practices all become methods of training or attuning the soul, making it able to receive knowledge and pursue wisdom, not as an object separate from it, but as a process in which the self is transformed in relation to both itself and its other.

This is not to say that Heidegger's diagnosis of the pivotal role played by the myth of the cave is simply wrong. The metaphysical tradition in the West finds its origin in Platonism as a specific form of abstraction from the Platonic text.

That abstraction as refined in Neo-Platonism becomes the intellectual bedrock of Augustinian Catholic theology and of the understanding of the individual soul's relation to both a timeless realm of god or the forms and a fallen separate world of objects, which it was both that soul's duty and right to use, manipulate and subjugate, to technologize in a series of discrete actions that could then be assessed as separate from the experience of that subject. This gradual refinement and separation of the metaphysical subject in many ways reaches its apogee with Descartes's *cogito*, the point at which Foucault observes the definitive separation between any concept of philosophy and that of a spiritual practice. But what we clearly see in the concept of *tribē* in Plato's "Seventh Letter"—that is, the "labour" between master and student, but also the "rubbing" or "friction" that creates a "spark"—is that there is simultaneously present within the history of Western thought an alternative tradition of wisdom as embodied practice, as ritual, as song, as poetry. It is this conception of knowledge/wisdom/education that we observe in the lengthy and odd discussion of the Athenian institution of the symposium at the beginning of Plato's final reflection on politics, the *Laws*. Likewise, even the famous simile of the divided line—in which a theory of knowledge is proposed as completely separate from the realm of appearance, from likeness and representation, a realm of pure ideas, according to the classical reading of Plato, a notion which must be formulated before the myth of the cave can have its full effect—is shown to dwell in the realm of appearance, not only owing to its status as a *simile* but also in the very formulation it makes of it highest noetic stage. The realm of *noesis* comes into being not as the pure contemplation of a divine essence but as a mode of action achieved through the placing of assumptions, which take the form of likenesses, under the subject. These *hypotheses* allow the subject to ascend to a point wherefrom they can themselves be questioned rather than, as in *dianoia*, descend from those assumptions, through a series of de-ductions, in order to reach a set of firm conclusions about objects in the world and their proper use.

Anyone familiar with Buddhist meditation practices or various forms of yogic practice will instantly see a parallel between these Eastern traditions of wisdom and the concept of spiritual practices as outlined by Foucault, and as traced by him, and his main influence in this regard, Pierre Hadot, throughout the ancient Western philosophical tradition (Hadot 1995). What is perhaps most telling about Foucault's work in this regard is that he demonstrates the presence of an alternative tradition within the very citadel of what Heidegger would term Western metaphysics, showing the presence of a counterhegemonic tradition within the dominant from the very beginning, and indeed one that

I would argue becomes all the more visible when the Western philosophical tradition is read with/against/alongside its supposed other.

The notion of true wisdom as embodied action rather than pure noesis, while at times problematic in the history of philosophy, is found strongly attested within the rhetorical tradition. We can see this in Callicles' response to Socrates in Plato's *Gorgias*, but even more clearly in the philosophical and theoretical works of Cicero, where he is always at pains to distinguish the enlightened Roman *orator*—speaker, lawyer, politician, thinker—from the idle Greek philosopher. This is not a simple matter of prioritizing the practical over the theoretical or even the Roman over the Greek, but rather a profound calling into question of these very oppositions in a way that has often gone unappreciated.

Thus if we look at the opening discussion of the *De Oratore* (1942), the opening question is: why are there so many generals in Rome, yet so few true orators? The orator is not merely the slick talker, the man who can argue both sides of any question, the sophist who can make the weaker argument the stronger. He is a leader. But he is also not the man of unreflective action, of brute force, of *vis* rather than *virtus*. The status of action as an end in itself is problematized from the beginning of the dialogue, which Cicero dedicates to his brother Quintus, who seemingly has no time for his elder brother's intellectual preoccupations (1942: 1.5–8). Yet any notion of pure knowledge as separate from embodied action is equally problematic for Cicero. Ciceronian oratory, when properly executed, is not a mere knack or craft, nor is it the simple and opportunistic manipulation of the audience, but it is rather a synthesis of all the lower arts, a kind of *summum studium* (Cicero 1942: 1.17).

In Book One of the dialogue, Crassus, the archetypical Roman orator who has no time for intellectual speculation for its own sake, none the less demonstrates a detailed knowledge of a wide range of Greek philosophy and particularly of the *Gorgias*. Unlike Plato, who contends in the *Phaedrus* that a true *rhetor* must be a philosopher, Crassus argues that philosophers, in so far as they are persuasive, must be orators. Thus, even if Socrates carries the day against his rhetorically trained adversaries in the *Gorgias*, he does not, according to Cicero, thereby demonstrate the superiority of philosophy over rhetoric, but rather that the ideal philosopher and the ideal orator are ultimately one. Indeed, Crassus suggests, the ideal orator would ultimately trump the figure of the pure philosopher, since real eloquence, as Plato argues, of necessity assumes a knowledge of the truth, but the converse is not necessarily the case, as attested by any number of dry and unpersuasive philosophical proofs (Cicero 1942: 1.42–50). Thus Crassus directly contests what he argues to be Socrates' claim that it is sufficient to know the truth to be eloquent and convince others (Cicero 1942: 1.63–5). Antonius, the other main speaker in the dialogue, replies with a defence of philosophy as being necessary to rhetoric, arguing that projection of *ethos* demands ethics, which in turn demands a systematic psychology (Cicero 1942: 1.87–8). In short, where pure philosophy is rejected as an idle pursuit, rhetoric without it is shown to be empty. The ideal orator of the dialogue is one who transcends the opposition between action and reflection, persuasion and knowledge, practice and theory, rhetoric and philosophy. Truth for Cicero is not a property of propositions formulated by detached subjects in relation to a set of previously delimited objects, but a form of action, even a weapon, by which the man of thought produces effects within the public realm when the philosopher returns to the cave: a moment when knowledge manifests its resistance to the rule of the generals, when the man of speech is the man of action who forms both himself and others.

Cicero's political philosophy reveals much the same pattern as his rhetorical theory. If we look at the opening pages of the *De re publica*, the complex dance between action, reflection, speech, and wisdom becomes if anything even more intricate with each term coming to qualify and relativize the other. Thus Cicero in his preface to the dialogue makes clear that the mere possession of abstract virtue, in the manner of some art or technique, the knowledge of which in and of itself sufficed without being actualized in the world, is a contradiction in terms (Cicero 1942: 1.2–3). True wisdom, he argues, cannot be separated from the constitution of the state, from politics, and hence from the practice of rhetoric. A knowledge that exists separately from the deed that instantiates it is no knowledge at all, but is either a kind of self-delusion or low entertainment.

At the same time, the *De re publica* (1928) is no defense of cynical pragmatism or of Roman anti-intellectualism. Indeed, the importance of a knowledge of geometry, mathematics, and astronomy to the ideal statesman is repeatedly stressed, and Socrates' authority is invoked for support (Cicero 1928: 1.16). Thus when Philus, one of the minor interlocutors, is challenged by the elder Laelius concerning the relevance of such abstract forms of knowledge when men have not yet acquired a perfect knowledge of what goes on in their "own homes," he replies:

> Do you not think it is important for our homes that we should know what is happening and being done in that home which is not shut in by the walls we build, but is the whole universe, a home and a fatherland which the gods have given us the privilege of sharing with them? (Cicero 1928: 1.19)

Laelius's challenge to Philus to demonstrate the immediate utility of these kinds of knowledge when so much is left to be done on the practical level is met not by a refutation, nor by a defense of the pursuit of knowledge in and of itself, but by an enlargement of our understanding of the immediate to include the transcendental. This kind of shift is typical of the dialogue as a whole, which famously ends with the "Dream of Scipio" and the contemplation of the music of the celestial spheres. On the one hand, there is an insistence on the claim that the only real knowledge, the only true wisdom, is that which takes the form of action in the world, and that action reaches its fullest flowering at the level of the governing of the household, the state and the fatherland; on the other, the delimitation of the realm of human action is in no way separated from even the most abstract of human knowledge: pure mathematics and speculative cosmology. The ultimate household, the true fatherland is not the patriarchal *domus* of the Roman aristocrat nor the land that falls within the *pomerium*, the traditional boundary that marks the limits of the *urbs aeterna*, but the universe itself, the entire realm within which men share their lives with the gods.

Ciceronian political pragmatism, like Ciceronian rhetoric, is thus neither a cynical reduction of all forms of reflection to immediate utility nor an effete abstraction from the demands of immediacy to a realm of pure discourse and disinterested contemplation; but it is always a form of knowledge in action, and a form of action that achieves meaning only in light of reflection. As Scipio, the main speaker of the dialogue and a highly esteemed statesman, scholar, and general states:

> As far as our lands, houses, herds and immense stores of silver and gold are concerned, the man who never thinks of these things or speaks of them as "goods," because he sees that the enjoyment of them is slight, their usefulness scanty, their ownership uncertain, and has noticed that the vilest of men often possess them in unmeasured abundance—how fortunate is he to be esteemed! For only such a man can really claim all things as his own, by virtue of the decision, not of the Roman People, but of the wise, not by any obligation of the civil law, but by the common law of Nature, which forbids that anything shall belong to any man save to him that knows how to employ and to use it. (Cicero 1928: 1.27)

The good, then, is not determined by the number of goods possessed, but neither is it the mere object of an abstract proposition formulated by a disinterested subject. Rather, goods are precisely those things that one knows how to use; and in that use comes the understanding of the limitations of their possession and the necessity of viewing all goods from the perspective of our ultimate *domus*, the one beyond all walls and all possessions, the one in which we come to possess all things: "Only such a man can say of himself what my grandfather Africanus used to say according to Cato's account—that he was never doing more than when he was doing nothing, and never less alone then when he was alone" (Cicero 1928: 1.27).

I want to finish, then, by looking briefly at a small selection of Confucian passages that I think are consonant with this counterhegemonic tradition in the West. I would also want to contend that these passages, if read within the widest possible context, have the ability not only to open up future comparative dialogues but also to open students of the Western philosophical, rhetorical, and poetic traditions to a variety of practices of wisdom: practices that see truth not as something external to be either achieved or manipulated, but as a set of actions in which the knower/doer is always implicated in the act, in which a separation that allows for a kind of technological manipulation is increasingly seen as an illusion, and in which the profound interconnection between knower, known, and practices of being is highlighted. A recognition of this interconnection is, moreover, crucial in a world in which our ability to separate ourselves from the consequences of our actions, and in which knowledge as a disembodied set of data is key to that separation and has the very real potential to lead to the end of human civilization through ecological disaster and various means of mass destruction. This task, I would submit, has never been more urgent.

Central to this inquiry is the Confucian notion of *li* 理 or ritual propriety, a vision of proper action and the knowledge of proper action as recognized in a set of practices that both mark the person performing them as knowing and make it possible for that person *to* know, to be wise. I take no position here on the origin and authenticity of the Confucian texts themselves, any more than I take a position on the age-old Socratic question. Both are philosophers who most likely did not write, and through whom others speak, but they are also the names assigned to the repositories of two discursive traditions that have been profoundly formative of their respective civilizations.

The first passage I want look at is from the third dialogue of Book Two of the Analects.[2] It is a statement on political leadership. It contends that a radical separation between leader and led produces political chaos, that effective political life comes from shared communal practices and the force of exemplarity:

> The Master said: Lead them by means of regulations and keep order among
> them through punishment, and the people will evade them and will lack

any sense of shame. Lead them through moral force and keep order among them through rites, and they will have a sense of shame and will also correct themselves. (de Bary and Bloom 1999: 2:3)

I do not wish to contend that there is nothing problematic in this statement. There is much one could debate; but I want to draw attention to the subjective stance it assumes for the political leader. It is not one of the commanding subject who creates and enforces a code on the objects of his rule—whether that be a feudal lord or a modern university administrator—it is one in which there must be constant negotiation to create a shared culture, and a culture that is transmitted and negotiated not simply as a set of propositions but also through ritual: through rhythms, images, narratives, and practices—even symposia.

The practices referred to by Confucius may include sacrificial rituals, special forms of food preparation, the serving of tea, or the performance of songs. In passage 1:15, thus, we find the master engaged with one of his disciples, Zigong, in trying to define virtue:

> Zigong said, "'Poor yet free from flattery; rich yet free from pride.' How would that be?"
>
> The Master said, "That would do, but it is not as good as 'poor yet finding joy in the Way, rich yet loving the rites.'"
>
> Zigong said, "The Ode says, 'As with something cut, something filed, something carved, something polished.' Does this resemble what you were saying?"
>
> The Master said, "With … [Zigong] one can begin to talk about poetry. Being told what is past, he knows what is to come."

Zigong starts by defining virtue as the absence of traditional vices. The poor flatter because they must; and the rich feel unwarranted pride based on their possessions. Those who rise above these common failings exemplify right behavior. The master responds to Zigong by upping the ante. The poor man who not only avoids his generic vice but who actively follows the Way—that is, the set of practices centered around filial devotion (*xiao* 孝), humanness (*ren* 仁), and ritual decorum (*li* 禮) that define the gentleman (*junzi* 君子)—is truly virtuous. Likewise it is not sufficient that the rich man eschew pride. He must actively love the ritual life of the community and subject himself to its rules.

This discussion of the relation of virtue to communal practices leads next, not to the pursuit of a set of abstract definitions or to a disembodied idea, but to the authority of the traditional Chinese book of *Songs* or *Odes*, which are said to have been collected and edited by Confucius himself (although this seems unlikely). The image cited from the poem doubles that of the move toward poetic refinement, "As with something cut, something filed, something carved, something polished." The virtuous person is one who has been cultivated or shaped, who subjects himself to a technology of the self or, to use another Foucauldian term, to an aesthetics of existence. The virtuous person's life is a block of stone, or a jewel that has been shaped, polished, cut, like the language of the poem itself.

The Master replies to Zigong, and again he ups the ante. He acknowledges his student's refinement and knowledge of the poetic tradition and then pivots off that to make a larger generalization. Through knowing poetry one knows the past, not simply as a set of isolated names, dates, or facts, but as a set of feelings, forms, and experiences. In acquiring this knowledge, one comes to be able to predict the future, the texture of its existence, its range of feeling. The virtuous man follows the Way, loves the rites, and knows the poetry that informs them. In doing so, he knows how to act appropriately. This is what defines nobility, neither accidents of birth nor disembodied knowledge in the form of a code, but right action.

The *junzi* is described neither as a means to an end nor as a moment of exclusion, but precisely as the person who is most inclusive in his or her pursuit of full humanity. To borrow Cicero's terms, the *junzi* is the person who recognizes that his or her house is ultimately the universe.

> The Master said, "The noble person is not a tool."
>
> The Master said, "The noble person is inclusive not exclusive, the small person is exclusive not inclusive." (de Bary and Bloom 1999: 2:12, 2:14)

None of this is to say that knowledge within the Confucian system has no content, or that knowledge is simply whatever anyone does; but rather it is to recognize that all knowledge is embedded, that it is social, that it is even rhetorical, and that this is a good thing. Of course, without a provisional—I would say "ironic"—separation of knower from known there can be no criticism, there can be no judgment, there can be no knowledge per se. But each moment of provisional separation is precisely a set of actions taken within the world, within a set of practices, and within the language of the statement, and never allows the subject to stand in opposition to the world to be known:

The Master said, "Without knowing what is ordained [by Heaven], one has no way to become a noble person. Without knowing the rites, one has no way to take one's stand. Without knowing words, one has no way to know other people." (de Bary and Bloom 1999: 20:3)

And I would add, one comes to know what is ordained only through knowing the ordinations of others; one comes to know the rites only through participating in the rites of others; and one only learns one's own language through experiencing the words of others. This is why the practice of comparison is crucially important. This is why translation, and not only on the level of the interlingual, is crucially important. And this is what the act of education, as opposed to mere technical mastery in accord with a given set of regulations or codes, truly embodies.

I am a literary scholar. But I am also a university administrator. My colleagues in Education, Business, Psychology, and the social sciences possess a vision of knowledge as a set of accurate propositions formulated by freestanding subjects in relation to a set of clearly delineated and clearly separate objects. They are even, at their most empirical, very Cartesian. When students know the things they are taught, they are able to formulate these same propositions. If they are advanced students, they should be able to form new propositions about those things. If they are truly doing original research they may even formulate new propositions concerning new objects. But in no case, within these disciplinary protocols, does the act of formulating those propositions implicate the subject in a pregiven world of meanings, which make possible both their propositions and their perceptions, nor does it implicate them in the world of the objects themselves. Within this understanding of truth, learning objectives can be assessed, forms of cognitions mapped, and consumer preferences charted, without ever compromising the observer's separation from the observed, without ever calling into question the definitional boundaries of either the self or the ontic world from which it emerges. This is precisely the technological world that Heidegger saw as the *telos* of metaphysics. But, as we have argued, within the very Platonic philosophy from which that system is abstracted there exists an alternative discourse that Foucault labels "spiritual practice." As time goes on, these practices become increasingly divorced from philosophy and its definition of science. They become marginalized, shunted off to the ambiguous realms of ritual, poetry, and the rhetoric. What I hope this paper has shown is that a comparative reading of our own tradition of wisdom practices with those of the Confucian and other Asian traditions can help to make the closure of our own system and its potential blind spots increasingly evident, and provide the tools necessary for rethinking such basic concepts as truth, knowledge, and wisdom, and for proposing a more humane and more inclusive relation to the world.

Notes

1   Cf. Plato 1997: *Republic* 511b4, where the hypotheses are not simply assumptions, but are that which you place (*tithēmi*) under (*hupo*) yourself, that you then step off as you approach being.

2   All references to the Analects are taken from de Bary and Bloom 1999.

Works cited

Bary, W. T. de and Bloom, I. (eds) (1999), "Confucius and the Analects," I. Bloom (trans.), *Sources of Chinese Tradition: From Earliest Times to 1600*, 2nd edn, New York: Columbia University Press, 41–64.

Cicero, M. T. (1928), "De re Publica," in C. W. Keyes (trans.), *De re Pubicla, De Legebus*, Loeb Classical Library 213, Cambridge, MA: Harvard University Press.

Cicero, M. T. (1942), *On the Orator [De Oratore], Books I-II*, E. W. Sutton and H. Rackham (trans.), Loeb Classical Library 348, Cambridge, MA: Harvard University Press.

Derrida, J. (1993), *Khôra*, Paris: Galilée.

Foucault, M. (1984), *L'usage des plaisirs. Histoire de la sexualité*, vol. 2, Paris: Gallimard.

Foucault, M. (2001), *L'Herméneutique du sujet: Cours au Collège de France, 1981–82*, F. Gros (ed.), Paris: Gallimard/Seuil.

Gadamer, Hans-Georg (1991), *Plato's Dialectical Ethics: Phenomenological Interpretations Relating to the Philebus* (trans.), Robert M. Wallace. New Haven: Yale University Press.

Hadot, P. (1995), *Qu'est-ce que la philosophie antique?*, Paris: Gallimard.

Heidegger, M. (1962), *Being and Time*, J. Macquarrie and E. Robinson (trans), San Francisco: Harper San Francisco.

Heidegger, M. (1982), "The Age of the World Picture," *The Question Concerning Technology and Other Essays*, W. Lovitt (trans.), New York: Harper Torchbooks, 115–54.

Heidegger, M. (1998), "Plato's Doctrine of Truth," in W. McNeill (ed.) and T. Sheehan (trans.), *Pathmarks*, Cambridge: Cambridge University Press, 155–82.

Irigaray, L. (1984), *Ethique de la différence sexuelle*, Paris: Minuit.

Jones, R. (2011), *Irigaray: Towards a Sexuate Philosophy*, Cambridge: Polity.

Mortensen, E. (1994), *The Feminine and Nihilism: Luce Irigaray with Nietzsche and Heidegger*, Oslo: Scandinavian University Press.

Oudemans, T. C. W. and Lardinois, A. P. M. H. (1987), *Tragic Ambiguity: Anthropology, Philosophy, and Sophocles' Antigone*, Leiden: Brill

Plato (1997), *Plato: Complete Works*, J. M. Cooper and D. S. Hutchinson (eds), Indianapolis: Hackett Press

Sallis, J. (1999), *Chorology: On Beginning in Plato's Timaeus*, Bloomington: Indiana University Press.

Wolff, F. (1992), "Trios: Deleuze, Derrida, Foucault, historiens du platonisme," in B. Cassin (ed.), *Nos Grecs et leurs modernes: Les Stratégies contemporaines d'appropriation de l'antiquité*, Paris: Seuil, 232–48.

Zuckert, C. H. (1996), *Postmodern Platos: Nietzsche, Heidegger, Gadamer, Strauss, Derrida*, Chicago: University of Chicago Press.

6

Anonymous Sages: Wisdom and Fame in Greco-Sino Philosophy

Geir Sigurðsson

Introduction

All the indications are that people of every culture and all times have regarded fame as desirable. This should come as no surprise, since fame, obviously, has the potential to offer advantageous social and economic opportunity. As Max Weber (1972: 531) pointed out almost a century ago, "social status (prestige) can be and very often has been the basis of power, also of economic power." With his notion of social status, Weber had hereditary titles primarily in mind, but fame can certainly be regarded as another form of social status. In this sense, however, fame has in general been associated with deserved merit. The degree and scope of the fame enjoyed by any given person has been popularly understood to be an indication of the individual's exceptional achievement, abilities, and—often—wisdom. In this sense, again, fame can be seen to be external evidence of a desirable inner potency. As Mark Rowlands (2008: 13) has observed, "fame, in the descriptive sense, used to track respect, in the normative sense."

In the contemporary world, however, fame is not what it used to be. The advent of the mass media, to say nothing of the digital age, seems to have made the reason for one's fame—one's talent or ability—largely secondary, or even altogether irrelevant. What matters now is fame itself: the extensive attention of others. The object of desire is the consequence without a cause or the fruit without a plant. Famous people are admired and envied not principally for their abilities but for their very fame. In the contemporary global media, millions watch famous people, read about them, follow their every move, and dream of being them or, at least, of living lives like theirs. From a popular perspective, they appear in the guise of "exemplary persons," worthy of emulation.

The multitude seeks to join their ranks. Thousands of people camp for days outside venues for auditions for talent shows such as American Idol and The X-Factor, although to most of the contestants it is (or should be) obvious that they themselves are far from talented as entertainers (Rowlands 2008: 3). They engage in every variety of outrageous but largely meaningless undertaking, purely to gain attention.[1] And even in the case of the majority, the non-participants in this aspiration, a certain micro-version of the phenomenon is played out in contemporary social media, where efforts are made by almost any means available to secure attention.

The desire to gain the attention of others of course can be entirely understandable and even legitimate. My fourteen-year-old daughter told me that even at her school they have "celebs" (she used the English word). Whether or not one is a celeb, she explained, is determined by the number of "likes" received on one's Facebook profile. Those receiving the greatest number become the school's "celebs." "So what is so desirable about being such a 'celeb,'" I asked, "what are the advantages?" "Well," she said, "everyone wants to be your friend and to hang out with you." This might call for further investigation into friendship and what it means but, in the meantime, in acquiring such social status there are clearly concrete gains to be found, especially for teenagers who, struggling to form their own identity, seek recognition from their peers.

The race for this sort of micro-fame is not, however, limited to teenagers. Adult Facebook users, also, take note of how many "likes" they receive. In some areas of social media, so-called "Klout scores" have been introduced that supposedly measure one's social influence, and are determined by the number of one's followers, likes, retweets, shares, and so on. Countless articles on the Internet instruct us on how to increase our Klout scores (cf. Bischoff 2013). These scores are even listed, or indexed, so that anyone is able, potentially, to become a sort of "web" celebrity simply by dedicating him- or herself to posting multiple opinions, and thereby advancing on the list of Klout scores.

As Weber observed, prestige tends to promote power or authority, and celebrities are frequently consulted on their insights, opinions, and views on a surprisingly broad range of topics, irrespective of the likelihood of their knowing anything about them: how to protect our environment, how to reduce poverty, how to spread tolerance, how to improve democracy, and so on. Certainly, we often consult the opinion of specific, prestigious, individuals who are either experts in a particular field or in a particular position to influence the matter in question. To ask Masoumeh Ebtekar about her views on environmental issues,

Ban Ki-Moon about poverty, and Alfredo Castillero Hoyos about democracy could only be seen as entirely reasonable.

The irony is that these individuals may not, themselves, be very famous. Indeed, they would not count as actual "celebrities", which confirms the observation that the phenomenon of fame has undergone radical change. Whereas in the past, famous people were admired for the achievement or quality that had brought them fame, their asset or talent, their wisdom or abilities, this is no longer necessarily the case. Experts may be well-known in their specific fields of expertise, but in general they are not famous. It seems that in modern times a contemporary version of fame has emerged, where we have a considerable number of people famous for nothing, or at least nothing in particular, but who are none the less often treated by the media as though they presided over profound wisdom. Indeed, wisdom is still explicitly attributed to them, as some kind of vestige of what fame used to mean.[2]

Undoubtedly, many celebrities are good at what they do. They may be excellent singers, actors, models, and so on. Others are famous, simply, as the expression goes, for being famous (Raiford 2014). But, whichever of these applies, it is at any rate clear that it is not wisdom that has brought them fame. In spite of this, they become role models solely by virtue of being famous, and then the public is anxious to know their views and opinions. Large numbers of people will listen attentively to what these celebrities say, take them seriously, and seek to follow their insights, *as if* they had some wisdom to share, while being reluctant to take advice from Masoumeh Ebtekar, of whose identity they are unaware.

This paper is a preliminary comparative philosophical investigation into the phenomenon of fame and its relation to wisdom. Although philosophical studies of this topic are not extensive, fame has nevertheless been a sufficiently important aspect of social living to have been addressed in the course of intellectual history by a number of diverse philosophers. It goes without saying that an overview of all of these cannot be provided in this short chapter, and its scope is restricted to seminal ancient Greek and Chinese philosophy. Indeed, since there is so much to choose from in these traditions, what is presented here can be seen as only a crude outline of ancient outlook. It is to be hoped that other, more detailed, treatments of the topic will follow.

Although many philosophers have referred to fame, few, whether past or present, have embarked upon a focused study of the phenomenon.[3] It seems almost as if they have tried to ignore fame. After the truly famous philosopher Socrates was sentenced to death and executed, perhaps philosophers

considered it wise to keep a low profile. Or perhaps the tendency of philosophers to snub fame is a version of Nietzschean slave morality. Certainly, there
are famous people within the camp of philosophy, but how many philosophers
are *really* famous? Possibly, because they cannot have it, they ignore it as being
worthless. And yet, even philosophers cannot entirely ignore the phenomenon
of fame, which has ever been a conspicuous object of desire among ordinary
people. Plato and Aristotle, Confucians and Daoists: all have something to say
about it.

Before closing this introductory section, we may remark that a certain key to
the notion of fame, especially as it manifests in contemporary times, is selfhood.
There is a modern tendency to attach enormous importance to the self; in fact,
we are fairly obsessed with self, especially our own. But, although the importance of self has probably reached unprecedented heights in the contemporary
West, and elsewhere, consciousness of self as such is of course nothing new.

In fact, the discovery of self has been interpreted even as being the origin
of philosophical thinking, most notably by Karl Jaspers (1949: 21) in his, not
uncontroversial, claim that the "Axial Age" involved a certain *Vergeistigung*,
a rise of a sense of individuality and selfhood, in Europe, India, and China.
In Jaspers' view, self-awareness is a necessary condition for philosophical
reflection. Psychologically, however, sustaining a sense of importance of self,
wherever it may be, is unlikely to succeed without the recognition, acknowledgment, and respect of others. If it is true that the "significant others ... are
not simply external to me" but "help constitute my own selfhood" (Taylor 1989:
509), it would be reasonable to expect that the more self-absorbed I am the
stronger will be my thirst for recognition.

In any case, the quest for glory, the desire for one's reputation to reach far
and wide, is to be found in most if not all ancient traditions and at all times. It
appears in other words to be very human to desire fame.

Let us start our journey in ancient Greece.

Wisdom and fame in ancient Greece

Glory, fame, and reputation are all treated as laudable goods in the Homeric
writings. Homer clearly understood fame as recognition of a notable talent,
ability, or, indeed, of wisdom. In *The Odyssey*, Telemachus, Ulysses' son, is
referred to as "the youth, whom Pallas destined to be wise and famed among the
sons of men" (Homer 2004: Bk. 3, 50). Towards the end of the epic, Telemachus

blesses this happy day "that shows me, ere I close my eyes, a son and grandson of the Arcesian name strive for fair virtue, and contest for fame" (Homer 2004: Bk. 24, 615).

References in both the *The Odyssey* and *The Iliad* to the desirability of honor, reputation, glory, and fame are numerous. As the quotations above show, however, fame is always associated with wisdom, virtue, and similarly admirable abilities. Acquiring fame, then, is unequivocally a challenge that requires genuine assets. Fame, like glory, is a value-laden term, and contrasted with shame.[4] While both attract the attention of others, the contrast made between them is quite clear. Glory is enjoying the admiration of others for some exceptional deed or ability, while shame refers to the condemnation of others for something deplorable. As we can see from *The Iliad*, where Glaucus on one occasion criticizes Hector for being cowardly in battle, reputation requires desert: "Hector—our prince of beauty, in battle all a sham! That empty glory of yours a runner's glory, a scurrying girl's at that" (Homer 1990: Bk. 17, 447). Undeserved reputation, in other words, is empty or worthless.

By the time the great philosophers come on the scene in ancient Greece, the rather clear distinction found in the Homeric writings between deserved fame and empty fame seems to have been undermined in Greek culture. In his typical bombastic style, Heraclitus still speaks of fame or glory as something that only exceptional individuals may enjoy: "The best choose one thing in exchange for all, everflowing fame among mortals; but most men have sated themselves like cattle" (Kahn 1979: 73). In this respect, Heraclitus could of course merely be expressing his aristocratic contempt for the masses by comparing them to beasts; or he might be referring to heroic deeds such as Achilles' choosing to die an honourable death in combat. But at the same time Heraclitus refers with no less contempt to those who undeservedly enjoy a reputation for being wise: "Of all those whose accounts I have heard, none has got so far as this: to recognize what is wise, set apart from all" (Kahn 1979: 114). As Charles H. Kahn (1979: 115) comments: "Those who passed for wise did not deserve the name: they did not know what wisdom is, and hence were separated from it." If we take Heraclitus' remark not simply as an arrogant attack on his Presocratic predecessors, it may indicate that the endeavor to make oneself appear as wise, perhaps chiefly in order to enjoy the concomitant privileges, was at any rate not unheard of in his time. It would seem, then, that fame and reputation were gradually becoming goods in themselves, independently of their foundations— the principal object of criticism, precisely, of the great philosophers Plato and Aristotle.

Jan Szaif (2011: 209) has recently pointed out that the "conventional pre-philosophical view" in ancient Greece "is that a life is ideally prosperous if it acquires and maintains great social, bodily and material goods: lasting reputation, a healthy and handsome body, wealth, a thriving family, etc." These external "goods" were certainly not rejected by Plato and Aristotle. Indeed, Aristotle (1984: 1360b) explicitly states that among the constituent parts of happiness are "fame, honour, good luck and excellence." But Plato and Aristotle approached them more critically than seems to have been the practice elsewhere. In addition, they tended to assign a greater value to the goods realized in the soul, which implied a more differentiated view of the status of external goods.

Plato, in the guise of Socrates, seeks wisdom through dialogue. It is natural, therefore, that he should want to engage in conversation with people who enjoyed prestige and were famous for being wise. While comparable examples can be found throughout Plato's dialogues, I intend to limit my discussion here to the relatively brief "Greater Hippias," which seems to me to sum up rather elegantly the Platonic attitude to fame and glory. It is worth mentioning that, while the authenticity of "Greater Hippias" as a work by Plato is in dispute, its content is generally acknowledged as genuinely Platonic (Cooper 1997: 899). In any case, the dialogue's authenticity does not matter much for my purposes.

The content of the dialogue suits the topic well. Socrates seeks advice from the sophist Hippias, famous for his wisdom, on what constitutes *kalon*, the quality of being fine, noble, or admirable, or, as defined by Hippias: "the sort of activities that would make someone most famous if he adopted them while young" (Plato 1997: 286b). Socrates is characteristically ironic in the dialogue, praising Hippias time and again for being "so finely dressed, finely shod, and famous for wisdom all over Greece" (Plato 1997: 291b), but, at the same time, mocking him as a money-making boaster. Following Hippias' description, at the beginning of the dialogue, of how busy he is, and how sought after by the various Greek cities, Socrates responds:

> That is what it is like to be truly wise, Hippias, a man of complete accomplish-
> ments: in private you are able to make a lot of money from young people (and
> to give still greater benefits to those from whom you take it); while in public you
> are able to provide your own city with good service (as is proper for one who
> expects not to be despised, but admired by ordinary people).
>
> But Hippias, how in the world do you explain this: in the old days people
> who are still famous for wisdom—Pittacus and Bias and the school of Thales of
> Miletus, and later ones down to Anaxagoras—that all or most of those people,
> we see, [are] kept away from affairs of state? (Plato 1997: 281b–c)

Socrates here points out a crucial difference between the "old days" and now in the behavior of those deemed wise. In earlier times they were reluctant to take office, seek power, and be the center of attention, whereas these are the goals, precisely, of their contemporary counterparts. In fact, fame and material prosperity have become the accepted criteria for the measurement of an individual's wisdom. A little further on in the dialogue, Hippias gives an account of the vast sums of money he has made from displaying his wisdom in the various Greek regions, to which Socrates responds:

> That's a fine thing you say, Hippias, strong evidence of your own and modern wisdom, and of the superiority of men nowadays over the ancients. There was a lot of ignorance among our predecessors down to Anaxagoras, according to you. People say the opposite of what happened to you happened to Anaxagoras: he inherited a large sum, but lost everything through neglect—there was so little *intelligence* [*nous*] in his wisdom. And they tell stories like that about other early wise men. You make me see there's fine evidence, here, I think, for the superiority of our contemporaries over those who came before; and many will have the same opinion, that a wise man needs to be wise primarily for his own sake. The mark of being wise, I see, is when someone makes the most money. (Plato 1997: 283a–b)

It is not necessary to go into more details of the dialogue. As we recall, its topic is what it means to be "fine," and essentially it is arguing for the classic Platonic objectivity of "fineness" against a relativist Sophist standard judged according to material profit, popularity, and fame. Plato seeks an objective criterion for deserved reputation and fame, giving precedence to wisdom, or other excellent attributes, as distinct from the application of an external appearance of success as a criterion for being fine. In other words, being rich, famous, and popular, or even being seen by many to be wise, is not a guarantee of one's having real wisdom and worth.

Aristotle is neither as ironic nor as harsh as Plato in this regard. Plato genuinely seems to despise vain people who seek fame and popularity on hollow pretence. Aristotle is much milder in his judgments. A likely reason for Plato's contempt rests on his charge that his beloved teacher, Socrates, was executed by vain, greedy, and power-hungry people who cared only for their own material interests and disregarded real truth and knowledge.

Aristotle is for the most part in agreement with Plato that fame, honor, or reputation must be deserved, and thus that there must be some objective criterion for worth behind it. "Honour," he says, "is the prize of excellence and it is to the good that it is rendered" (Aristotle 1984: 1123b). The proud man will accept honors "conferred by good men" and "be moderately pleased" with them, "but honour from casual people and on trifling grounds he will utterly despise" (Aristotle 1984: 1124a). The proud man seems to correspond with what Aristotle elsewhere calls "greatness of soul", which is described thus:

> A mean between vanity and littleness of soul, and it has to do with honour and dishonour, not with honour from the many but with that from the good, or at any rate more with the latter. For the good will bestow honour with knowledge and good judgement. He will wish then rather to be honoured by those who know as he does himself that he deserves honour. For he will not be concerned with every honour, but with the best, and with the good that is honourable and ranks as a principle. Those, then, who are despicable and bad, but who deem themselves worthy of great things, and besides that think that they ought to be honoured, are vain. (Aristotle 1984: 1192a)

Thus, it is certainly blameworthy conduct to be "aiming at honour more than is right and from wrong sources" (Aristotle: 1984b, 1125b). But Aristotle is not particularly severe in his judgment of someone seeking acknowledgment by others:

> He who claims more than he has with no ulterior object is a contemptible sort of fellow … but seems futile rather than bad; but if he does it for an object, he who does it for the sake of reputation or honour is … not very much to be blamed, but he who does it for money, or the things that lead to money, is an uglier character. (Aristotle 1984b: 1127b)

The reason for Aristotle's different attitudes to these two contrasting individuals is that the one who boasts just for show is not in fact depriving others of anything they have, whereas the individual who promotes himself for money does so precisely with the ulterior motive in mind of profiting from others. In this respect, Aristotle refers in particular to those individuals who charge money for exercising special powers they claim to possess, such as prophets, seers, and others.

To summarize, then, the Greek masters emphasize the importance of desert. Being acknowledged or famous for one's wisdom, as in the case of Hippias, is far from being a sufficient condition for actually being wise. Plato seeks to reveal that the reputation of certain people is overrated, and to show that a popular measurement of a person's worth is simply not reliable.

Wisdom and fame in ancient China

Ancient Chinese thinkers are largely in agreement with their Greek counterparts that fame requires some underlying quality or asset to make it deserved. In this sense, then, they acknowledge that fame and prestige are an important social good and a source of social power. This view applies in particular to Confucian thinkers, who are explicitly meritocratic, believing, not unlike Plato, that political and social affairs should be in the hands of the most competent members of society. Thus, wisdom is an important, indeed necessary, prerequisite for deserved fame. Confucians seem to fear, much as Plato, that power-hungry individuals who may be clever but are not really wise will manipulate popular sentiment in such a way as to be considered wise and therefore worthy of political or other kinds of power. Fame is in this sense quite uneriable as a criterion of worth, and must be thoroughly scrutinized.

As we shall see below, Daoists, too, are wary of fame, although for rather different reasons. But we shall begin by looking into the Confucian warning about superficial popular evaluation based on appearance.

It ought to be noted first, however, that Confucius has nothing in principle against being known, and rather to the contrary: "The Master said: 'Exemplary persons [*junzi* 君子] worry about leaving this world without having established a name for themselves'"(Confucius 1997: 15.20, 135).[5] Since the aim of (Confucian) learning is to improve society, it is natural that Confucian scholars should aspire to take office. Without doubt, being well known for one's wisdom and abilities will facilitate this objective. In one's endeavor to establish a name for oneself, however, it is not the case that anything goes. The point is that the name, or the fame, is precisely not the point. It is merely a convenient tool. Consider the following two passages, both of which essentially express the same thought: first, "The Master said: 'Wealth and honour are what people desire; but if they are obtained by deviating from the proper way, I won't have anything to do with them'" (Confucius 1997: 4.5, 25–6);[6] second, "wealth and honour obtained through inappropriate means are to me like floating clouds" (Confucius 1997: 7.16, 55).[7]

One's reputation or fame must therefore be acquired for the right reasons. They require desert. Confucius and his followers are altogether conscious of the danger that certain individuals may seek acclaim for qualities or abilities which they do not actually possess. External appearances can be quite deceptive, and there are those who can be quite proficient in making others believe that they command some kind of superior ability.

From a Confucian point of view, one's external appearance or one's physical bearing can be definite indicators of one's level of sophistication. Mencius, for instance, states quite explicitly that "junziness," the high Confucian status of sophistication, manifests itself in outward appearance:

> To the natural dispositions of exemplary persons [*junzi* 君子] belong humaneness [*ren* 仁], a sense of appropriateness [*yi* 义], a sense of propriety [*li* 礼], and wisdom [*zhi* 智], which are rooted in their thoughts and feelings [*xin* 心]. These manifest themselves in the mildness of their faces, amplify themselves in their backs and extend to their limbs, which, in turn, instruct them without uttering a single word.[8] (Mencius 1966: 7a.21)

However, one's outward appearance and demeanor are primarily a reflection of one's internal status, but not necessarily vice versa. There may be individuals who are good at portraying themselves as commanding true wisdom and a high level of sophistication, but this can all be appearance, an art of dissimulation, based on very little or even nothing at all. Confucius makes a clear distinction between being *da* 達, distinguished, eminent, or prominent, and being *wen* 聞, known or famous:

> Zizhang asked, "How can the scholar achieve designation as 'prominent' [*da* 達]?" "What do you mean by 'prominent'?" the Master replied. "Certain to win fame [*wen* 聞], whether serving the state or in the house of a ruling family", answered Zizhang. "That is being 'famous'", the Master said, "not being 'prominent'. The prominent are naturally disposed to be upright and fond of what is appropriate [*yi* 義]. ... Those who are merely famous put on airs to appear humane [*ren* 仁], which their conduct clearly belies. Confident in their role, however, they are certain to win fame, whether serving the state or in the house of a ruling family".[9] (Confucius 1997: 12.20, 108)

Consider also this poignant metaphor, suggested by Mencius:

> Xuzi said, "Confucius often praised water by saying, 'Oh water, water!' What was it he saw in water?" "Water from an abundant source", said Mencius, "rolls on day and night without stop, surging forward only after all the holes on its way are filled, and then moving on into the sea. Anything having an abundant source is like this. This is what Confucius valued in water. Anything without a source is like the rainwater that gathers after pouring rainfalls in the seventh and eighth months will fill all the gutters. However, we can just stand and wait for it to dry up. Thus exemplary persons are ashamed of a reputation beyond their merits."[10] (Mencius 1966: 4b.18)

The recently discovered *Wuxing* 五行 document, or *The Five Kinds of Conduct*, a pre-Qin text excavated in China for the first time in 1973 and possibly written by Confucius' grandson, Zisizi 子思子, or his disciples, is quite clear about the distinction between conduct that is merely externally appropriate and conduct emanating from within. In its very first paragraph, it says that "where wisdom [*zhi* 智] takes shape from within, it is called virtuous conduct [*de* 德]; where it does not take shape within, it is called mere (proper) conduct" (Li Ling 2002: 78).[11] The same argumentative pattern is afterward repeated in the passage for the other core Confucian notions, such as *yi* 義 (appropriateness conduct), *li* 禮 (propriety) and *sheng* 聖 (sagacity).

An important implication here is that actions executed with wisdom, skill and authenticity, on the one hand, or by sheer imitation, on the other, are bound to be vastly and noticeably different. A mere imitation of external form, the latter will be hollow, at least to anyone having the capacity to distinguish between them. And this appears to be the issue in question: the general public does not have this capacity. Hence, popular sentiment, and thus the level of fame enjoyed by a given person, cannot be a criterion for that person's worth. Aristotle's insistence that there must be an objective criterion, according to which a person may be acclaimed or blamed, an objective criterion that only the best will be able to use, is clearly shared by Confucius: "Zigong inquired, saying, 'What do you make of someone who is loved by everyone in his village?' 'It is no good,' said the Master. 'How about someone who is hated by everyone in the village?' 'It is no good either. It is best if the good villagers love this person and the bad hate him'" (Confucius 1997: 13.24, 115).[12]

The more agreement there is between people's views, the more suspicious Confucius becomes. Like Plato, Confucius is meritocratic and not democratic, and certainly not a spokesperson for regarding popular sentiment as being the criterion of truth: "The Master said, 'Where everyone hates a person, the matter must be looked into carefully; where everyone glorifies a person, the matter must be looked into carefully'" (Confucius 1997: 15.28, 136).[13]

Thus, while Confucius understands that fame and popularity can be powerful factors, he would rather like to diminish their value and influence. It is probably not far-fetched to understand the following remarks by Confucius as a kind of mockery of the popular idea and perceived value of fame: "A villager of Daxiang said, 'Confucius is indeed great! He is so broad of learning. A pity he never acquired much fame.' When the Master heard this, he called his disciples, saying, 'Now, what should I specialize in? Charioteering perhaps? Or maybe archery? No, I think I'll go for charioteering'" (Confucius 1997: 9.2, 70).[14]

A later Han dynasty Confucian thinker, Yang Xiong 楊雄 (53 BCE–18 CE), sums up the Confucian view on this issue quite succinctly in his *Yangzi fayan* 揚子法言: "The good reputation that one makes without seeking it is best. The reputation one makes by seeking after it is merely second best" (Yang Xiong n.d.: Bk. 13, §8).[15]

The Confucian take on fame and reputation is in many ways close to the views of Plato and Aristotle. Their similarity derives to some extent from their comparable attitude to political life—that the wise person is expected to take office and play her or his part in governing society. Reputation can certainly be helpful, as it makes it possible to have some social influence, but merely aiming for reputation, either for its own sake or for the sake of gaining wealth and power, is nothing but hypocrisy, and potentially detrimental to society.

Turning finally to Daoism, we come across slightly different approaches and views. To be sure, Daoists are for the most part in agreement with Plato and the Confucians that it is best for the state to be ruled by wise people. At the same time, however, they cast doubt on the wisdom of engaging at all in such affairs, and instruct us instead to stay away altogether from politics, public office or anything that would bring us into the spotlight. Despite this, the *Laozi* appears to be written largely as a manual for wise rulers. Such a ruler, it says, will seek to downplay the social celebration of fame, because the hunger for fame and prestige is bound to cause social perturbation: "Not to extol the worthy will prevent people from contending" (Laozi 1998: §3, 4).[16] The aim is thus to prevent fame, and, similarly, expensive goods, from being desired. The less people value such things, the less they strive for them, and the more tranquil society will be. The *Laozi* may appear to present a rather patronizing view of ordinary human beings: the more they are kept in ignorance, the better they will behave (which may make us think of the official policy in contemporary North Korea). However, the point is not just politically pragmatic, but much more substantial than that: striving for fame will simply not make our life better. We will waste both time and energy on anguish, disappointment, and other emotions detrimental to our wellbeing, leading to disharmony with our surroundings. And, should we be so unfortunate as to succeed in becoming famous, we are even worse off, never able to find tranquility. Indeed, the *Laozi* likewise advises a wise ruler to keep a low profile, to aim at simplicity, and not to be misled by superficial values such as fame and glory. "Your name or your person," it asks, "which is dearer?" (Laozi 1998: §44, 27).[17] It is probably a challenge for a ruler to be wholly unknown, but, the more a ruler goes unnoticed, the better for both society and for the ruler as an individual.

Zhuangzi, who develops Daoism as a philosophy of life, takes this thought further. Zhuangzi's overall consideration is that since we enjoy this one opportunity to live in the form of a human being, with the particular privileges and abilities that it entails, it is unwise to waste it on aims and worries that prevent our making the most of it. Laozi and, especially, Zhuangzi make a strong case to the effect that we need to overcome the social influences imposed on us by our upbringing and socialization, and reveal the futility, indeed harmfulness, of many of our most mundane and widespread social values.

A few examples from the *Zhuangzi* are sufficient to clarify this view. A passage from the very first chapter, "Rambling Without a Destination" 逍遙游, sets the tone: "The perfect person has no (thought of) self; the spiritual person none of success; the sage person none of fame" (Zhuangzi 1998: 53).[18] A comprehensive explanation of these rather enigmatic claims would require a lengthy discussion, but, briefly stated, they mean that such a person, a person commanding real wisdom, has both comprehended and thoroughly absorbed in her or his being (or rather becoming) the impermanence, coincidence, and uniqueness of human living here and now. Thus, she or he naturally overcomes mundane social valuations pursued by individuals primarily for the sake of boosting their own self-confidence. A sagacious person has transcended such level of selfhood. The strongest individualism is one that has no need for recognition from others.

The Zhuangzi often attacks, or rather mocks, the dependency on acknowledgment by others, often by making use of the character of Confucius. In chapter 14, "Heavenly Revolutions" 天運, Lao Dan reprimands Confucius for being too obsessed with social valuations: "The snow-goose does not take a bath every day to make itself white, nor does the crow blacken itself every day to make itself black. The natural simplicity of their black and white does not afford any ground for dispute; and the pandemonium of fame and praise does not make people greater than they naturally are" (Zhuangzi 1998: 195–6).[19]

Lastly, in chapter 20, "The Mountain Tree" 山木, Confucius is instructed, again by a Daoist sage, on how to prolong and nurture life:

> Previously, I heard a highly commensurate person say, "boasting is a sign of no success. Success obtained is bound to overthrow. Fame obtained is bound to harm." Who can rid himself of (the ideas of) merit and fame, return and put himself on the level of the masses of men? His *dao* flows, but he does not care to dwell where it can be seen; his virtue moves, but he does not wish to dwell in fame. Simple and commonplace, he may seem mad. Obliterating his footprints, giving up his power, he aims not at merit and fame. Therefore, he does not

blame others, and they do not blame him. The perfect person does not seek to be renowned; how is it that you delight in doing so?[20] (Zhuangzi 1998: 248)

Immediately after hearing this advice, as the text tells us, Confucius abandoned his disciples, retired to a great marsh where he lived in solitude with animals, dressed in skins, and fed on acorns and chestnuts.

In concluding this section, I should go to the length of saying that merely the prospect of being famous is an occasion for Daoists to withdraw. Fame is regarded as downright evil; it "overflows into violence," as it says in chapter 26, "External Phenomena" 外物 (Zhuangzi 1998: 332).[21] It leads one to be absorbed by the most insignificant affairs of the day, whereby there will be no time or occasion for authentic participation in the transformation of things. To seek fame, according to Daoists, is simply unwise. Those who are genuinely wise are unknown and nameless: true sages remain anonymous.

Afterthoughts

The ancient Greek and Chinese thinkers could not possibly have imagined how an obsession with fame, treated only marginally in their own writings, would grow so out of proportion in our modern times. They would undoubtedly be appalled by the present state of affairs, by the vanity and hypocrisy it engenders, and by the general tension, perturbation and misery ordinary people bring upon themselves when they enter this absurd and meaningless spinning wheel. In the introduction to this chapter, I remarked that the advent of mass media and digital technology had significantly exacerbated the pervasive striving for fame and acknowledgment. It has certainly added to the superficial glamor and appeal of the lives of the famous by increasing their overall visibility, while at the same time creating new and diverse global and local sites where others seek their own personal micro-fame. But the technology is not entirely to blame. For a more far-reaching explanation we must look at other cultural and historical factors. In his short but insightful and entertaining book on fame, Mark Rowlands argues that in our contemporary hunger for fame and the related loss of a sense of quality is a particular kind of cultural degeneration. He traces this primarily to the Enlightenment project, to the rise of individualism and objectivism, and last (but not least) to their degenerate forms, relativism and fundamentalism, which he describes as having produced a variant of fame that he calls "vfame" (Rowlands 2008: 20). Vfame is distinguished from fame proper in that the former "is not, in its essence, a matter of quality. Vfame has nothing to do with value" (Rowlands 2008: 91). It is, in fact, the kind of fame or attention sought after by so many today, a kind that requires no special talent, asset, capacity, or wisdom. Toward the end of his book, Rowlands says:

> The existence of vfame is evidence of a culture whose individualism has lost its objectivist counterbalance, and as a result is constantly buffeted between a facile form of relativism and a chilling form of fundamentalism. In this culture, each way of developing yourself as a person is just as legitimate and valuable as any other. Therefore, it doesn't matter why you are famous, just that you are. And having no independent and objective values with which to measure our lives, we think that validation is to be found in the simple—and largely baseless—recognition of our peers. The result is vfame. (Rowlands 2008: 113)

A final consideration: are the celebrities we deem to be famous for just being famous perhaps wiser than we think? Is it conceivable that they are feigning ignorance "like an infant that has not yet learned to smile" (Laozi 1998: §20, 13)?[22] "I don't really think, I just walk" (Koman 2013), Paris Hilton has been quoted as saying. These seemingly mysterious words, had they appeared in certain contexts, might have inspired many a Daoist scholar to compose long and profound commentaries. Are they perhaps the words of a sage? Hilton herself seems confident: "I'm very intelligent. I'm capable of doing everything put to me. I've launched a perfume and want my own hotel chain. I'm living proof blondes are not stupid." The anonymous commentator then continues: "As final proof of her great intelligence, Hilton offered some advice for coping with the global financial crisis. She said: 'You should wear happy colours'" (stuff. co.nz 2008).

Zhuangzi might very well concur. Perhaps there is more to celebrities than we are wont to assume.

Notes

1   *Guinness World Records* (n.d.) is probably the best known venue for such acts, listing records such as "most straws stuffed in the mouth (hands off)," "largest collection of sick bags," and "most rotations hanging from a power drill in one minute."

2   Consider the following examples: Hicklin 2014, Donovan 2011, and The *Independent* 2013.

3   Rowlands 2008 is a notable exception.

4 Cf. Homer (2004: Bk. 5, 136): "Had some distinguish'd day renown'd my fall / (Such as was that when showers of javelins fled / From conquering Troy around Achilles dead), / All Greece had paid me solemn funerals then, / And spread my glory with the sons of men. / A shameful fate now hides my hapless head, / Unwept, unnoted, and forever dead!"

5 子曰：「君子疾沒世而名不稱焉。」 Translations of Chinese sources are my own unless otherwise noted. As here, above, and in all cases, the original Chinese text is included in the corresponding endnote.

6 子曰：「富與貴，是人之所欲也；不以其道得之，不処也。」

7 不義而富且貴，於我如浮雲。

8 君子所性，仁義禮智根於心，其生色也，睟然見於面，盎於背，施於四體，四體不言而喻。

9 子張問：「士何如斯可謂之達矣？」子曰：「何哉，爾所謂達者？」子張對曰：「在邦必聞，在家必聞。」子曰：「是聞也，非達也。夫達也者，質直而好義，察言而觀色，慮以下人。在邦必達，在家必達。夫聞也者，色取仁而行違。居之不疑，在邦必聞，在家必聞。」

10 徐子曰：「仲尼亟稱於水，曰：『水哉，水哉！』何取於水也？」孟子曰：「原泉混混，不舍晝夜。盈科而後進，放乎四海，有本者如是，是之取爾。苟為無本，七八月之閒雨集，溝澮皆盈；其涸也，可立而待也。故聲聞過情，君子恥之。」

11 智形於内﹐谓之德之行；不形於内﹐谓之行。

12 子貢問曰：「鄉人皆好之，何如？」子曰：「未可也。」「鄉人皆惡之，何如？」子曰：「未可也。不如鄉人之善者好之，其不善者惡之。」

13 子曰：「眾惡之，必察焉；眾好之，必察焉。」

14 達巷黨人曰：「大哉孔子！博學而無所成名。」子聞之，謂門弟子曰：「吾何執？執御乎？執射乎？吾執御矣。」

15 不為名之名，其至矣乎！為名之名，其次也。

16 不上賢，使民不爭。

17 名與身孰親？

18 至人無己，神人無功，聖人無名。

19 夫鵠不日浴而白，烏不日黔而黑。黑白之朴，不足以為辯；名譽之觀，不足以為廣。 In translating this passage, I have partly followed Watson 2013: 115.

20 昔吾聞之大成之人曰：「自伐者無功，功成者墮，名成者虧。」孰能去功與名而還與眾人！道流而不明居，德行而不名處；純純常常，乃比於狂；削跡捐勢，不為功名。是故無責於人，人亦無責焉。至人不聞，子何喜哉？

21 名溢乎暴。 This translation may admittedly be contested. I interpret 暴 as referring here to *bao* (violence, cruelty) and not *pu* (manifestation, show).

22 如嬰兒之未孩.

Works cited

Aristotle (1984), *The Complete Works of Aristotle*, J. Barnes (ed.), vol. 2, Princeton: Princeton University Press, 1984.

Bischoff, K. (2013), "How I Increased my Klout Score by 6 Points in 2 Weeks with 7 Tweets a Day," *Huffington Post*. Available from http://www.huffingtonpost.com/ kirsten-bischoff/i-increased-my-klout_b_2398400.html (accessed 5 February 2015).

Confucius (1997), *Lunyu zhijie* 論語直解 [*Confucian Analects with annotations*], Zhang Weizhong 張衛中 (annot.), Hangzhou 杭州: Zhejiang wenyi 浙江文藝.

Cooper, J. M. (1997), "Foreword" to "Greater Hippias," in J. M. Cooper (ed.), *Plato: Complete Works*, Paul Woodruff (trans.), vol. 3, Indianapolis and Cambridge, MA: Hackett, 898–9.

Donovan, L. (2011, 12 May), "Kim Kardashian has Words of Wisdom, Advice for Bristol Palin," *Daily Caller*. Available from http://dailycaller.com/2011/05/12/ kim-kardashian-has-words-of-wisdom-advice-for-bristol-palin/ (accessed 2 February 2015).

Guinness World Records (n.d.), *Guinness World Records*. Available from http://www. guinnessworldrecords.com/ (accessed 1 February 2015).

Hicklin, A. (2014), "The Wit and Wisdom of Mariah Carey," *Guardian*, April 26. Available from http://www.theguardian.com/music/2014/apr/26/wit-wisdom-mariah-carey-savvy-diva-self-aware-pop-star (accessed 2 February 2015).

Homer (1990), *The Iliad*, R. Fagles (trans.), New York: Penguin Books.

Homer (2004), *The Odyssey*, A. Pope (trans.), Grandview: The Write Direction.

Independent, The (2013), "The Sly Wisdom of Action Hero Sylvester Stallone." Available from http://www.independent.co.uk/voices/iv-drip/the-sly-wisdom-of-action-hero-sylvester-stallone-8474646.html. 31 January (accessed 2 February 2015).

Jaspers, K. (1949), *Vom Ursprung und Ziel der Geschichte*, Munich: Artemis-Verlag.

Kahn, C. H. (1979), *The Art and Thought of Heraclitus: An Edition of the Fragments with Translation and Commentary*, Cambridge: Cambridge University Press.

Koman, T. (2013), "11 Life Lessons from Paris Hilton," *Cosmopolitan*, October 2. Available from http://www.cosmopolitan.com/entertainment/celebs/news/a4859/ paris-pearls-of-wisdom/ (accessed 5 February 2015).

Laozi (1998), "Laozi zhijie 老子直解" [*Laozi with annotations*], in *Laozi Zhuangzi zhijie*, Chen Qinghui 陳慶惠 (annot.), Hangzhou 杭州: Zhejiang wenyi浙江文藝.

Li Ling 李零 (2002), *Guodian Chu jian jiao du ji* 郭店楚簡校讀記, Beijing: Beijing daxue.

Mencius 孟子 (1966), *A Concordance to the Meng Tzu*, Taipei: Chinese Materials and Research Aids Service Centre.

Plato (1997), "Greater Hippias," in J. M. Cooper (ed.), *Plato: Complete Works*, P. Woodruff (trans.), Indianapolis and Cambridge, MA: Hackett, 898–921.

Raiford, T. (2014), "20 Celebrities Who Are Famous for Being Famous," *Celebrity Toob*. Available from http://celebritytoob.com/

did-you-know/20-celebrities-famous-famous/. 16 October (accessed 3 February 2015).

Rowlands, M. (2008), *Fame*, Stocksfield: Acumen.

stuff.co.nz (2008), "I'm not a dumb blonde," *stuff.co.nz*, December 12. Available from http://www.stuff.co.nz/entertainment/759155/I-m-not-a-dumb-blonde (accessed 5 February 2015).

Szaif, J. (2011), "Aristotle on friendship as the paradigmatic form of relationship," in R. A. H. King and D. Schilling (eds), *How Should One Live? Comparing Ethics in Ancient China and Greco-Roman Antiquity*, Berlin and Boston: De Gruyter, 208–37.

Taylor, C. (1989), *Sources of the Self: The Making of the Modern Identity*, Cambridge, MA: Harvard University Press.

Watson, B. (trans.) (2013), *The Complete Works of Zhuangzi*, New York: Columbia University Press.

Weber, M. (1972), *Wirtschaft und Gesellschaft*, Tübingen: J. C. B. Mohr (Paul Siebeck).

Yang Xiong 楊雄 (n.d.), *Yangzi fayan* 揚子法言, Chinese Text Project. Available from http://ctext.org/yangzi-fayan/juan-shi-san (accessed 3 February 2015).

Zhuangzi (1998), "Zhuangzi zhijie 莊子直解" [*Zhuangzi with annotations*], in *Laozi Zhuangzi zhijie*, annot. Chen Qinghui 陳慶惠, Hangzhou 杭州: Zhejiang wenyi 浙江文藝.

7

Seeking Wisdom with Aristotle and Zhu Xi

May Sim

Philosophy as the love of wisdom is characterized by Aristotle as the pursuit of the first principle or cause of all things, also known as the primary *ousia*—a one that precedes the many things that exist. Similarly, the Neo-Confucian, Zhu Xi (1130–1200 CE) holds that one achieves wisdom/knowledge when one knows the one principle *li* 理 that causes everything else. Put otherwise, the love of wisdom for both Aristotle and Zhu takes the form of questioning the Being or First Principle of everything. Such questioning into the source of everything is what Aristotle calls "first philosophy" or metaphysics. Since both Zhu and Aristotle theorize about the relation between a One first principle and the Many it causes in pursuing wisdom, the question of being or the object of wisdom is one for them. Wisdom is not only about how a One principle can cause the many for Zhu and Aristotle but how an attempt to understand the many things inevitably leads to a One principle. Put otherwise, the substance, function, or goodness of the many, that is, all questions about the norms and natures of all things, lead to one question: What is being?

Is there a single question of being which can take various forms like "what is being/*ousia*?" and "why is there something rather than nothing?" Or do these different formulations indicate multiple questions of being? One way of addressing these issues of the one and the many surrounding the question of being is to examine how Aristotle and Zhu Xi responded to them, as the metaphysics of both focus on a first principle/being of everything, and theorize about how it relates to multiple beings. Both discourse about "substance" and "function," and substance as the cause/reason for why particulars are what they are.[1] Despite their affinities about the one and the many, differences in their accounts are rife. For instance, whether first principle is inherent in everything or transcendent; whether first principle is an ultimate of nonbeing *and* being or only being; whether it is tranquil or always active; and whether it is material or immaterial: just to name a few. If I can show that even their different answers to the question of the one and the many are attempts to resolve the question, *"what is being?"* there is compelling evidence for a single question of being for them, whose answer someone with wisdom will possess. How else can we account for their similar questions when they come from radically disparate philosophical, historical, geographical and linguistic backgrounds?

Let me begin with Zhu Xi. Even though Zhu asserts that the Principle *li* of creation is one (Zhu Xi and Lü Zuqian 1967: 10), he distinguishes it into an "ultimate of nonbeing" (*wuji* 無極) and the "great ultimate" (*taiji*太極). While the former is tranquil and unmanifested, the latter is active and manifested.[2] Zhu distinguishes the one first principle into two ultimates to explain change and transformation, for he thinks that transformation cannot issue from a unity. Yet, he does not think that there are two first principles, saying, "Therefore 'the Ultimate of Nonbeing and also the Great Ultimate' [quoting Zhou Dunyi]. It does not mean that outside of the Great Ultimate there is an Ultimate of Nonbeing" (Zhu Xi and Lü Zuqian 1967: 5).[3] Contrasting Zhu's analysis of the two ultimates with Aristotle's *ousia*/God (who is always active [see Aristotle 1935: 1074b35], and a unity [Aristotle 1935: 1074a37] that moves everything else), I shall show that both authors are concerned with the same question, "what is being?". Because they understand being as immaterial and the first cause, each explains how immaterial being can cause material things. Since both stress the oneness of being in causing the many, it shows that the problem of being is one for them. Moreover, I shall show that their concerns regarding the substance, function, and goodness of the many and our knowledge of them are traceable to being as a first principle. As Aristotle puts it, "it is from the concept of substance that all the other modes of being take their meaning" (1933: 1045b29–30). And Zhu says, "Principle is one. It is called destiny in terms of what Heaven has imparted to the myriad things, and is called nature in terms of what they have received from Heaven. Actually, the different names express different points of view. That is all" (Zhu Xi and Lü Zuqian 1967: 10). In other words, all questions about the norms and natures of things lead to the one question, "what is being?", showing again that this is the question of being for them, whose answer will eventually satisfy our desire for wisdom and truth.[4] If these two are agreed on the singleness of the question of being despite their different views about the one and the many, comparing them can help us to understand why there is only one question of being and yet multiple manifestations of it.

Let me begin with Zhu's first principle of nature *tian li* 天理 or *dao* 道. Zhu speaks of a heaven-endowed nature or principle that is in all things, making them what they are, which is the form or essence of *dao*. He says, "The essence of *dao* is an all-encompassing wholeness which contains everything, and which is contained in everything" (Zhu Xi 1991: 1.2, 59).[5] That everything contains the principle of *dao* is clear when Zhu says, "Principle is not something generated forcibly from outside; rather, the principle of *dao* is the principle which is innate in ourselves" (Zhu Xi 1991: 2.35, 78). The pervasiveness of *dao* is evident when he says, "*Dao* exists in the world in all places and at all times, and that's it" (Zhu Xi 1991: 1.65, 69). Again, he says, "Like flying hawks and leaping fish, the substance of *dao* is everywhere. You need not forget it or help it, for the universal principle of *dao* just flows along. This is simply the way it is" (Zhu Xi 1991: 1.64, 69).

More elaborately, Zhu maintains that the *dao* in everything is one principle that is universal and the same even though its manifestations are many (Zhu Xi 1991: 1.3, 59). He says, "The universal principle of *dao* is the same, but its manifestations are different. Therefore, there is a principle for ruler-subject relationships as well as for father-son relationships" (Zhu Xi 1991: 1.74, 70). Put otherwise, the particular principles that govern particular relationships and things are different, for example, how sons are to relate to fathers is different from how subjects are to relate to rulers, even though they are caused by the same principle of *dao*, the effect of which is that things are what they are because of the principle of order. For instance, Zhu claims that the following remark by Cheng I is too general: "Humanity (*ren* 仁) is the correct principle of the world. When the correct principle is lost, there will be no order and consequently no harmony" (Zhu Xi and Lü Zuqian 1967: §17, 17). Instead, Zhu says, "humanity is the perfect virtue of the original mind and consequently there is the principle of nature (*tian li*) in it. If the principle of nature is absent, human desires will run wild. How can there be any order or any resultant harmony?" (Zhu Xi and Lü Zuqian 1967: §17, 17). Zhu means that *tian li* is ultimately responsible for any order and harmony in the human mind and the world. Thus, as Kwong-loi Shun points out, while explaining Zhu, "The task of self-cultivation is to enlarge one's heart/mind, until one sees everything as connected to oneself" (Shun 2005: 2).

Even though Aristotle has a functional equivalent of Zhu's principle of nature in his form that causes everything to be what it is (Aristotle 1933: 1032a22–3), unlike Zhu, Aristotle's form is not universal nor the same in every-thing (Aristotle 1933: 1033b20–2). Aristotle's form is neither an encompassing wholeness that contains the different manifestations of everything, nor the same form contained in everything. Rather, form as the principle of nature of a thing is particular to the thing. He says, "formal [*logos*] causes coexist with their effects" (Aristotle 1935: 1070a22). Form (*eidos*), for Aristotle, is the shape (*morphê*) that in a material thing or a form–matter composite makes it what it essentially is. For example, the shape of a plate makes the clay matter into a plate while the shape of a bowl makes it into a bowl. In each case, the form of plate or bowl is not just a manifestation of one and the same form or nature that exists in everything else. But, as it is for Zhu, form for Aristotle is the principle of order that exists in each thing and organizes it into what it essentially is.

For Aristotle, to the extent that the form that causes this plate and others can be generalized into a kind of thing, it is a universal form or definition of plate, and qua kind is common to all plates. It is this formula of plate in the craftsman's mind that causes each plate to be a plate. Aristotle says, "essence will belong to nothing except species of a genus, but to these only; for in these the predicate is not considered to be related to the subject by participation or affection, nor as an accident" (Aristotle 1933: 1030a12–14). Put otherwise, only the species has a predicate that expresses the essence of something rather than an accident. The form of plate in the craftsman's mind in an artificial production, or the form of man in the parent, in a natural generation, is not one in number with the generated plate or man, respectively, but one in formula or definition for Aristotle (Aristotle 1933: 1033b33). He says, "Moving causes are causes in the sense of pre-existent things, but formal [*logos*] causes coexist with their effects" (Aristotle 1935: 1070a21–2). Because the form used to generate the particular thing is not one in number with the form in the generated thing, Aristotle's form is unlike that of Zhu. Put otherwise, Aristotle's universal form is not like Zhu's: it is a generalization of particular plates or men, expressing the species in a definition, rather than in Zhu's principle of nature that is the Great Ultimate (*taiji*) that actually inheres in all things, or the Ultimate of nonbeing (*wuji*) which, although unmanifested, contains the concrete principles of all things.

Just as Aristotle contrasts the particular form in something with its species form that is universal, let us examine Zhu's contrast between the universal principle of *dao* with the particular principles in things. Contrasting the particular principles in things with the universal principle of *dao*, Zhu says, "*Dao* means a roadway. Roughly speaking, it is that road which all men travel on. Each principle has a linear system and circumscribed limits … *Dao* is the Way. It has no form, though when we travel it we can see it in affairs" (Zhu Xi 1991: 1.53, 67). The universal principle of *dao* has no form in the sense that it has no particular order, nor is it a particular path even though its essence of order in general is present in each particular principle, making each thing what it is. Zhu tells us that the principles for particular things and relationships exist before these concrete particulars, and they originate from the same source. He says:

> Before the existence of things and affairs, their principles are already present. All our handlings of affairs and responses to things, however momentary, are manifestations of this principle. A track is a path on which one should travel. Such things as deep love on the part of the father and filial piety on the part of the son are but one track. They all come from one source. (Zhu Xi and Lü Zuqian 1967: §32, 26)

In short, *dao* is the one universal principle in everything, giving rise to the particular principles that manifest the one order of everything.

Aristotle would agree with Zhu about the determinateness and limits of his particular principles specifying the particular orders of everything, as this is akin to the way that particular forms work. He would even agree that the principles of particular things must in a sense exist before the concrete things. For example, the form of bowl must already exist in a craftsman's mind before he can make a clay bowl. Likewise, the form of man must already exist in a parent before a child can be generated. But he would disagree with Zhu that the particular principle of the generated thing is the same as, or one in number, with the principle in the craftsman's mind, the parent, or the *taiji*. Rather, Aristotle holds that the particular form that organizes each particular thing is individual to the thing.[6] In his words, "the causes of things in the same species are different, not in species, but because the causes of individuals are different: your matter and form and moving cause being different from mine, although in their universal formula they are the same" (Aristotle 1935: 1071a27–9).

Aristotle would also disagree with Zhu's characterization of the universal principle of *dao* as being devoid of any form or order even though it is the cause of order in all things. Whether we compare Zhu's *dao* to Aristotle's universal species form, or, more appropriately, to Aristotle's first cause or unmoved mover/God, their accounts are quite different. While Zhu thinks that his *dao/li* 道/理 cannot have any form in order to be the encompassing wholeness that contains the particular principles of all things, or inhere in them, Aristotle's species form is determinate and limited. Only by being limited can universal form be definable to specify the essence of something. An examination of Zhu's *dao/taiji/li*, and its functional equivalence in Aristotle, namely, God, will reveal more differences than similarities.

Just as Zhu's *dao*, Aristotle's God is the cause of the natures/substances of all things. They differ in that *dao* acts as a cause by inhering in everything and containing their concrete principles even before they exist, whilst this is not the way of Aristotle's God. Rather, God works by being the primary substance that causes everything else; by being an unmoved mover that is an actuality that exists necessarily. Unlike *dao* that is directly related to everything by inhering in each, Aristotle's God is indirectly related to its effects by being transcendent. For concrete things that are combinations of form and matter to exist for Aristotle, we need some sort of matter, form, and an efficient cause that instills the form into the matter to make the resulting thing.[7] Additionally, there must be something else, that is neither the matter nor form of the thing, but which causes the motion, say, of the efficient cause. He says:

> The cause of a man is (i) his elements: fire and earth as matter, and the particular form; (ii) some external formal cause, viz. his father; and besides these (iii) the sun and the ecliptic, which are neither matter nor form nor privation nor identical in form with him, but cause motion. (Aristotle 1935: 1071a14–18)

More specifically, the sun and movements of the heavenly bodies are responsible for the generation, growth, and motion of everything in the universe. However, because these celestial bodies are themselves moved, Aristotle thinks that there must be an unmoved mover, a first complete reality (*to prôton entelecheia* [Aristotle 1935: 1071a37]), a principle (*archên*), a substance (*ousia*) which is an actuality (*energeia*) that exists eternally (Aristotle 1935: 1071b20–1) and necessarily, to move them. Aristotle insists on the actuality of an unmoved mover to explain the movement of the universe, for he denies that a mover that is moved can be the first principle. This is because a moved mover, like the first heaven (*prôtos ouranos*), requires a mover to move it (Aristotle 1935: 1072a21–5).

Apart from being an unmoved mover that causes motion in the universe and everything in it, and is thus prior in causality and time, Aristotle's God also causes by being the one primary substance by which all other substances are defined, for they are more or less united as substances, depending on how nearly they can approximate God's characteristics. Even though physical substances have the sources of motion in themselves, they are not prior in motion and causality because they depend on a prior mover. Similarly, although mathematical substances are immovable, they are not like God for they are not capable of separability or independence, and hence cannot be primary substances. Only God satisfies the conditions of immovability and separability required of a primary substance. God is the one substance that is most stable and definable because he is immovable, prior in cause, time, and separability. Consequently, God is the primary substance that is most knowable (Aristotle

1933: 1028a31–b3). The conditions that characterize God's existence are the standards of oneness by which we measure the substantiality of all things. Things that are more knowable, stable, and definable accord more to the one (*pros hen*) God, and thus are more substantial than others that are not as united because they fail to satisfy these conditions of knowability, stability, and definability. With these characteristics in mind, God and *taiji* differ, in that, while God is most definable, *taiji*, being without limit and formless, is indefinable. Aristotle's understanding of God as the *pros hen* cause of substances, namely, as the one separate and immovable substance toward which all other substances are defined, is also different from Zhu's *taiji*, since the latter is neither separate from everything in which it inheres nor immovable.

More elaborately, since Aristotle's unmoved mover is transcendent and unmoved, it is different from Zhu's *taiji*, which moves. *Taiji* relies on *qi* 氣 (material energy that is common to mind and matter) for its activity. Zhu says, "The Great Ultimate [*taiji*] exists only in the *yin* 陰 and *yang* 陽, and cannot be separated from them" (Chan 1963: 630). He explains the relation between *taiji* and the *yin* and *yang qi* in the process of generation as follows:

> Principle attaches itself to *yin* and *yang* as a man sits astride a horse. As soon as *yin* and *yang* produce the Five Agents (*wu xing* 五行), they are … fixed by physical nature and are … differentiated into individual things each with its nature. But the Great Ultimate is in all of them. (Chan 1963: 641)

Aristotle would say that if *taiji* relies on the *yin* and *yang qi*/matter to exist and generate, Zhu's *taiji* cannot be the first principle.[8] Zhu's system, for Aristotle, would look more like a composite substance, because of the combination of *taiji* with the material *qi*.

A further difference is that Zhu seems to rely on matter to distinguish things, since he talks about the same principle inhering in everything. Zhu also says that, apart from a *taiji* that is unable to exist without *yin* and *yang qi*, the kind of *qi* in which principles must inhere to become active is the mind (*xin* 心). He says, "The mind embraces all principles and all principles are complete in this single entity, the mind" (Chan 1963: 606); and, "There must be mind before nature can be gotten hold of and put into operation" (Chan 1963: 616). Despite the fact that the same principle of nature completely inheres in everything, only human beings who have mastered their *qi* and can control their desires can access it completely. What inhibits the complete access of anything to principle is its *qi*. As I put it elsewhere:

> Something's limited access to *li* is due to its *qi*. Depending on the clarity or turbidity, purity or impurity of *qi*, something will be more or less obstructed

from *li*. In spite of how men, animals and things are born with the same *tian li*, the *qi* of things and animals obstruct their access to *li*; they can never penetrate this obstruction. Zhu says, "The principle received by things is precisely the same degree as the material force received by them .... the physical constitution of dogs and horses being what it is, they know how to do only certain things. (Sim 2010: 87)

Contrary to Zhu's view, in which *qi* individuates things and obstructs their ability to know the principle of nature (*tian li*) that inheres in them, Aristotle's view is that both form and matter individuate things. For Aristotle, both form and matter make up a man and are unique to him.

Nor would Zhu's Ultimate of nonbeing (*wuji* 無極) be the functional equivalent to Aristotle's God. This is because even though *wuji* is independent of matter, it is also inactive. By contrast, Aristotle's God is always active in thinking of himself, as he is the best object of thought; he would not be independent and prior if his thoughts were of things other than himself.

Despite the differences between Zhu's *taiji* and Aristotle's God, respectively, as the first principles, they are similar in claiming that there is one first principle, and in attempting to explain how everything is caused by the first principle. Both are agreed that the first principle must be prior to everything, be immaterial, and yet affect matter to create the many material things. These agreements show that the question of being can be summed up in the question "what is being?" This question is in turn related to questions such as: "is being one or many?", "why is there something rather than nothing?", and "how is being related to the many?". For both authors, what being is not only raises these questions but provides the answers to them. This is also why answering questions regarding how the one and the many are related and, ultimately, the question regarding the nature of being, will lead to wisdom and truth. More specifically, the answers are as follows: because being is ultimate, it must be one; because being exists, there is something rather than nothing; because being is good and immaterial, it manifests itself in the many material things that exist because of being, and are good because they share in being's goodness.

To elaborate on the relation between metaphysics and ethics,[9] Zhu's principle (*li*) that inheres in everything is "invariably good" (Chan 1963: 597). He says, "The nature is the same as principle. Traced to its source, none of the principles in the world is not good" (Chan 1963: 606; see also Zhu Xi and Lü Zuqian 1967: 1.38, 28). Because *li* is good and responsible for the nature of everything by inhering in them, everything is governed by moral principles. He asserts: "That which is inherent in things is principle. That by which things are managed is moral principles" (Zhu Xi and Lü Zuqian 1967: 1.15, 16). Again: "Of the thousands and tens of thousands of human beings and all things, there is none independent of these moral principles" (Chan 1963: 617). Because for Zhu the same principle of nature exists in everything, everything, regardless of whether it is human, is endowed with moral principles. However, since only the human mind has the kind of *qi* that can access the principle of nature completely, it is man's function to purify his nature in order to know the *li* and act according to the moral principles. Specifically, because man is endowed with the moral principles of humaneness (*ren*), appropriateness (*yi* 義), ritual propriety (*li* 禮), and wisdom (*zhi* 智) as his substance, his proper function is to feel commiseration, shame, deference, and compliance, and to act by distinguishing between right and wrong respectively. In short, human beings are to act morally because their minds are "basically good" (Zhu Xi 1991: §16, 107).[10] Zhu holds that just as the minds of Heaven and Earth produce things without ceasing, man's mind is to use the four virtues of *ren*, *yi*, *li*, and *zhi* to "love people gently and to benefit things" (Chan 1963: 595). Human beings then, for Zhu, being endowed with these particular moral principles, have the function of acting morally toward other human beings and things in the universe.[11] What is normative for human actions stems from the same source of normativity for heaven's and earth's function, and that is the first principle of *li/taiji*, which is invariably good.

By the same token, Aristotle's unmoved mover "is necessarily [*anankê*] good [*kalôs*] and is thus the first principle [*archê*]" (Aristotle 1935: 1072b11–12). He continues:

> Life belongs to God. For the actuality of thought is life [*nou energeia zôê*], and God is that actuality [*hê energeia*]; and the essential actuality of God is life most good and eternal. We hold, then, that God is a living being [*zôon*], eternal [*aidion*], most good [*ariston*]; and therefore life and a continuous eternal existence belong to God; for that is what God is. (Aristotle 1935: 1072b27–31)

Similar to Zhu's *li*, as the norm of goodness for everything, Aristotle's God, being life most eternal and good, is the standard of goodness for everything. Aristotle's God is the one end toward which everything is ordered. When considering whether the supreme good/God is related to the universe as something separate and independent, or as the whole whose parts are ordered, Aristotle says that it is both, even though it is more the former, that is, God is separate and independent. Comparing God's relation to the universe to that of a general to his army, Aristotle maintains that just as the general is the reason for the order of the army, yet is not in any way dependent upon the army, God, too, is responsible for the order of the universe while being independent of it. Just as Zhu assigns a special status to human beings for being able to know the *taiji* and act according to the moral principles endowed in them by *taiji*, Aristotle, likewise, privileges human beings in knowing the first principle and achieving the good because of their nature. Only human beings have the speculative part of the soul (*nous*) that is immortal and separable, and which, hence, is most like God when it contemplates eternal truths. Even though things like fishes, birds, and plants are also ordered to God as the one end, they are not ordered toward Him like human beings.[12] Aristotle illustrates the difference in the ordering of human beings and these other creatures to God by citing the order in a household. He says that, in a household, free persons "have the least liberty to act at random, and have all or most of their actions preordained for them, whereas the slaves and animals have little common responsibility and act for the most part at random; for the nature of each class is a principle as we have described' (Aristotle 1935: 1075a20–3). In short, because human nature consists of the rational part of the soul, which is divided into the speculative part and the deliberative part, the human function is to know the truth with the speculative part, and perform right and good actions with the deliberative part. Put otherwise, human wisdom is inseparably bound up with the truth of human nature. Only knowledge of the latter can lead to wisdom.

Two differences between Aristotle's and Zhu's accounts of the human substance and function are: (i) Aristotle separates the theoretical/speculative part of the soul from the deliberative part so that the former is directed at the truth or falsehood of invariable objects while the latter is directed at good actions concerning variable objects. In contrast, Zhu does not separate theory from practice, as he thinks that the investigation into things in the universe will enable us to know their concrete principles and issue in proper actions. Because the same *li* inheres in everything, knowledge of the concrete principles of things can also lead to knowledge of the moral principles in human beings. Thus, theory and practice are continuous for Zhu, while they are separate for Aristotle. (ii) Whereas the perfection of the deliberative part of the soul results in *phronêsis* that is restricted to moral actions toward other human beings for Aristotle, the possession of the four moral principles (*ren, yi, li,* and *zhi*) for Zhu leads to virtuous actions not only toward human beings but also toward everything else in the universe. Thus, Zhu's view of the function of morality is different from that of Aristotle, in being more cosmic in scope.

In conclusion, I have shown that, despite the differences between Aristotle's and Zhu's specific views regarding their first principles, they agree that these first principles are prior to, and the causes of, everything else. Each offers an account of how his first principle answers the question of what being is, and how the one being relates to the many in the universe. Ultimately, apart from explaining why everything in the universe exists, what being is for each also accounts for the truth and nature of each thing and what is good for each. That is, for both authors, answering the metaphysical question of being will provide wisdom because one will not only be wise about the truth but also possess practical wisdom with respect to actions. Whereas Zhu answers these questions by asserting that the *li/taiji* inheres in everything, Aristotle answers them by positing a transcendent God who moves without itself being moved. The answer of each author results in a different account of knowledge of the first principle, as well as a different account of human actions. Nevertheless, it is clear from comparing them that there is a single question of being for both. The answer to this single question—"what is being?"—is also the answer to other questions that can be asked about being. For Aristotle and Zhu, then, desiring the answer to the question of being or first principle is also a desire for wisdom.

Notes

1   Aristotle says, "the primary and unqualified definition (*haplôs horismos*) and the essence (*to ti ên einai*), belong to substances (*tôn ousiôn*)' (Aristotle 1933: 1030b5–6; see 1032a1–2 for the identity of essence, substance, and *logos*). Speaking of the mind of Heaven and Earth which produces and reproduces all things, Zhu Xi says, "When it is tranquil and has returned to its original state, it exists as substance before it is manifested. When it is active and penetrates everything, it exists as function after it has manifested itself" (Zhu Xi and Lü Zuqian 1967: 12). Again, Zhu Xi says, "Permeating the world there is a single mechanism which vitalizes things. It flows out and issues forth as function and not for a moment does it cease" (Zhu Xi 1991: 70).

2   Tranquility, for Zhu Xi, "is not non-being as such. Because it has not assumed physical form, we call it non-being. It is not because of activity that there is being. Because (activity makes) it visible, we call it being" (Chan 1963: 629, 44:6b–7a).

3   See Dorter 2009: 257 for how the Great Ultimate is identical with the Ultimate of Nonbeing when he says, "'The operations of heaven are not beings, if beings are what can be perceived by the senses; therefore they can be considered non-being. Thus too, the Great Ultimate, which is prior not only to sensible qualities but even to differentiation, is the ultimate of non-being."

4   I address how both Zhu's and Aristotle's metaphysics yield not only wisdom about everything but a practical wisdom that offers resources for alleviating environmental problems, in Sim 2010.

5   All substitutions of Pinyin for Wade-Giles, and minor modifications, are mine. In-text references to Zhu Xi (1991) will be in the following format: Author, date: chapter number, section number, page number (e.g. Zhu Xi 1991: 1.2, 59). References to Zhu Xi and Lü Zuqian (1967) will be cited in the same format, though section number may sometimes be inapplicable: e.g. (Zhu Xi and Lü Zuqian 1967: §74, 70) *or* (Zhu Xi and Lü Zuqian 1967: 1.38, 28).

6   For a detailed explanation of Aristotle's view of particular form, see Sim 2007: 136 and 145.

7   I compare the necessity of matter in a concrete thing such as a man for both Aristotle and Zhu in Sim 2010: 80.

8   For a critical examination of Zhu's metaphysics and its weaknesses in comparison to a Daoist account in Laozi's *Daodejing*, see Sim 2015b.

9   For a discussion of the essential relation between metaphysics and ethics in early Confucianism, see Sim 2015a.

10   Compare these principles with Mencius's remarks, "The feeling of compassion is the sprout of benevolence. The feeling of disdain is the sprout of righteousness [appropriateness]. The feeling of deference is the sprout of propriety. The feeling of approval and disapproval is the sprout of wisdom" (Mencius 2009: bk. 2A, 6.5), thus his conclusion that human beings are by nature good.

11   Patt-Shamir explains the objective source of these principles in Heaven by saying that Heaven is an ultimate that "is 'objective' in the sense in which it can be known to human beings, insofar as it offers standards that prevent the relativism that could be the outcome of a theory that centers on human beings and their powers. By knowing Heaven, we can improve human practice in such a way that Heaven becomes human, rather than that humans become 'heavenly'" (2004: 353).

12   For an account of how plants, animals and nature in general are ordered toward God differently than human beings, see Dorter 2009: 259: "Human beings could not fulfill the goal of nature if we were not supported by the animal, plant, and mineral realms. It is not that plants grow and rivers flow out of love for the mind of God, but that nature as a whole does what is necessary for its highest manifestation, human beings, to achieve that goal. We are like the fruit of a tree, which could not exist without all the other parts. Only human beings are capable of reaching the goal and achieving consummate happiness (N. E. X.8.1178b24–32.), but lower forms of life, in seeking to thrive, seek to emulate the actualization of God as far as their natures allow. Their efforts to survive are a love of life, and implicitly of the most actualized life, which is God (Meta. Λ7.1072b26–30), and they emulate God's eternality in their desire to reproduce themselves through procreation (De Anima 2.4.415a–26–b2)."

Works cited

Aristotle (1933), *Aristotle: Metaphysics, Books I-IX*, H. Tredennick (trans.), Cambridge, MA: Harvard University Press.

Aristotle (1935), *Aristotle: Metaphysics, Books 10-14. Oeconomica. Magna Moralia*, H. Tredennick and C. G. Armstrong (trans), Cambridge, MA: Harvard University Press.

Chan, W. T. (ed.) (1963), *A Sourcebook in Chinese Philosophy*, Princeton: Princeton University Press.

Dorter, K. (2009), "Metaphysics and Morality in Neo-Confucianism and Greece: Zhu Xi, Plato, Aristotle, and Plotinus," *Dao: A Journal of Comparative Philosophy* 8/3, 255-76.

Mencius (2009), *The Essential Mengzi*, B. W. Van Norden (trans.), Indianapolis: Hackett Publishing Co., Inc.

Patt-Shamir, G. (2004), "Moral World, Ethical Terminology: the Moral Significance of Metaphysical Terms in Zhou Dunyi and Zhu Xi," *Journal of Chinese Philosophy* 31/3, 349-62.

Shun, K.-L. (2005), "Zhu Xi on Gong 公 (Impartial) and Si 私 (Partial)," *Dao: A Journal of Comparative Philosophy* 5/1, 1-9.

Sim, M. (2007), *Remastering Morals with Aristotle and Confucius*, Cambridge: Cambridge University Press.

Sim, M. (2010), "From Metaphysics to Environmental Ethics: Aristotle or Zhu Xi?" in R. Engel, L. Westra, and K. Bosselmann (eds), *Democracy, Ecological Integrity and International Law*, Newcastle: Cambridge Scholars Publishing, 77-90.

Sim, M. (2015a), "From Metaphysics to Ethics: East & West," *Review of Metaphysics* 63, 487-509.

Sim, M. (2015b), "Laozi and Zhu Xi on Knowledge and Virtue" in J. Tiwald (ed.), *Oxford Handbook of Chinese Philosophy*, Oxford: Oxford University Press (forthcoming).

Zhu Xi (1991), *Further Reflections on Things at Hand*, A. Wittenborn (trans.), Lanham: University Press of America.

Zhu Xi and Lü Zuqian (1967), *Reflections on Things at Hand: The Neo-Confucian Anthology*, W. T. Chan (trans.), New York: Columbia University Press.

8

Wisdom as Realization: Heidegger and Zhuangzi on Belonging in the World[1]

Steven Burik

Once and for all, there is a lot that I don't want to know.—Wisdom sets limits even to knowledge (Nietzsche 1997: 5).

Introduction

There is a common conception of the difference between knowledge and wisdom where the latter is understood to entail something more than just knowledge, and seems to have a practical component in the sense that wise people are generally considered those who not only know a lot of things but more importantly know how to live. For example, the *Oxford Guide to Philosophy* has it that wisdom is a "form of understanding that unites a reflective attitude and a practical concern" (Honderich 2005: 959). This suggests that knowledge in itself is "not enough." I argue in this chapter that both Heidegger and Zhuangzi are in similar ways concerned that philosophers of their respective times were too concerned with the artificiality of mere knowledge, and forgot about wisdom. Although obviously separated by enormous rifts of time, culture, and philosophical background, Heidegger and Zhuangzi share a commitment to a kind of thinking that is profoundly this-worldly, and consequently focus on wisdom with its practical component more than on abstract knowledge. They both seek to realize (in both senses of the term) their ways of thought within the confines of our concrete existence.

A number of related similarities in their approach will be discussed. First, Heidegger and Zhuangzi both articulate forms of criticism on the more established theories of their times. These criticisms, although set in vastly different circumstances and times, amount to the accusation that wisdom, or the right kind of thinking, is lacking because of the dominant focus on knowledge systems built on artificial distinctions. Not only are such knowledge systems inadequate, they also form an obstacle for gaining wisdom. Heidegger criticizes representational or propositional thought with its subject–object distinction, which he sees as responsible for the forgetfulness of Being, and Zhuangzi criticizes the artificiality of making distinctions on many levels, which he sees as responsible for the losing of *dao* 道. Second, both see thinking as experiential and thoroughly connected to concrete experience. In that sense both will claim that wisdom lies in the thoughtful acknowledgment of this connection to concrete experience, and that wisdom thus includes know-how rather than just factual knowledge. This will be supported with Heidegger's examples of localized knowing and Zhuangzi's examples of skilful craftsmen. Connected to this, the dispositions or attitudes of the wise (or those who think properly), *Gelassenheit* (releasement), *ziran* 自然 (so-of-itself), and *wu wei* 無為 (non-assertive action) are shown to convey a form of belonging to the world. Both Heidegger and Zhuangzi show us the contextuality of our thoughts and existence, and urge us to realize a relational understanding of the continuity of ourselves and the rest of the world. Lastly, both Heidegger and Zhuangzi think that, when we think properly, we do in fact realize a world, rather than just correspond to it. This is the other sense of "realization," and I will argue that both Heidegger and Zhuangzi think that mankind plays, or rather could play, a crucial role in this kind of realization, and is not just a passive observer. In conclusion, this means that both actively sought wisdom as realization rather than knowledge.

Knowledge versus wisdom

Let me start with some clarifications: It seems that neither Heidegger nor Zhuangzi is very interested in the specific terms "knowledge," "wisdom," or classical Chinese equivalents, if there are such. Certainly Heidegger (and I think also Zhuangzi) rarely uses the term in a more than ordinary way. Although this may be the case, it is in fact within their way of thinking that wisdom finds a place.

For both Heidegger and Zhuangzi, the distinction between knowledge and wisdom is played out through a distinguishing between the wrong and the right kind of thinking. We should realize this when we are discussing this in English, as many translators have used the terms "knowledge" and "wisdom" interchangeably, both in the case of Heidegger (for example to translate *Wissen*) and in Zhuangzi (for example to translate *zhi* 知). So instead of discussing the terms per se, I discuss them indirectly. I will argue that in the case of Daoism, there are really two kinds of knowledge or wisdom: one that is abhorred and attacked by most Daoists, and another that is revered. I will refer to the first, which is considered the wrong kind of knowing, as "knowledge," and to the second, which is the right kind of knowing, as "wisdom." I must mention this to defuse the seeming tension in such passages as *Zhuangzi* Chapter 7: "do not be a proprietor of wisdom" (Watson 2003: 94–5). In this sense my contribution builds only loosely on the traditional idea of "wisdom," and will play freely with the different "wise" persons of Daoism, be they the sages, the authentic persons, or the daemonic persons. My focus in talking about "wisdom" is really on how people ought to live and think, according to Heidegger and Zhuangzi respectively.

The next clarification concerns the term "realization" or to "realize." There are two meanings of "realization." We are said to realize something when we become aware of it, when we come to know something. This first meaning is closely related to (plain and simple) knowledge, but even here we need to make a distinction, in that "realization" suggests something a bit more or something different than just knowledge. We can know that it is raining, but if we say we realize it is raining we are making a slightly different assertion. Realization seems to entail a closer connection to the thing realized than "knowledge" has. This difference between knowledge and realization will hopefully become clearer in what follows. More importantly, the second meaning of "realization" is concerned with making real, actualizing, applying, or implementing. When one realizes one's goals, they become actuality, and not just things dreamed of in the future.

Based on these clarifications, my claim will be that both Heidegger and Zhuangzi think that proper thinking (wisdom) is intimately connected to both senses of "realization." First of all, in the sense where just knowing things is definitely not enough, and even detrimental to proper thinking, and second, in the sense that wisdom is indeed the application in real life which actively creates a world rather than merely observes it.

Daoism

In classical Chinese philosophy, knowledge is not always universally praised. Although we could say that in the Confucian tradition knowledge is fairly well regarded, those of a more Daoist bent do not fancy knowledge much. But even within the Confucian tradition there is the understanding that knowledge will get you only so far. Confucius himself qualified knowledge to the extent that "to truly love it is better than just to understand [or know] it, and to enjoy it is better than simply to love it" (Ames and Rosemont 1998: 108). Knowledge here seems to be seen as a preliminary that is insufficient on its own, without application or accompaniment by a different attitude (love or enjoyment).[2] And even Xunzi, a great proponent of learning, does not think that knowledge is always good, and advocates that "great wisdom consists in not deliberating over certain things" (Chan 1963: 118).

Daoism in general seems to militate against knowledge: in one part of his definition of wisdom in classical Chinese thought, Graham argues that, for Daoism, wisdom lies in "the mirroring of the particular situation without forcing it into classifications by naming" (Graham 1989: 385). By naming things, we abstract them from their immediate situation. This being so, knowledge (*zhi*) is frowned upon since it is understood to be intimately linked to classification by naming, and therefore knowledge artificially breaks the whole of a situation into different components, as well as distracting our attention from that situation. In the *Daodejing* it is said that one must "cut off sagacity (*sheng*) and get rid of knowledge (*zhi*)" (Ames and Hall 2003: 104 ["wisdom" changed to "knowledge"]). The Guodian text of the *Daodejing* is, as we shall see, more in line with Zhuangzi, as it has "Cut off knowledge and get rid of discrimination"[3] here. The *Daodejing* also militates against the cumulative nature of knowledge, saying that "In studying, there is daily increase, While in learning of way-making (*dao*), there is daily decrease: one loses and again loses to the point that one does everything noncoercively (*wu wei*)" (Ames and Hall 2003: 151). Artificial knowledge or information-gathering is an obstacle rather than an aid. It clutters a person with unnecessary information, while distracting from what is actually important. Other passages from the *Daodejing* that convey the uselessness of knowing, or even its character as obstacle to "real," that is "unprincipled" knowing, are found in chapters 56 and 81, where it is argued that to talk or to be erudite is not to know truly, and in chapter 65, where knowledge is said to be bad for ruling the state.

With this criticism of knowledge, the *Daodejing* advocates a different approach, through its use of the *wu*-forms. In their discussion of these *wu*-forms, prevalent in the *Daodejing*, Ames and Hall put the idea of *wuzhi* 無知 in the following way:

Wuzhi ... actually means the absence of a certain kind of knowledge—the kind of knowledge that is dependent upon ontological presence: that is, the assumption that there is some unchanging reality behind appearance. Knowledge grounded in a denial of ontological presence involves "acosmotic" thinking: the type of thinking that does not presuppose a single-ordered ("One behind the many") world, and its intellectual accoutrements. It is, therefore, *unprincipled* knowing. (Ames and Hall 2003: 40)

Zhuangzi

So, knowledge that is intent on fixating references based on ontological presence is frowned upon in the *Daodejing*. And when we come, finally, to the *Zhuangzi*, the story is no different and Zhuangzi seems even more adamant to be rid of the idea of knowledge. Throughout the *Zhuangzi* this theme returns in various passages, and knowledge is almost invariably discredited, especially abstract knowledge or the knowledge that classifies, makes distinctions.

Let us consider some examples: In the first chapter, Zhuangzi already states that "Little understanding cannot come up to great understanding" (Watson 2003: 24), and that one must move beyond the superficiality and artificiality of "common" or "normal" knowledge, which for Zhuangzi means the level of discrimination and representation. Elsewhere in the inner chapters (chapter 4), it is said that one must "expel knowledge from the heart" (Graham 2001: 69) in order to achieve the disposition that is ideal for the Daoist. Graham's comments on this passage suggest again that knowledge is an obstacle, rather than a help to the spontaneous character of the Daoist sage: "the heart will be emptied of conceptual knowledge, the channels of the senses will be cleared, and he will simply perceive and respond" (Graham 2001: 69). Put in other words, in chapter 2 of the *Zhuangzi*: "Great wit is effortless, petty wit picks holes" (Graham 2001: 50). Zhuangzi further mentions that, for the sage, "knowledge is a curse" (Graham 2001: 82), something that the sage has no need for, since the spontaneous nature of her or his actions does not need any planning or deliberation based on representational knowledge. Wisdom, or living as a Daoist sage according to Zhuangzi, definitely entails giving up on the common sense or normal idea of knowledge: "Ignorance is profound, knowing it is superficial" (Graham 2001: 163). Indeed, Zhuangzi quite literally says that you should "smash to pieces your knowledge" (Graham 2001: 132).

Based on the aforementioned, we can say a couple of things about the kind of knowledge discredited in Daoism in general. This is (i) the kind of knowledge that seeks to halt the process character of *dao*, by fixing references based on some kind of metaphysical principle akin to Platonic ideas or forms, and (ii) knowledge that seeks to make artificial distinctions between things, where the Daoist rather seeks to understand there to be a continuity not to be divided into separate parts.

But is that all? Fortunately not. All these diatribes against discriminating knowledge are preliminary to taking "the step beyond knowledge" (Graham 2001: 90). The Daoists understand wisdom to entail a going beyond knowledge. The difference lies mostly in the fact that the wise, the sages, do *not* discriminate but focus their attention on the whole situation. This means that wisdom is a kind of non-knowing awareness, in touch with reality. In fact, for Zhuangzi this kind of wisdom seems to lie in the realization that there is some profound interdependence or relationality between ourselves and the world:

> The men of old, their knowledge had arrived at something: at what had it arrived? There were some who thought there had not yet begun to be things—the utmost, the exhaustive, there is no more to add. The next thought there were things but there had not yet begun to be borders. The next thought there were borders to them but there had not yet begun to be "That's it, that's not". The lighting up of "That's it, that's not" is the reason why the Way is flawed. (Graham 2001: 54)

When people still made absolutely no distinction between themselves and other things, that is, that "things" had not begun to exist as "things" for them yet, but people were wholly immersed in and interdependent with their surroundings, that was when *dao* was properly attended to. What "knowledge" does is to alienate us from this kind of interdependence, and pretend that we can isolate ourselves from the world by abstracting and discriminating, or, in more Western metaphysical terminology, by generalization, classification, and categorization of "things." For Zhuangzi this approach is highly unsatisfactory:

> To "divide", then, is to leave something undivided: to "discriminate between alternatives" is to leave something which is neither alternative. "What?" you ask. The sage keeps it in his breast, common men argue over alternatives to show it to each other. Hence I say: "to 'discriminate between alternatives' is to fail to see something". (Graham 2001: 57)

And this is because "the greatest discrimination is unspoken" (Graham 2001: 57). Here the episode in the "Autumn Floods" chapter featuring Gongsun Long is instructive: the clearest representative of artificial knowledge and distinction-making has to acknowledge that his way of thinking fails to even come close to

Zhuangzi's, and Gongsun Long is left to wonder "whether my arguments are not as good as his, or whether I am no match for him in understanding" (Watson 2003: 108).

Heidegger

So what is it that we normal people fail to see? Let me hold on to that question, and first turn my focus to Heidegger in order to see if we can become clearer on the distinction between wisdom and "mere" knowledge. Heidegger has ideas similar to those of the Daoists. Yet, in Heidegger, the dichotomy between superficial knowledge and wisdom is discussed on a different playing field: the distinction between *Wissenschaft* and *Vorstellen* (calculative or scientific thought and representational thought) on one side, and *Denken* (thinking) and *Besinnung* (mindfulness or reflectiveness) on the other. But in this different field, Heidegger sounds remarkably similar to the Daoists. For example, he states: "we moderns can learn only if we always unlearn at the same time. Applied to the matter before us: we can learn thinking only if we radically unlearn what thinking has been traditionally" (Heidegger 1993: 374). Heidegger further says that "science itself does not think, and cannot think" (Heidegger 1993: 373), pointing to the limitedness of the subject–object approach and of rational deliberation.

Heidegger also discusses the distinction between *Wissenschaft* and *Besinnung* (mindfulness) in *Science and Reflection*, where he argues that far from being "objective" and "neutral," scientific thinking imposes its categories upon the world, in that the subject sets up (*stellt vor*) the world, in terms of objectness or *Gegenständigkeit*.[4] And in the "Letter on Humanism" Heidegger argues that ever since the "characterization of thinking as *theoria* and the determination of knowing as 'theoretical' behaviour ... 'philosophy' has been in the constant predicament of having to justify its existence before the 'sciences'. It believes it can do that most effectively by elevating itself to the rank of a science. But such an effort is the abandonment of the essence of thinking" (Heidegger 1993: 218–19).

Through these examples we can see that Heidegger makes a clear distinction between the knowing of science (*Wissenschaft*) and "real" knowing or thinking (*denken*). This is similar to Zhuangzi's distinction between artificial knowing and "real" knowing. For example, in *Mindfulness*, one of the more meditative works of Heidegger, he sounds very much like Zhuangzi: "we stay in the leap ahead of any yes and no. Certainly we are never the knowing ones, yet in knowing-awareness we are those who *are* ... We do not know goals, and are only a pathway" (Heidegger 2006: 5–6).

In *Mindfulness* the good kind of knowing (*wissen,* not to be confused with *Wissenschaft*) is translated as "knowing-awareness," for example: "to philosophy belongs the serenity of the mastery of imageless knowing-awareness" (Heidegger 2006: 42). Such forms of *Wissen* and *Weisheit,* which are related, denote a form of wisdom rather than conventional knowledge. They have to do with an immediacy that in an essential way connects the "knower" to the situation. And for Heidegger, such "wisdom" must, of course, be related to Being, and his hopes are pinned on retrieving or finding anew the meaning of Being, and a way to live accordingly. This way of living is described in terms of *Gelassenheit* and *Ereignis,* and I will focus on these terms later in this chapter. For now, sticking with knowing and wisdom, this is what Heidegger has in mind: "When *knowing as preserving* [*Verwahrung*] the truth of what holds true ... distinguishes future man (*vis-a-vis* the hitherto rational animal) and lifts him into the guardianship of be-ing, then the highest knowing is that which is strong enough to be the origin of a *renunciation*" (Heidegger 1999: 43). As with Zhuangzi, the first step to wisdom is a step back, a renunciation. But, according to Heidegger, such a renunciation is not negative, but should again be thought of in terms of *Gelassenheit.*

Beyond knowing

So both Heidegger and Zhuangzi are talking about the distinction between "conventional" and "real" knowledge, and I use the term "real" very loosely here. In that sense, for both, wisdom is understood as that kind of thinking that goes beyond all knowledge, all conventional worldviews, and indeed, beyond the idea of "worldview" itself, by first of all taking a step back from it.

So wisdom does not entail only the still rather facile distinction between "real" and "superficial" knowledge. The passages from both Heidegger and Zhuangzi mentioned so far would make it easy to think that the wisdom of the sages lies in making the right kind of distinctions between "good" wisdom and "bad" knowledge. But Zhuangzi and Heidegger go further than just making distinctions themselves between the appropriate and the inappropriate kind of knowing or thinking. The making of a distinction between "little knowledge" and "great knowledge" itself still remains a thinking in dichotomies, reminiscent of the dualist approach that both Heidegger and Zhuangzi loathe, although in different ways. And both of them are very aware of this problem. Zhuangzi for example, in the "Autumn Floods" chapter, observes that "the wisest, because they have a full view of far and near, do not belittle the smaller or make much of the greater, knowing that measuring has no limit" (Graham 2001: 145–6). "Real" wisdom is to let go of artificial distinctions and abstractions, and to (re-)turn to a situational and inclusive understanding of oneself. Zhuangzi shows contempt for those who think they can separate things one from the other, but ultimately also for those who think that "greater knowledge" is intrinsically better than "smaller knowledge."

The steps both Heidegger and Zhuangzi have taken so far thus reflect only the initial stage of a process. In the case of Heidegger we can surely say that calculative and representational thought cannot live up to *Denken* (thinking) or *Besinnung* (meditative thought), but this does not mean there is no space for such representational thought. Heidegger has said on many occasions that representational or calculative thinking is not only valuable in its own right[5] but also part of Heidegger's *aletheia* (truth), and thus also a way of unconcealing or revealing: "Technology is a mode of revealing. Technology comes to presence [*west*] in the realm where revealing and unconcealment take place, where *aletheia*, truth, happens" (Heidegger 1977: 13). In other words, there are "two kinds of thinking, each justified and needed in its own way: calculative thinking and meditative [*besinnliches*] thinking" (Heidegger 1966: 46).

So it seems that, according to Heidegger, we should refrain from seeing such conventional thinking as all bad. It has its place and time, but the real problem arises when such a restricted form of thinking claims exclusive rights to truthfulness to the detriment of other ways of thought, when representational and calculative thought override "wisdom".

A similar thing appears to be the case in the *Zhuangzi*. The first chapter sets up the difference between small knowledge and great knowledge, and recognizes that there is a need to overcome the more restricted way of thinking. The bird Peng and the fish Kun have many more capabilities than their counterparts, the smaller animals. Yet Peng and Kun, too, are in some fundamental way restricted, as is Liezi's flying exercise. And their hugeness effectively prevents their being able to do what the small animals can do. In the Autumn Floods chapter, any seriously dichotomous view of great and small is squarely discredited:

> A beam or a pillar can be used to batter down a city wall, but it is no good for stopping up a little hole—this refers to a difference in function. Thoroughbreds like Qiji and Hualiu could gallop a thousand li in one day, but when it came to catching rats they were no match for the wildcat or the weasel—this refers to a

difference in skill. The horned owl catches fleas at night and can spot the tip of a hair, but when daylight comes, no matter how wide it opens its eyes, it cannot see a mound or a hill—this refers to a difference in nature. Now do you say that you are going to make Right your master and do away with Wrong, or make Order your master and do away with Disorder? If you do, then you have not understood the principle of heaven and earth or the nature of the ten thousand things. This is like saying that you are going to make Heaven your master and do away with Earth, or make Yin your master and do away with Yang. Obviously it is impossible. (Watson 2003: 103)

Although the preference thus often leans quite heavily to one side of the dichotomy and there is a definite inclination towards the "bigger picture," we must understand Zhuangzi as warning us that thinking in this way is not the whole story. The "bigger picture" is really just another picture.

In another crucial instance, at the beginning of chapter 6, Zhuangzi seemingly assents to the distinction between real knowledge, which comes from *tian* 天, and superficial knowledge, which comes from humans themselves. But he immediately complicates such an approach. It seems that only knowledge of the distinction between what is from *tian* and what is from man is the final wisdom, but, by complicating the distinction between *tian* and man, Zhuangzi succeeds in arguing that real knowledge or wisdom lies in exactly forgetting about this distinction, and in taking "the step beyond knowledge" (Graham 2001: 90). So Zhuangzi first sets up a dichotomy between *tian* and man, but in the end convinces us that "someone in whom neither *tian* nor man is victor over the other, this is what is meant by the True person" (Graham 2001: 85, modified). I must now show how such a true person could be perceived. The next sections will focus on two interlinked ideas of such a person: wisdom as belonging in, or being at one with, the world, and wisdom as realizing the world.

Wisdom as belonging

Both Heidegger and Zhuangzi agree that "knowledge" abstracts us from the world, and that the right kind of thinking, or wisdom, brings us back into it. Wisdom, then, should be understood as the opposite of abstracting, so, rather, as resonating with the world. In this sense, we should understand that wisdom can never be the possession of a subject with regard to an object, since it is exactly that kind of thinking that denies the belonging of ourselves to the world, and seeks to abstract or isolate us from it. Instead, Heidegger and Zhuangzi are concerned about a thinking and way of being that lies in between people and the world, that connects us with the world, with the further realization that we were never separate from it to begin with.

Belonging to the world: Heidegger

Let me start with Heidegger this time. Already in *Sein und Zeit*, Heidegger employs a number of terms that demonstrate his commitment to a thinking that sees humans as continuous with their world. For example, the term "Dasein," for humans, is specifically designed to not understand man as subject. Instead, Dasein, if translated, becomes "being-there," and as such is understood as "*that belongingness that, holding unto the ab-ground, belongs to the clearing of be-ing*" (Heidegger 2006: 286, italics in original). The knowledge of the subject is descriptive since the subject distances itself from the world, whereas the wisdom of the Dasein lies in the awareness of belonging to the world, to Being.

Furthermore, Dasein is always already *Mitsein* and *Beisein*, being (together) with things. And Dasein is always already thrown into a world (*Geworfen*), finds itself always somehow attuned (*Befindlichkeit* and *Stimmung*). So Dasein is not to be understood as some entity aside from this world. In fact, the whole phenomenological approach of Heidegger in *Sein und Zeit* could be said to show that humans are not distinct from the world, but always find themselves in the world, and, in contradistinction to the metaphysical approach, we should not struggle to escape this world, but rather acknowledge and celebrate our belonging in it.

However, in *Sein und Zeit* Heidegger still thought all this from Dasein. In his later work Heidegger becomes increasingly aware of the interdependence of Dasein and Being, and now attempts to think more from Being than from Dasein. He still sees representational thought as abstracting and distracting, but now seeks that wisdom that is found in the *Gelassenheit* of Dasein and in the belonging to the earth in the constellation of *Geviert*, the fourfold, in an *entsprechen* or *gehören* (belonging) to the world, and in the *Ereignis*.

Another key term Heidegger uses in this regard is *Inständigkeit* or "in-abiding," also occasionally translated as "in-dwelling." The authentic person stands, abides or dwells *in* the world, and not outside of it in any way. In Heidegger's words: "'*Wisdom*' is foundational knowing-awareness [*wesentliches wissen*]; is inabiding the truth of be-ing" (Heidegger 2006: 52). Also, in "The Origin of the Work of Art" Heidegger puts it in the following way: "This 'standing-within' of preservation [*Bewahrung*], however, is a knowing. Yet knowing does not consist in mere information and notions about something. He who truly knows beings knows what he wills to do in the midst of them" (Heidegger 1993: 192). In-abiding is knowing what to do in the midst of a situation, is responding to the *Geworfenheit* one finds oneself in. This, Heidegger ties to the notion of existence [*Ek-sistenz*]: "in existence, man does not proceed from some inside to some outside; rather, the essence of *Existenz* is out-standing standing-within the essential sunderance [*Auseinander*] of the clearing of beings" (Heidegger 1993: 192). What Heidegger means, with apologies for the Heideggerean jargon, is that properly existing entails a knowing of the essential characteristic of being in a world, rather than having a world. In laymen's terms this would be a form of know-how rather than of know-that or know-why. And such knowing, or rather wisdom, finds itself in releasement and in-abiding.

Releasement or *Gelassenheit* points to a different kind of thinking, removed from representational, calculative thought: "Perhaps there is a thinking ... more sober-minded still than scientific technology, more sober-minded and hence removed, without effect, yet having its own necessity" (Heidegger 1993: 449). Releasement involves keeping an open attitude towards the transformational nature of the world and of our existence in it. It is aimed at creating the space in which things can "be" what they are; it is a letting-things-be as they are. In Heidegger's words:

> [Releasement] is in no way a matter of weakly allowing things to slide and drift along ... Perhaps a higher acting is concealed in releasement than is found in all the actions within the world and in the machinations of all mankind ... which higher acting is yet no activity. (Heidegger 1966: 61)

In "Discourse on Thinking" (which is the translation of Heidegger's original German *Gelassenheit*), *Inständigkeit* and *Gelassenheit* are linked in the following way: "The in-dwelling [*Inständigkeit*] in releasement [*Gelassenheit*] to that-which-regions [*Gegnet*] would then be the real nature of the spontaneity of thinking" (Heidegger 1966: 82). In normal English, abiding in the world through releasement is what real thinking is about. Other terms Heidegger uses in this connection are *weilen* and *verweilen*, both roughly meaning abiding/enduring with the things of the world.

A further aspect of Heidegger's thought, important in this regard, is that he always understands thinking as experience, connected to *Ereignis*. Experience for Heidegger is not the inner *"erlebnis"* of a subject, but refers to the whole situation or constellation of *Ereignis*. In other words, any idea of a self or subject would only be a function of the more originary *Ereignis* or event of appropriation, and would have meaning only within this *Ereignis*. In similar ways, the *Geviert*, or fourfold, is meant to bring mortals, divinities, heaven, and earth together in their original configuration. Not as four separate things that have a relation to each other, but as the configuration which first produces those relatively separate things.

In *On the Way to Language* Heidegger says the following: "Experience means *eundo assequi*, to obtain something along the way, to attain something by going on a way. What is it that the poet reaches? Not mere knowledge" (Heidegger 1971a: 66). Proper thinking appropriates, and we must think this in terms of *Ereignis*. The thinker does not gain knowledge which she then applies to the world, but thinking directly experiences the world in which it is generated, it sees itself as appropriated by and appropriately in the world, since as mentioned before, the separation of these two (thinking and the world) is what is artificial.

Heidegger also thinks along these lines when he discusses Parmenides' saying that "thinking and being is the same" in *Vorträge und Aufsätze*.[6] It is important to note that for Heidegger, the "same" is not the identical, but refers rather to a form of belonging together:

> The same never coincides with the equal, not even in the empty indifferent oneness of what is merely identical. The equal or identical always moves toward the absence of difference, so that everything may be reduced to a common denominator. The same, by contrast, is the belonging together of what differs, through a gathering by way of the difference. We can only say "the same" if we think difference. It is in the carrying out and settling of differences that the gathering nature of sameness comes to light. (Heidegger 1971b: 216)

Proper thinking or wisdom, then, lies in the acknowledgment of the belonging together of ourselves as thinking beings to Being. Not in order to become identical with the world, but to see our "sameness," or continuity with it.[7]

Belonging to the world: Zhuangzi

Zhuangzi similarly disparages knowledge in favor of the wisdom that sees oneself as "one" or continuous with the world. In similar fashion, originally the separation was not there, "knowledge" (*zhi*) arises only when man artificially separates himself from the world. Abstract knowledge literally separates man from the world, subject from object, mind from matter and so on. So both Heidegger and Zhuangzi seek to undo the separation of man and world, and, by pointing to their deeper togetherness, both seek to rethink the issue as a matter of reuniting what was wrongly separated in the first place. But such a reuniting does not take place in the form of reversing a hierarchy, but by pointing out that the separation is only a separation when thought within the confines of conventional knowledge, which in Heidegger's case is the dominant metaphysical way of thought, and in Zhuangzi's case the dominant Confucian and Mohist methods of discrimination or distinguishing or deeming.

In Zhuangzi the thinking experience is thus one of continuity with the rest of the world. But this experience is always from a particular locality. Wisdom, then, is insertion into a situation in full awareness of its particularity. There is a passage in chapter 23 of the *Zhuangzi* which quite literally describes the intimate connection of wisdom and the world: "'Knowing' is being in touch with something, 'knowledge' is a representation of it" (Graham 2001: 190). Graham elucidates that "'Knowing' (which is a good thing) is being in touch with things as they come and go, 'knowledge' (which is a bad thing) is preserving fixed representations of them" (Graham 2001: 190). That is why Zhuangzi can say: "I know it from up above the Hao [river]" (Graham 2001: 123). Such knowing experience is *wuzhi*, and thus not "normal" knowing. As Ames and Hall put it: "Ultimately, *wuzhi* is a grasp of the *daode* 道德 relationship of each encountered item that permits an understanding of *this* particular focus (*de*) and the field that it construes" (Ames and Hall 2003: 41, italics and Pinyin in original).

Since in Chinese thought in general knowing and doing are intimately related, so are *wuzhi* and *wu wei*. The Daoist terminology of *ziran* 自然 (spontaneity, so-of-itself) and *wu wei* 無為 (non-assertive action) seeks to express the idea that we are part of the world and should not impose our "knowledge" on it. Our responsiveness to the world entails an attitude of openness to how things inherently are, and this entails a respectful responsibility to the world that we also see in Heidegger's *Gelassenheit*. *Wu wei* is not a non-doing, but a certain kind of doing which seeks not to impose or interfere with the natural inclinations of things to be themselves. In the words of Hall and Ames, *wu wei* "involves the absence of any course of action that interferes with the particular focus (*de* 德) of those things contained within one's field of influence" (Ames and Hall 2003: 39).

The point of all this seems to be that wisdom as realization is connected to an awareness and involvement in the changing processes of the world without artificially trying to halt such processes with rigid structures of "knowledge" or by artificially distinguishing *pian* 辨 and deeming *wei* 為. Graham also argues that the discriminations made by "chop logic" are really not conducive to understanding and acting in a situation, and that rather the sage has to be absorbed in the situation (Graham 2001: 12).

Such absorption takes a different kind of knowing, and the wisdom of the sages is exactly that they can display "impersonal calm" (Graham 2001: 14) to respond to a situation, and thus the absorption does not reduce them to nothingness. Zhuangzi is thinking of a particular way of being in *this* world. The idea is neither to try to escape the world nor to fully lose oneself in it, but to immerse oneself within and reflect the changing nature of this world, and that is wisdom. "The utmost man uses the heart like a mirror; he does not escort things as they go or welcome them as they come, he responds but does not store" (Graham 2001: 98). In the "Below in the Empire" chapter, Zhuangzi says this about the Daoist sage:

Within yourself, no fixed positions:
Things as they take shape disclose themselves.
Moving, be like water,
Still, be like a mirror,
Respond like an echo.
Blank! As though absent;
Quiescent! As though transparent.
Be assimilated to them and you harmonise,
Take hold of any of them and you lose. (Graham 2001: 281)

In other words, assimilation to the process character of the world and reflecting the situation accurately means harmony, whereas insisting on a fixed position and attaching to such fixation means you lose out on something.

In the *Huainanzi*, the resonance of the wise person with the world, or the understanding that everything is indeed connected, is again said to be impossible to gain through mere "knowledge": "That things in their [various] categories are mutually responsive is [something] dark, mysterious, deep, and subtle. Knowledge is not capable of assessing it; argument is not capable of explaining it" (Major et al. 2010: 216). In short, the *Zhenren* 真人 or utmost person is one who in full awareness of her or his continuity with the world mirrors its transformational nature. After all, as Zhuangzi says: "Heaven and earth were born together with me, and the myriad things and I are one" (Graham 2001: 56).

When we think of this in terms of *wu wei* and *Gelassenheit*, the dispositions that such properly thinking persons should exhibit, we see also that it is imperative not to change the propensities of the situation, or at least not in any drastic ways. And this is why both Zhuangzi and Heidegger are averse to technology and artificial knowledge, since these lead us astray from our true provenance. Too much "knowledge" is a bad thing, and the quest for such knowledge makes us forget Being (Heidegger) or *dao* (Zhuangzi), and with that we would be imposing on the inherent tendencies of things to be what they are. Wisdom is not knowledge that seeks to change things, but lies in a way of living that seeks to be in resonance with the changing things.

This idea that wisdom is connection to this changing world is found also in how both thinkers think about death. Both Heidegger and Zhuangzi[8] spend considerable time on this topic, and both argue that one of the defining features of the really wise lies in the reconciliation with death. The ways they get there are quite different, though, although we can fairly say that in the "normal" world of both Heidegger and Zhuangzi people fear death and want to live. Heidegger's overcoming of this fear lies in the notion of *Angst*, or anxiety, as a way to becoming authentic, through facing up to our own mortality. Zhuangzi takes a slightly different approach, in that he does not think it necessary to go through the anxiety phase, but instead seems to quite calmly accept mortality as a necessary part of living. But it has been suggested that the realization of continuity with the world did create, or rather was created by, an existential crisis in Zhuangzi, with the episode of the strange Magpie and the gamekeeper.[9] Whatever the differences amount to, it is clear that both Heidegger and Zhuangzi seek to infuse the sense of mortality into the way we live our life, and that, at least partly, wisdom lies in doing exactly that. And in that sense they both seek to connect us with the world we live in, and both shun recourse to other-worldly considerations.

Wisdom as local connection

If wisdom is understood as resonating with the changing things, it is not surprising that both Heidegger and Zhuangzi see it in persons who display a very intimate connection with their surroundings, often through the practice of a craft or skill. Heidegger, for example, says in "What is Called Thinking": "Perhaps thinking, too, is just something like building a cabinet. At any rate, it is a craft" (Heidegger 1993: 380).

There are plenty of examples in Heidegger of such localized wisdom, and this suggests that wisdom, in its practicality, is indeed "provincial," but not in the negative sense of the word, but in the positive sense of being connected to the direct experience of the land and environment. Indeed, Heidegger is famous, or infamous, for being "provincial," something which he gladly acknowledged in his "Why do I Stay in the Provinces?" (Heidegger 1934), where he says that his work "is intimately rooted in and related to the life of the peasants."

Some other examples of this include "Building Dwelling Thinking," which has a section on a Black Forest farmhouse, and how it gathers the fourfold and gives a sense of place, of intimate connection to the land or context (Heidegger 1993: 361–2). And in *The Origin of the Work of Art* Heidegger dedicates some time to the painting of a pair of peasant shoes by Vincent van Gogh. Here, Heidegger says something which I think is both intuitively understandable and right. The scientific approach, the rational consideration of a pair of shoes in their objectivity, can never "know" those shoes for what they are. The shoes are worn, rather than being mere objects. "The peasant woman wears her shoes in the field. Only here are they what they are. They are all the more genuinely so, the less the peasant woman thinks about the shoes while she is at work" (Heidegger 1993: 159). Knowledge is universal, or aspires to be so in its objectifications, abstractions and generalizations; but, while it is quite successful in seeking out general features in this sense, it fails miserably in really knowing things intimately within their situation or context in this attempt. On the other hand, wisdom then should be local and come from or reflect a situational point of view that seeks to understand things in and from their context.

In the *Zhuangzi* a large selection of people and other creatures display a similar kind of behavior pertinent to wisdom. I will not rehearse all those stories, of which the Cook Ding story is the most famous. But we can see that, at least in a metaphoric way, the skilled craftsmen act in such a way that they become continuous with the situation; and that their success, for example in the case of the swimmer, depends very much on not going against the current, against what the situation demands. Such people are considered "wise" within the confines of their profession or activity, within their situation, and this situational wisdom is then extended in the sage, who would presumably display such skill and attention to the demands of situation in all she or he does. In short, wisdom is mindfulness in application to situation, using not a fixed principle but being able to vary according to circumstance.

Realizing *dao* and being

But Heidegger and Zhuangzi in another way can be said to think of wisdom as realization. Both *dao* and *Sein* are nothing without the proper attention from, or thinking by, humans. For Heidegger, it is Dasein especially and beings in general that make up Being, and Being is not without Dasein's correct approach to it. "Be-ing needs [*braucht*] man in order to hold sway [*wese*]; and man belongs to be-ing so that he can accomplish his utmost destiny as Da-sein" (Heidegger 1999: 177). So Dasein realizes or could realize Being, and the forgetfulness of Being is such that, when the last thinkers are gone, so will Being be erased from the human world. This can be seen in things like the death of God, the fleeing of the gods, and man's powerlessness with regard to, or dependence on, technology, all of which signal a completion of metaphysics that does away with Being in favor of beings. Heidegger counters with terms such as *Andenken, gehören, logos* as gathering humans and Being together, the *Geviert*, jointure, *Ereignis*, all of which seem to aim at our "reconnection" to Being. "Being ... is a call to man and is not without man" (Heidegger 1993: 211).

Thus, not only is there a form of interdependence of humans and world, but it is also humans, or in Heidegger's case Dasein, who create a world. Here I must resort to Heidegger's German: "Wissen ist nicht Wissenschaft im neuzeitlichen Sinne. Wissen ist das denkende Gewahren der Wahrnis des Seins" (Heidegger 1994b: 349). In English this would be translated as: "wisdom/knowing is not scientific/science in the modern sense. Wisdom/knowing is thoughtful preserving/making true of the preservation/preserve of Being." The terms *Gewahren* and *Wahrnis* are difficult to translate, but crucial to understanding Heidegger's intention here. *Gewahren* has connotations with preserving, with making *wahr* (true), *Wahrheit* (truth), to be understood in Heidegger's sense of *aletheia*, and with guarding. So has *Wahrnis*, which Heidegger explicitly connects to *Hut*, "guarding," "keeping," some paragraphs earlier (Heidegger 1994b: 348). Elsewhere in "The Question Concerning Technology," Heidegger says that man "may be the one who is needed and used for the safekeeping (*Wahrnis*) of the coming to presence of truth" (Heidegger 1977: 33). So I take Heidegger to be saying that wisdom lies in the keeping and guarding of the truth/preserve of Being, and thereby providing through *Gelassenheit* the openness in which things can manifest themselves.

So humans make Being come true, or guard it, if they think wisely. This means that "[t]hinking is not a means to gain knowledge. Thinking cuts furrows into the soil of Being" (Heidegger 1971a: 70). Thinking does something to Being, it could open Being up, in the same way as the land is opened up by cutting furrows into it for planting. And yes, another farming metaphor that displays an intimate connection to the land. So humans are capable of providing the space in which things can "be" what they are, that is, for Being to come to presence through beings.

In Chinese philosophy in general it is also man that makes the way. It is not something laid out for us to find, at least not for the more thoughtful. In what follows, we should take care not to read "knowing" as the artificial knowing, but now start to see it more in line with my interpretation of wisdom as realization. This is already found in Confucius: "It is the person who is able to broaden the way (*dao*), not the way that broadens the person" (Ames and Rosemont 1998: 190). Ames has also discussed the nature of "real knowledge" or wisdom in classical Chinese thought in terms of "tracing": "This Chinese 'knowing' is resolutely participatory and creative—'tracing' in both the sense of etching a pattern and following it. To know is 'to realize,' to 'make real'" (Ames 1993: 57).

This kind of thinking is also present in the *Daodejing*. Ames and Hall's translation of *dao* with "way-making" makes this aspect clear, and they mention that in terms of Daoist knowing: "Such performative 'knowing' is for one to actively interpret and realize a world with healthy, productive effect" (Ames and Hall 2003: 42). Also consider this passage from the *Daodejing*: "Way-making is moreover enhanced by those who express character, just as it is diminished by those who themselves have lost it" (Ames and Hall 2003: 112).

In the case of Zhuangzi, it is also clear that *dao* is present only when certain people live according to it. The way can be absent from this world, or it can come to presence. As Zhuangzi says: "the *dao* comes about as we walk it" (Graham 2001: 53, modified). This entails that if we walk "the wrong way," we will lose the *dao*. As Ames puts it: "for Zhuangzi, knowledge is performative, a function of fruitful correlations. Thus, it is something done—a qualitative achievement. Knowing a situation is the 'realizing' of it in the sense of 'making it real'" (Ames 1998: 220).

And it is of course the firm belief of most Daoist classics that the ruler who embodies *dao* is not only at one with the world but also can make sure that the world is properly and effectively governed (preferably through non-interference [*wuwei*]), which, although maybe not for Zhuangzi himself but certainly for other Daoists, is the ultimate application of wisdom in the world. For Zhuangzi, it is the sage or authentic person who embodies such wisdom, in the way that she or he goes about in the world in general. And such application always takes the form of *wuwei*, where a realization of the world takes form in letting things be what they inherently are, without obstruction.

Conclusion

I have argued that although neither Heidegger nor Zhuangzi seems very interested in the terms knowledge and wisdom, they nevertheless make a clear distinction between the right kind of "knowing" and the wrong kind. Hence, we have seen that both Heidegger and Zhuangzi consider common, conventional knowledge with its artificial distinctions to be inadequate for, and even a hindrance to, understanding the position of man in the world. Thus, both philosophers agitate against conventional knowledge and argue that a higher or better "knowing," wisdom, is needed to transcend the limitations of representational thinking. Although both conceive of such a "greater" knowing, they also realize that such wisdom is in the end not fundamentally different from the "smaller" knowledge; so ultimately both Heidegger and Zhuangzi seek to overcome the dichotomy between small and great knowing. They try to do so by understanding wisdom as an intimate belonging to this world, and as a realization that, by "knowing" in the right way, we could actually make real and not just observe the world we belong to. This "realization" should inform the way we are and the way we treat everything around us.

Notes

1   The author wishes to acknowledge that this chapter was written as part of a study funded by the Singapore Management University through a research grant (no. 14-C242-SMU-023) from the Singapore Ministry of Education Academic Research Fund Tier 1.

2   Wing-tsit Chan translates the same passage as: "To know it is not as good as to love it, and to love it is not as good as to take delight in it" (1963: 30).

3   As translated by Ames and Hall 2003, 208 n.46.

4   See Heidegger 1994a: 52 and Heidegger 1977: 155ff.

5   See for example Heidegger 1971a: 58–9, or Heidegger 1966: 45–6.

6   Heidegger 1994a: 223ff.

7   Other ideas Heidegger uses in this connection are those such as "*gehören*" and "*Stimmung*," belonging and attunement, or when he discusses the ancient Greek *Logos* to mean "gathering" rather than having anything to do with "logic."

8   But this is also present for example in the *Liezi*. See Graham 1990: 26.

9   See for example Graham 1989: 109.

Works cited

Ames, R. T. (1993), *Sun-tzu: The Art of Warfare*, New York: Ballantine Books.

Ames, R. T. (1998), *Wandering at Ease in the Zhuangzi*, Albany: SUNY Press.

Ames, R. T. and Hall, D. L. (trans) (2003), *Daodejing, Making This Life Significant*, New York: Ballantine Books.

Ames, R. T. and Rosemont, H. Jr (1998), *The Analects of Confucius: A Philosophical Translation*, New York: Ballantine Books.

Chan, W. (1963), *A Source Book in Chinese Philosophy*, Princeton: Princeton University Press.

Graham, A. C. (1989), *Disputers of the Tao: Philosophical Argument in Ancient China*, La Salle: Open Court.

Graham, A. C. (1990), *The Book of Lieh-tzŭ*, New York: Columbia University Press.

Graham, A. C. (2001), *Chuang-Tzu: The Inner Chapters*, Indianapolis: Hackett Publishing Co.

Heidegger, M. (1966), *Discourse on Thinking*, J. M. Anderson and E. H. Freund (trans), New York: Harper & Row.

Heidegger, M. (1971a), *On the Way to Language*, P. D. Hertz (trans.), New York: Harper & Row.

Heidegger, M. (1971b), *Poetry, Language, Thought*, A. Hofstadter (trans.), New York: Harper & Row.

Heidegger, M. (1977), *The Question Concerning Technology and Other Essays*, W. Lovitt (trans.), New York: Harper & Row.

Heidegger, M. (1981), "Why do I Stay in the Provinces?" in T. Sheehan (ed.), *Heidegger: the Man and the Thinker*, Chicago: Precedent Publishing, 27–9

Heidegger, M. (1993), *Basic Writings*, D. F. Krell (trans.), New York: HarperCollins Publishers.

Heidegger, M. (1994a), *Vorträge und Aufsätze*, Stuttgart: Günther Neske.

Heidegger, M. (1994b), *Holzwege*, Frankfurt a. M., Klostermann.

Heidegger, M. (1999), *Contributions to Philosophy (from Enowning)*, P. Emad and K. Maly (trans), Bloomington: Indiana University Press.

Heidegger, M. (2006), *Mindfulness*, P. Emad and T. Kalary (trans), London & New York: Continuum International Publishing Group.

Honderich, T. (ed.) (2005), *The Oxford Guide to Philosophy*, 2nd edn, Oxford: Oxford University Press.

Major, J. S., Queen, S. A., Meyer, A. S., and Roth, H. D. (eds and trans) (2010), *The Huainanzi*, New York: Columbia University Press.

Nietzsche, F. (1997), *Twilight of the Idols*, R. Polt (trans.), Indianapolis: Hackett Publishing Company.

Watson, B. (trans) (2003), *Zhuangzi: Basic Writings*, New York: Columbia University Press.

Part Three

Contemporary Wisdom

9

Philosophy as a Spiritual Practice: An Old Idea Whose Time has Come

Sean J. McGrath

Above all else, guard your heart, for everything you do flows from it
(Proverbs 4.23)

The love of wisdom has become in today's situation a political matter, for it signifies a defection from the political-economic ideology that now dominates the globe: consumer capitalism. In order to defend this thesis, it is necessary to first recognize how philosophy today is threatened on all sides. Never in the modern era has philosophy had to contend with such an obdurately un-philosophical culture as it does today, in the era of the homogenous state, the globalized developed world, which I will describe as the *consumer-capitalist juggernaut*. The exterior life of communities is now highly regulated by carefully monitored global market forces while the inner life of the human being is effectively colonized by media-driven consumer desire. There is no longer a coherent space, a civil-society, within which we might debate the best and worst possible ways to live on the planet; the space has already been set up and catered by a half-dozen multi-national companies eager to exploit whatever potential consumer interests are coming into expression. And we are only too ready to comply, for our subjectivities are increasingly moved and motivated by a common set of inner ideals. We are all members of the same church and practice the same religion, the theology of consumption (McGrath 2013, 2014).

And yet, philosophy has always thrived in adversity. Think only of Socrates surrounded by Sophists, the Stoics in Hedonist Alexandria and Rome, or, more recently, existentialism during the Second World War. These examples prove that philosophy does not need cultural or institutional support. Indeed official endorsement is often the death knell of authentic philosophical life. Today, when academic philosophy has reached a degree of irrelevance unprecedented in its recent history, at a time when the global culture appears to be held entirely captive by consumerism, to the point of refusing to recognize how its unsustainable lifestyle imperils its own existence, when academics routinely surrender all questions of knowledge to the high priests of the science-technology industry, philosophy is in a good place. For it can no longer avoid the question, which must always remain alive within it, the question: What is philosophy? What is its purpose? Why does it continue to attract followers even when apparently it has been proven to be scientifically and politically irrelevant?

The situation

A juggernaut is a huge, human-powered wagon that carried an image of a Hindu god through crowded Indian streets. The devotees were encouraged to throw themselves beneath its wheels in an act of hysterical self-sacrifice. A juggernaut refers, then, to an unstoppable force of destruction, something that demands blind devotion and merciless sacrifice. To describe the consumer-capitalist society as a juggernaut is to say: No one can stop its progress. It is not driven by a central intelligence but moves, inexorable, by force of a collective mania for technical progress at all costs and unregulated human appetite. It has destroyed natural and human environments and will not stop until there is nothing left. The juggernaut is fueled by consumerism, the absurd belief that the individual's seemingly endless freedom to upgrade his identity through the purchase of mass-produced products leads inexorably to beatitude, a belief for which we are willing to sacrifice the better part of our lives and the life of our planet, and which we know on some level to be false.

The freedom of the consumer is endless because it is purely negative: it consists in an unlimited capacity to choose on an ontologically limited plane: we are free to choose not the structure of our society or good and evil but from an endless variety of material goods. The good of consumption is not one of the options. As Žižek has put it, the denizens of late capitalism labor under a super-ego injunction to enjoy, at all cost. From a pervasive anxiety, perpetuated by advertisement, that we do not measure up to what society expects of us, we *must* enjoy our distracted and endlessly unsatisfying lives of constant consumption. We must, if we are to enjoy the privileges of consumerism, lose ourselves in the distraction of constant upgrading.

According to Žižek, the absence of real decision is crucial to the logic of consumerism, which demands of us absolute devotion to the infinite effort to find satisfaction in that which somehow we know can never satisfy:

It's no surprise that Coca-Cola was first introduced as a medicine. Its strange taste seems to provide no particular satisfaction. It is not directly pleasing, however, it is as such, as transcending any use-value, like water, beer or wine, which definitely do quench our thirst, that Coke functions as the direct embodiment of 'IT', the pure surplus of enjoyment over standard satisfactions. It is the mysterious and elusive X we are all after in our compulsive consumption. The unexpected result of this is not that, since Coke doesn't satisfy any concrete need we drink it only as supplement, after some other drink has satisfied our substantial need—it is rather this very superfluous character that makes our thirst for Coke all the more insatiable. Coke has the paradoxical quality that the more you drink it, the more you get thirsty. So, when the slogan for Coke was 'Coke is it!', we should see in it some ambiguity—it's 'it' precisely insofar as it's *never* IT, precisely insofar as every consumption opens up the desire for more. The paradox is thus that Coke is not an ordinary commodity, but a commodity whose very peculiar use-value itself is already a direct embodiment of the auratic, ineffable surplus ... The more profit you have, the more you want, the more you drink Coke, the more you are thirsty, the more you obey the superego command, the more you are guilty. In all three cases, the logic of balanced exchange is disturbed in favour of an excessive logic of 'the more you give the more you owe', or the 'more you possess what you are longing for, the more you are missing and thus the greater your craving', or the consumerist version, 'the more you buy the more you must spend' (Žižek 1999).

The hysteria of consumption is a situation of maximal unhappiness, for we are like the gerbil on the wheel which can never get anywhere no matter how fast he runs, and at the same time, and by virtue of that unhappiness, it is a situation of maximal profit. In so far as the economics of consumerism presumes that consumption will not depend on material need—the consumer will infinitely produce new trans-material needs that demand satisfaction—consumerism is basically idealist and theological, even as it represents the perfection of capitalist logic. Think only of our addiction to information technology. We can never stop with the recent version of the smart phone or last year's iPad because next year's version will be so much better, and in the meantime our lives, which we negotiated easily enough without the internet in our pocket only a few years ago, are now unthinkable without these devices. Even more, the processing these machines are required to do is always increasing in such a way that no one generation of the device could ever be definitive. The mountain of discarded machines grows ever higher, proportionate to the exponential growth of Apple's profits, while we stare mesmerized at the shiny new machine, fresh out of the box, when it still has its aura of transcendence. In three months, we will be tired of our new toy and eagerly awaiting the release of the next generation.

Let us not be deceived into thinking that the consumer-capitalist juggernaut is simply the global application of nineteenth-century liberalism. In fact, consumer-capitalism has killed liberalism as a philosophy. Equality and liberty are precisely what cannot survive the conjunction of consumerism and capitalism, for the corporate oligarchy that rules the planet is always outside the political equation—by definition not bound by any social contract—and the much-touted liberty of the individual is qualified by the commandment that all you hold most dear must be relegated to a private, politically innocuous space. And we have not even mentioned the state of slavery presumed by consumer-capitalism, for it is clear that not all can enjoy the carnival of consumption: there must be a slave labor force hidden away in some unspeakable hole somewhere, making our clothes and devices in the sweat shops of South East Asia for rock bottom prices.

But we must not overlook the crucial and still unnamed third that makes the consumer-capitalist juggernaut move: technology. Here we touch on the other obstacle to a genuinely public philosophy (consumerism, which limits the sphere of ethical questioning being the first): scientism, which limits the sphere of ontological questioning.

Consider an early text announcing the victory of scientism over ontology: Wilfrid Sellars' seminal 1962 piece, "Philosophy and the Scientific Image of Man" (Sellars 1963). In this text, Sellars distinguishes between the "manifest image" and the "scientific image" of the world. The manifest image includes subjective intentions, thoughts, and appearances, the world as it appears from a first-person perspective; the scientific image describes the world in terms of the theoretical physical sciences, the world precisely as it *does not appear* to a first-person but the structure of which we indirectly indicate through notions such as causality, particles, and forces. The manifest image includes practical or moral claims, whereas the scientific image does not. While Sellars appears to be endeavoring to carve out a space for philosophy as a discourse about norms in a situation in which the all-important task of ontology has now been taken over by the sciences, in his own words, "to formulate a scientifically oriented, naturalistic realism which would 'save the appearances'" (Sellars 1975: 289), the historical effect of his article was precisely the opposite (think of the Churchlands' effort to create a philosophical language in which the first person, with its reference to a non-existent interiority, is never used, or even simply the ethical and political ineffectuality of analytical philosophy): far from empowering philosophy, Sellars has emasculated it. Of course, it was not Sellars who made the final cut: as a good analytical philosopher he is merely giving an account of "how things in the broadest possible sense of the term hang together in the broadest possible sense of the term" (Sellars 1963: 1); but the game is already up when Sellars presupposes, "In the dimension of describing and explaining the world, science is the measure of all things, of what is that it is, and of what is not that it is not" (Sellars 1956: 253).

Sellars believes, somewhat desperately, that philosophy could still play a normative role when all ontological questions are now closed, for describing and explaining are not the only "dimensions" of linguistic activity. There is still "the manifest level" of subjective experience, which is wildly at variance with the non-manifest level that science alone describes. Ostensibly there is still work to be done on the manifest level, work that science cannot do; evaluating questions of the human good, for example. It is science's job to uncover the structure of empirical reality, the causal nexus within which we live, but, since we do not live our lives at subatomic levels, we continue to need philosophy, which deals with the "how" of life rather than the "what," the pragmatic problem of getting along in a world, which science alone progressively discloses to us.

But this was 1962. Things have gotten considerably worse for philosophy since then, and it seems to some that this normative task of philosophy, however marginal it truly was, is now taken from it. For it would appear that liberal capitalism, now apparently freed from all theological baggage and tethered to technology, has achieved a decisive triumph over all other ethical and political systems. At least, this was Fukuyama's argument in 1992. In spite of the ridicule heaped on Fukuyama's association with neoliberal triumphalism, in spite of the resurgence of nationalism, the resistance of Islam to the West, and the emergence of new economies in the developing world, has anything *substantial* changed since 1992? The "end of history" might have been prematurely proclaimed. However, this much Fukuyama got right: the events of September 11 and the 2008 economic crisis have confirmed that what might have previously appeared to be a primarily American approach to political economy and secularization is now a global agenda and concern.

Looking back on his 1989 article, "The End of History," written significantly at the moment of the collapse of the Soviet Union, that is, at the moment of the unmasking of Marxism as an impossible fantasy of a purely secular human cooperation, Fukuyama summed up his argument in the following words:

A remarkable consensus concerning the legitimacy of liberal democracy as a system of government had emerged throughout the world over the past years

... liberal democracy may constitute the "end point of mankind's ideological evolution" and the "final form of human government", and as such constitute the "end of history". That is, while earlier forms of government were characterized by grave defects and irrationalities that led to their eventual collapse, liberal democracy was arguably free from such fundamental internal contradictions. That was not to say that today's stable democracies, like the United States, France, or Switzerland, were not without injustice or serious social problems. But these principles were ones of incomplete implementation of the twin principles of liberty and equality on which modern democracy is founded, rather than flaws in the principles themselves ... the ideal of liberal democracy could not be improved on. (Fukuyama 1989: xi)

Fukuyama adds that the crucial catalyst in this achievement of what Kojeve, interpreting Hegel, first called the homogenous state, is technology; and with it comes a hypothetical imperative. Modern technology introduces a new level of military threat that places pressure on the country that is out of pace with its neighbors to technologize itself. And this technologization requires a market economy, in Fukuyama's words, "a uniform horizon of economic production possibilities." Such a market cannot tolerate cultural and ethnic diversity. "All countries undergoing economic modernization must increasingly resemble one another: they must unify nationally on the basis of a centralized state, urbanize, replace traditional forms of social organization like tribe, sect, and family with economically rational ones based on function and efficiency, and provide for the universal education of their citizens" (1989: xiv–xv). The punishment for not modernizing is isolation: without a link to global markets and consumer culture, the recalcitrant anti-modern state will have no chance of producing the capital required to develop a technological system of defence, Hence Fukuyama's infamous conclusion: a "universal evolution in the direction of capitalism" has been proven in our era (1989: xv).

If ontological questions are now settled by science (Sellars), and ethical-political questions are increasingly moot since de facto there is only one political system left standing and its ethical and anthropological presuppositions can be regarded as settled (Fukuyama), philosophy can be forgiven for thinking that there is nothing left for it to do. But this would be a mistake. What has collapsed in our era is not philosophy as such. Philosophy will always remain as the product of a universal human need to use the mind in a non-utilitarian application, which is neither merely play nor art. But the *idealist* notion of philosophy, which is more or less synonymous with modern philosophy, is no longer defensible. Philosophy as *knowledge of knowledge* (idealism) is the dream of a meta-science, a comprehensive, self-justifying account of reality that makes sense of all partial accounts, be they scientific, theological, or political, of the various domains of existence. This idea appears in Descartes, Leibniz, and Spinoza, becomes basic to German Idealism, and survives up to the heyday of phenomenology, Husserl, and the early Heidegger. But the idea apparently cannot survive the contemporary moment, the conquest of scientism, and the triumph of the consumer-capitalist juggernaut.

The contemporary situation has given us pause to consider that perhaps philosophy has a deeper *raison d'être*, one that can in the demise of the idealist aim of a comprehensive knowledge of knowledge still offer a vantage point from which to critique scientism and consumerism. This deeper *modus operandi* was basic to ancient philosophy and medieval theology, but has become forgotten in academic philosophy. It is philosophy as *spiritual practice*, that is, philosophy as a reflective caring for the self, which the philosopher undertakes in light of his best guess at the truth about things and what ought to be done both collectively and personally to promote human flourishing. Our contemporary situation is dire, and no obvious solutions present themselves. But as the Canadian philosopher George Grant put it, "It always matters what each of us does" (Grant 2005: 98).

Practical philosophy

We are brought back, then, to the oldest ideal of philosophy, what we might describe as the first ideal of philosophy, that which animated Socrates and the major schools of Hellenistic philosophy (the Stoics, the Epicureans, and the Neo-Platonists), and lived on for millennia within the institutions of Christian monasticism until it was eclipsed by the new model of philosophy as "knowledge of knowledge" that emerged in the seventeenth century. Philosophy before Descartes was not universally considered to be a comprehensive science, not even by the most scientifically inclined of pre-modern philosophers, for example the medieval Aristotelians. As the love of wisdom, philosophy was originally a practice of attending to oneself, on the assumption that one was not yet wise, not yet knowing, and needed to undergo a transformation before one could even consider oneself capable of knowing.

This forgotten history was retrieved by Michel Foucault in his late lectures at the College de France (1981–2). The late Foucault qualifies the largely negative view of human subjectivity developed in his *History of Sexuality* with a positive, even prescriptive, account of "the technologies of the self" widely practiced in Hellenistic philosophy (Foucault 2005). In *The History of Sexuality*, the so called interiority of the subject is in fact an entirely politicized space constituted by a discourse of confession, obedience, and punishment: I am only a subject on the condition of my total subjection to the Other (Foucault 1978). While indications of the Hellenistic alternative appear in volume three of *The History of Sexuality* in a small chapter entitled "The Cultivation of the Self" (Foucault 1986: 37–68), it is in Foucault's *Hermeneutics of the Subject* (Foucault 2001) that he explores how another option for interior freedom comes to light in Stoicism, Epicureanism, and Neo-Platonism, a different notion of the self that emerges out of a practice of making oneself *capable* of the truth.

At work in Hellenistic philosophy, argues Foucault, is not only a different kind of subject but a different conception of truth, a personal conception of truth, which forbids access to the uninitiated and which demands of the subject a practice of self-care: attending to that in our experience which is still our own, to our representations, desires, and judgments of value, which can facilitate or obstruct our experience of truth. This pre-modern subject constitutes itself by means of techniques of the self, rather than being constituted by techniques of domination (Power) or discursive techniques (Knowledge).

In the course of these remarkable analyses, Foucault offers us a definition of "spirituality," which effectively liberates it from both Roman Catholicism (on the conservative side) and New Age (on the progressive side) and re-situates it at the very heart of pre-modern philosophy. "Spirituality," Foucault writes, is "the pursuit, practice, and experience through which the subject carries out the necessary transformations on himself in order to have access to the truth" (Foucault 1986: 15). Thinkers such as Socrates, Plotinus, Epictetus, Epicurus, Origen, and Augustine were spiritual teachers in addition to being teachers of philosophy. Indeed, for each of them philosophy was, if not exclusively a spiritual practice, none the less a discipline that was intimately connected with spiritual practices. The ancient philosopher was above all a contemplative. To revise Marx, the point of philosophy was not to change the world but to change the self so as to be able to know the truth, on the assumption that our spontaneous experience of the truth is skewed by self-deception, wishful thinking and addiction. After the seventeenth century, philosophy became identified with the scientific ideal of truth, which Foucault describes as an indifferent truth, a truth that is indifferent to the state of the subject cognizing it: it is knowledge of knowledge. As such, philosophy did not and could not include personal transformation as a condition for experiencing the truth. After the Enlightenment, knowledge becomes the automatic result of abstracting the mind from its spiritual life. As Foucault writes: "The modern age of the history of truth begins when knowledge itself and knowledge alone gives access to the truth, that is to say, when the philosopher (or the scientist, or simply someone who seeks the truth) can recognize the truth and have access to it in himself and through his acts of knowledge alone, without anything else being demanded of him and without his having to alter or change in any way his being as subject" (Foucault 2005: 17). No personal, spiritual, ethical, or philosophical transformation is required of the modern knower. All that is needed to arrive at pure objectivity is strict obedience to a method that anyone can practice.

Against the dominant current of modern philosophy, Foucault asks: "Can you have access to the truth without bringing into play the very being of the subject who gains access to it? Can you have access to the truth without paying for it with a sacrifice, an *ascesis*, a transformation, a purification which affects the subject's very being? Can the subject have access to the truth just as he is? (Foucault 2005: 522). Philosophy as "care of the self," or practical philosophy, moves through the Stoics, Epicureans, and Cynics toward such non-academic domains of self-formation or "spiritual exercise" as catechesis, political training, and what we might broadly if somewhat anachronistically describe as pre-modern psychological counseling ("spiritual direction," "confession," "spiritual formation"). If the modern notion of truth is scientific and epistemological, the pre-modern notion of truth is the harmony or coherence that obtains between the sage's (or the saint's) life and teaching.

Pierre Hadot, the historian of Hellenistic philosophy and Foucault's colleague at the College de France, concurs, and argues that almost without exception classical philosophy was primarily formative rather than informative in character.[1] The wisdom the philosopher loves, that is, longs for and does not possess, is to be understood as a way of life rather than as a systematic discourse. The achievement of truth in this sense is not a matter of moral indifference. Care of the self makes the greatest demands possible on the one who would pursue the truth: it demands an absolute commitment, a conversion of life. This truth is not primarily cognitive but moral; it is not something one has but, as Socrates put it in *The Apology*, a way one is (Plato 1961: 36b–c).

What exactly are the spiritual practices associated with practical philosophy in the Hellenistic and Medieval period? Hadot follows the Stoics in distinguishing three branches of philosophy: physics, ethics, and logic. But we should not understand these as departmental divisions of philosophy in a modern sense. They do not concern three different domains of knowledge, which the philosopher is to comprehend and synthesize. Rather, Stoic physics, ethics, and logic are three directions for reflection which philosophy takes in its practice of self-care. Thus the imperative to care for the self undergirds all three and makes of each branch a practical arena for spiritual exercise. Physics concerns the philosopher's place in the universe and is associated with practices whereby the philosopher reminds himself of his finitude, of his dependence of the body, on materiality, on the impermanence of physical existence and his enmeshment in the web of space and time. Ethics concerns the principles that governed his conduct and the imperative of justice; logic concerns the consistency of his beliefs. But the point of each series of reflections is to engender *apatheia*, or "rule over the passions." Hadot sums up the practical philosophy of Marcus Aurelius as follows: philosophy concerns "attempting to practice objectivity of judgment, attempting to live according to justice in the service of the human community, and attempting to become aware of our situation as belonging to the universe" (in Flynn 2005: 615). Practical philosophy is thus occupied with spiritual practices such as meditation, control of one's appetites and desires, training one's memory, examination of conscience—rather than with encyclopedic surveys of the various kinds of knowledge. But this is not to say it is indifferent to knowledge. Rather, knowledge will be considered from various sources and judged on the basis of practical criteria. To what degree is this knowledge confirmed in my life and to what degree can I in turn live from it?

The temptation to reduce philosophy to talk about talk was well known to ancient philosophers. The way to guard against this reversal of ends and means in ancient philosophy, at least as Hadot reads it, was to ensure through practice that one's philosophical discourse takes its origin in one's choice of a way of life.

The lesson of the ancients, according to Hadot, is that way of life and discourse need not be opposed as they are today. The two do not correspond to practice and theory. Discourse in the ancient world was thought to have necessarily a practical aspect to it; if it did not it would be superfluous. The ancient philosopher engages in discourse in so far as it tends to produce a desirable effect in the listener or reader. In the forgetting of practical philosophy, discourse has become the *primary* work of academic philosophy, which continually justifies itself in the ever-embattled institution of the human sciences as another form of scholarship. When asked what philosophy was, G. E. Moore gestured to the wall of books behind him and said, "philosophy is what these books are about." One can easily move from this terse indexical definition to a justification of philosophy as a form of historical scholarship that has as its object the surveying, cataloguing, and expositing of what philosophers have said. And since philosophers have said a great deal in the twenty-five hundred years of the history of Western philosophy, the need for a specialist in every university to interpret this literature for new generations would seem to be as obvious (or as unjustifiable) as the need to have classicists, historians, and literary theorists in a university worthy of the name.

But philosophy is of course crucially different from any other academic discipline: it can never be reduced to scholarship. Always active within philosophical discourse, if only as a possibility, is the option to live philosophically; that is, to philosophize out of one's life and in one's own voice.

Hadot goes further than Foucault and recognizes the persistence of philosophy as a spiritual practice in medieval Christianity. Foucault recognizes that Hellenistic practical philosophy was largely absorbed by Christianity as a monastic discipline. For Foucault this was the beginning of the end, for when spirituality no longer answers to an explicitly philosophical imperative but has an institutional home within religion, philosophy at that point becomes an impersonal theoretical enterprise paving the way for the modern ascendancy of knowledge of knowledge. Hadot is more generous to the Middle Ages and sees the continuity of Hellenistic spirituality with medieval Christian spirituality as an indication that philosophy as a way of life never entirely disappeared from the West. Hadot refers to the way some Church Fathers spoke of Christianity as a philosophy, as in fact the true philosophy. He draws analogies between Hellenistic and monastic practices, for example the *memento mori*. The Stoic philosopher Epictetus says: "Let death be before your eyes every day, and you will never have any abject thought nor excessive desire" (Hadot 1995: 131). Anthony the Christian Hermit says: "Live as though you were dying every day, paying heed to yourselves" (Hadot 1995: 131). This reading of the Latin tradition allows Hadot to continue to find practical philosophy at work in early modern thinkers as diverse as Ignatius of Loyola, Spinoza, Descartes (noting how the *Meditations* are designed to bring about an existential change of perspective in the subject), Hegel (whose *Phenomenology of Spirit* is intended as an initiation into thinking), and twentieth-century existentialism.

Conclusion

Even if academic philosophy is doomed as an institution (and it appears to me that it is), philosophy itself can continue as a practice. Indeed, philosophy as a care of the self needs no institutional support and perhaps will fare better in its absence. Institutions sap the life of philosophy. Exercising vigilance over one's thoughts and desires is as relevant today as it was in first-century Alexandria. The urgency of existential questions is as keenly felt by undergraduates today as it was by the youth in Socrates' day.

Foucault's and Hadot's notions of practical philosophy could be developed in two directions—which neither of them take: on the one hand, in the direction of a critique of contemporary forms of institutional religion; on the other hand, in the direction of a critique of psychoanalysis.[2] For religion and psychiatry are the two institutions active in contemporary global culture in which the language of the care of the self is still at work. Whatever else the contemporary churches are doing, they are not creating harbors for contemplatives, even if their literature and liturgies abound with contemplative values. With the death of God, the evangelical churches are more than willing to become reduced to helpful agents of social work (however dressed up with theology). And, with the increasing marginalization of Christianity in the educational and scientific sphere, Roman Catholicism threatens to contract into a hard reactive knot, a club for those who for their own sense of security need to dogmatically deny history.

Psychoanalysis, on the other hand, is an anomaly in many ways. Here is a space where the idea of conversion as the condition for accessing the truth is still alive, or at least it was in the thought of its founders. Striking about psycho-analytical training is the insistence by each of the founders of the major schools of analysis (Freud, Jung, Lacan) on "the training analysis." The condition for becoming an analyst is not primarily a degree; it is the completion of a lengthy process of self-analysis under the guidance of a trained analyst. It is not recog-nized often enough that psychoanalysis is an initiatic practice, something that put it at odds with straightforward empirical science from the beginning. It is interesting to note how, today, with its marginal place in psychiatry, psycho-analysis is increasingly dogged by the pressure to medicalize its methods and to drag its practices of the "talking cure" into the canons of empirical science; a place where, in fact, it can barely exist.

Above all let us not interpret Foucault's and Hadot's call to practical philosophy in a liberal register. Let us not assume that what is meant here is that, with the occupation of the public sphere by scientism and consumerism, philosophy can still retreat to the apolitical space of private subjectivity, where each of us remains free to think what we will about life, death, good and evil, so long as it does not obtrude on public values. For practical philosophy respects no such distinction between the private and the public. It understands the care of the self to be an eminently political act, for out of the self flow all actions.

Practical philosophy aspires to change the self in its most intimate sphere of ownness (*Jemeinigkeit*), and such a changed self will inevitably change society, if only in a micropolitical way. Nor should we allow scientism to reserve all ontological questions to the scientists while the rest of us chatter on about norms on a manifest level that science will not even dignify with recognition of its existence. The fact–value distinction which scientism continues to live from is put into question by practical philosophy. Here practical philosophy can ally itself with critiques of science emerging from other corners, for example Latour's rejection of the apolitical, value-neutral nature of scientific work (see, for example, Latour 2004).

In the end, the call to practical philosophy is an extremely simple matter, so simple that its radical and counter-cultural implications are likely to be overlooked. In the era of the consumer-capitalist juggernaut, when our desires are the matter of a systemic, corporate-controlled manipulation, it makes eminent sense (psychologically, spiritually, ecologically, and politically) to attend to our thinking and desiring, our hopes and our fears.

I will give the last word to the poet. At the end of Eliot's *Waste Land*, the narrator, having drearily surveyed the decadence and emptiness of modern life, experiences a minor enlightenment: he can at least attend to the self.

> The boat responded
> Gaily, to the hand expert with sail and oar
> The sea was calm, your heart would have responded
> Gaily, when invited, beating obedient
> To controlling hands
>
>   I sat upon the shore
> Fishing, with the arid plain behind me
> Shall I at least set my lands in order? (Eliot 1922: lines 418–25)

Notes

1   For a comparison of Foucault and Hadot, see Flynn 2005 and Irrera 2010.

2   I have to some degree endeavored to retrieve the practical and spiritual origins of psychoanalysis in my *Dark Ground of Spirit* (McGrath 2012), but this is a field in which much works remains to be done.

Works cited

Eliot, T. S. (1922), "The Waste Land," *The Waste Land and Other Poems*, San Diego: Harcourt Brace Jovanovich.

Flynn, T. (2005), "Philosophy as a Way of Life: Foucault and Haddot," *Philosophy and Social Criticism* 31: 608–22.

Foucault, M. (1978), *The History of Sexuality, Vol. 1: An Introduction*, R. Hurley (trans.), New York: Random House.

Foucault, M. (1986), *The History of Sexuality, Vol. 3: The Care of the Self*, R. Hurley (trans.), New York: Random House, 37–68.

Foucault, M. (2005), *The Hermeneutics of the Subject*, F. Gros (ed.), G. Burchell (trans.), New York: Picador.

Fukuyama, F. (1992), *The End of History and the Last Man*, New York: Simon & Schuster.

Grant, G. (2005), *Lament for a Nation: The Defeat of Canadian Nationalism*, Montreal, QC and Kingston, ON: McGill-Queens.

Hadot, P. (1995), *Philosophy as a Way of Life: Spiritual Exercises from Socrates to Foucault*, A. I. Davidson (trans.), Malden, MA: Blackwell.

Irrera, O. (2010), "Pleasure and Transcendence of the Self: Notes on 'A Dialogue Too Soon Interrupted' between Michel Foucault and Pierre Hadot," *Philosophy and Social Criticism*, vol. 36, 995–1017.

Latour, B. (2004), *The Politics of Nature: How to Bring the Sciences into Democracy*, C. Porter (trans.), Cambridge, MA: Harvard University Press.

McGrath, S. J. (2013), "The Tyranny of Consumer Capitalism and the Third Age of Revelation," *Analecta Hermeneutica*, vol. 5. Available from http://journals.library. mun.ca/ojs/index.php/analecta (accessed 1 February 2015).

McGrath, S. J. (2014), "Secularization and the Tyranny of the Homogeneous State," *Bharatiya Manyaprad: Journal of Indian Studies*, vol. 2, 90–106.

Plato (1961), "Apology," *The Collected Dialogues of Plato*, E. Hamilton and H. Cairns (eds), H. Tredennick (trans.), Princeton, NJ: Princeton University Press, 1961.

Sellars, W. (1956), "Empiricism and the Philosophy of Mind," in H. Feigl and M. Scriven (eds), *Minnesota Studies in the Philosophy of Science*, vol. 1, Minneapolis, MN: University of Minnesota Press, 253–329.

Sellars, W. (1963), "Philosophy and the Scientific Image of Man," in W. Sellars (ed.), *Empiricism and the Philosophy of Mind*, London: Routledge, 1–40.

Sellars, W. (1973), "Autobiographical Reflections (February 1973)," in H. N. Castañeda (ed.), *Action, Knowledge, and Reality: Studies in Honor of Wilfrid Sellars*, Indianapolis: Bobbs-Merrill, 277–93.

Žižek, S. (1999), "The Superego and the Act: A Lecture by Slavoj Zizek," *The European Graduate School*, August. Available from http://www.egs.edu/faculty/slavoj-zizek/ articles/the-superego-and-the-act/ (accessed 1 February 2015).

10

Wise Questions

C. Wesley DeMarco

Ask a foolish question, get a foolish answer. Ask a wise question, and get what? Definitive solutions? Universal consensus? More questions? I shall argue that there are wise questions that are wise-making, and a way of wise questioning that turns entirely upon issues so far-reaching and thoroughgoing that we need a globe of world philosophies to burn away our personal fixations and socially sedimented assumptions and expose them. Wise questions pondered and practiced can integrate and orient all the questions of a lifetime.

By "wisdom" in this context I mean knowing the truth, especially the truth about the most important things, and living with and in the truth. This involves a practice of the perfusive presence of root realities. When we are wise in this sense, final truths shine through every truth; we sense the roots of things in everything, and opportunities to work for primary values are found at every practical turn. Wisdom in this sense is a harmony of the *lived* harmony of thought and life with the *thought* harmony of thought and life. There is a second sort of wisdom, an "ancillary wisdom," which consists not in knowing and living primary truths but in being open to every sort of truth, above all to the truth about the most important things, and enacting this openness. I shall argue that the way of wise questioning—the *via interrogativa*—is a way of wisdom in the secondary sense, and quite possibly in the first.

The claim that there is a way of wisdom that consists entirely or essentially of questioning is a claim that hangs on a distinction among fundamental orientations of the activity of questioning. These are discernible ways that different questions—or even the same question—might be entertained. I call these primitive interrogative attitudes, that orient the events of inquest, the *flavors of wonderment*. A lot of confusion can be avoided if we get clear about them.

Each interrogative attitude is distinguished by characteristic aims and expectations. Different things count as answers in each way of wondering; each sets standards for what counts as a legitimate question, and each is marked above all by a distinctive relationship between question and answer.[1] Since my home tradition is Socratic, I use Greek terms to mark these out.

The first is the *zetetic* flavor. It is the search mode that seeks determinate solutions to definite problems. Specifying the problem is much of the process, and in zetetic inquiry what matters above all is framing a problem in such a way that a number of distinct alternatives can be set out, the better to ascertain which is the best solution. A well-framed question is a stencil for a particular style of solution. Moreover the best solutions are those that prompt further zetetic questions.[2] In the simplest cases, the answer is selected from a number of separate alternatives; we want to know which of the candidate solutions is the best, all things considered, or simply is true, yes or no. To be sure, research is rarely so simple, but that marks a sort of ideal: the answer is *there* as a matter of fact, and we can and shall seek it out.[3]

In the zetetic flavor, what counts as a solution is an adequately determinate answer that is detachable from the questions that motivate the search. Questions in a zetetic flavor are instrumental; the questions we ask are the means to an end, and the end is some definite and determinate solution. Once an answer is in hand, the motivating question seems otiose. This kind of questioning is common to empirical science and humanistic research, despite their many differences. There is an answer; it is a matter of fact; we can find it and shall find it. It is a problem solving mode, familiar in practical life no less than in the theoretical disciplines that refine it.[4]

What counts as an answer in zetetic inquiry poses a question to the *aporetic* way of wondering. The aporetic flavor wonders typically about the meaning and value of proposed solutions or, more radically, of the questions themselves. Aporetic inquiry seeks elucidations of proposed answers or questions. Not satisfied by determinate and detachable solutions, this flavor is defined by a taste for *resolutions*.[5] Its answers relate claims to other claims—especially claims of larger scope—and relate these relations to norms of meaning or standards of argument and evidence. In this way, we resolve inquisitive situations in which different people are posing rival claims about putatively the same facts, or in which a particular claim is differently construed, or in which the framing of the questions themselves is at issue. The shape of the answer is a clue to the quality of the wonderment that prompts the question, but the wonder is prior, at least erotetically.

Questioners with a taste for aporetic wonderment delight in resolutions. Nevertheless, resolutions remain problematic because the clarification of one interrogative situation implies other actual or possible resolutions. A question coherently answered in one situation may not be so in another. If there were not multiple coherent resolutions, the inquiry would not be aporetic. To resolve these matters with respect to specific standards of evidence and norms of meaningfulness is answer enough for the aporetic taste.[6] It is an error to suppose that all wonderings that hang on norms of meaning and standards of evidence and argument can be settled by fact-finding, and an equal and opposite error to regard all fact-finding as tantamount to interpretation-smithing. It is false to regard "solutions" as the only legitimate answers, and false to regard all legitimate questions as those in a zetetic flavor. It is equally false to regard such solutions as merely materials for the humanizing interpretations whose problematics are the real grist of understanding. These are distinct forms of inquiry that turn on discernible flavors of wonderment, neither of which is reducible to the other.

In general, what makes a question aporetic is not the subject matter or the method of approach. Rather, it is the way of wondering which directs a questioner or community of inquest to the pertinent aspect of events. Usually we understand questions from answers. It is true that a set of answers can make explicit what is implicit in the mode of questioning which gives rise to it, and can thereby help us to understand it. But questions are prior to answers temporally, erotetically, epistemically, and otherwise; questions shape answers and the forecasts of satisfaction. Moreover there are important ways that the flavors of wonderment are prior to specific questions. Aporetic answers are distinctive because the questions are distinctive, and the questions are distinctive because the flavor of wondering is distinctive. Wondering is the root.

A third flavor of wonderment is satisfied neither by a solution that appears as the single best determinate option, a solution that leads to further research which can build upon it without revising it, nor by a resolution that clarifies rival conceptions each of which seems by its own lights best. It is satisfied by nothing less than dissolutions of pressing questions. The *ephectic* flavor is curiously neutral and counts the neutralization of a question as its success. "Dissolution" is this neutralization of the force of a question which presses for an exclusive answer and pushes us to take sides. Neutralization may be chosen or compulsory, and the dissolution may entirely undermine a question or may simply put it out of play.

Dismissing a question as a pseudo-problem is an example of a particular result of ephectic inquiry, not definitive of dissolution. In many cases, a question that is arguably central to a line of inquiry is bracketed so as to allow it to proceed unhindered. Mathematicians, to get on with their work, may set aside the question of the nature of numbers, while keeping the issue open in the background. Physicists may set aside the question of the applicability of math to matter, or remain agnostic about the nature of physical law. A question may be defused, as with interpersonal dialogue in which strong convictions are adjourned so that meanings may be more sensitively discussed. Suspensive wondering may open whole new areas of inquiry. Phenomenologists suspend the object-fascinated natural attitude and bracket questions of external existence to allow phenomena to appear as phenomena. That facilitates inquiry into the structures of appearance and the constitution of meaning. Madhyamika dissolve fixation on conceptual constructions to let them appear *as* constructions in the empty space of codependencies.[7] Pyrrhonians suspend judgment on philosophical questions for the sake of tranquil living. These quite different uses of the ephectic mode all hang on suspension of the answer via neutralization of the prior question on which that answer depends.

The ephectic way is critical and criterial. The style of criticism is internal, typically, to a criterion that specifies the quality of the state of wonder. This might be pure doxastic self-evidence, phenomenological immediacy, meditative luminescence, rational clarity and distinctness, or what have you. Critique is made in reference to and in light of the criterion. The state of not-knowing— suitably lit—is itself a state of wonderment, and its features define the satisfaction of the flavor and hence its characteristic sorts of answer. The pure ideal of ephectic wondering would be inquiry without beliefs, vision without views, thinking without posits, dialogue without discord. True to form, philosophers try nevertheless to milk this condition to support rival theories and partisan positions. It is, often enough, such attempts that have given suspensive wonder a bad name.

The other flavors are also critical. Zetetic critique includes charges of inaccuracy, inadequate evidence or method, failure to frame questions in suitably zetetic ways, and failure to attain non-revisability of the answers on which subsequent questions depend. Aporetic criticism includes the internal critique that a view is not coherent by its own standards or cannot cover all the pertinent facts, the external critique that a rival view can handle its questions better than it can, and the dialectical critique that combines internal and external critique in reference to some purpose that is implied by the contending views even if it is not recognized by them. Wondering in the ephectic flavor makes a specialty of criterial critique, and its central cases involve suspending in light of a criterion internal to the state of wonderment.

In some of the most interesting cases, the phenomena investigated are closely related to that on which one has suspended. Examples include linguistic irrealism in which it is left undecided whether effable patterns are imposed by nature on language or by language on nature, logical noneism in which existential import is neither ascribed to nor denied of existential quantification, and forms of idealism in which phenomena are explored *as* phenomena by suspending on the question of whether they are subjective or objective, generated by internal or external causes, or both. In this way the sunny neutrality of ephectic wonderment, far from marking the end of inquiry, cleans up existing lines of investigation and clears the way for new ones. In each such case, erotetic neutrality allows a certain sort of inquiry to move forward—into appearances, feelings, qualities, possibilities, structures of consciousness, or what have you—precisely because the probative force of looming questions has in some pertinent sense been dissolved. Phenomenology, Pyrrhonianism, Madhyamaka, and kindred lines of inquiry would be impossible without the ability to wonder in a specially neutral and neutralizing way, frame a criterion using some of its features, suspend pertinent questions in light of that criterion, and pursue the inquiry so defined.

Neutralization is not cancelation, though sometimes questions are annulled. Still, any sceptical position that rejects knowledge as impossible in principle is a degenerate form of ephectic inquiry. (I do not wish to deny that such scepticism is an honorable option, simply that it is ephectic *wonderment*.) Similarly, empiricism as a position that excludes other kinds of meaning or truth is a degenerate form of zetetic inquiry and hermeneutical conventionalism or semiotic constructivism are, as positions and theories, degenerate forms of aporetic inquiry. Still, the ephectic flavor of wondering hazards skepticism and nihilism, just as the aporetic flavor risks relativism and constructivism, and zetetic inquiry risks empiricism and positivism. All wonderings are risky—simply as wonderings.[8]

A fourth flavor of wonderment is more controversial still, and more central to my purpose in this chapter. Call it the *thaumasic* flavor—an ugly word for a lovely concept. This is a contemplative mode of inquiry that is fully interrogative and fully meditative.

Not satisfied by solutions or resolutions or dissolutions, what counts as an answer in thaumasic questioning is an absolution.[9] A question is absolved when it is realized as an exemplification of a maximally general question—a "final" question about fundamental realities or primary values, the nature of self, or what have you. The unrestricted issue glimpsed in the restricted and tractable one is a bottomless question. A bottomless question is not an unanswerable question, though in its unrestricted form it cannot be answered by solutions or dissolutions or resolutions.[10] It is the inexhaustible source of spinoff questions which are often taken—mistakenly—to replace the source question. These spinoffs are renderings needed to frame particular inquiries so that they may attain to solutions or resolutions or dissolutions. Endeavoring to provide any manageable answer for a bottomless question inevitably involves replacing it with some zetetic or aporetic or ephectic question. However, none of these more manageable spinoff questions can replace the bottomless question without remainder. History and analysis and experience show this. No numerable set of zetetic and aporetic and ephectic questions can replace a bona fide bottomless question.

Becoming receptive to all flavors helps us to appreciate how a particular question is a bounded rendering of an unbounded bottomless one. Contemplative inquest is *satisfied* by finding and meditating these "absolutions." They are not easy to come by, since they require specific recognition and not merely a nod to the general idea. The emergence of a bottomless thaumasic question of which zetetic and aporetic and ephectic questions are proper parts is the answer sought by contemplative wonderment. Absolution adds depth to the bounded question and enriches the bottomless one. Absolved, the question remains. Such a question is in a way an answer.

There are two ways that this sort of question is at the same time an answer. First, a bottomless question wondered in the thaumasic flavor is a question that can be lived. That makes it a practical answer. That it is practical can be seen once all attentive engagements, including bodily engagements, are regarded as kinds of questioning,[11] and once the bond between every question and one or more bottomless questions is recognized. The second way the question is an answer is that with contemplative wonderment the answer is inseparable from the question. Not only is the question that which is sought; we have here an authentic non-duality of question and answer.[12]

It is impossible that all the flavors of wonderment involve question–answer non-duality. For example, if the search mode were nondual, answers could never be detached from the questions and no *facts* could be, or be known (howsoever variably framed). Aporetics contextualize it. Ephectic experience may be nondual in relation to appearances, but only in virtue of a bracketing which defers dualities. Certain sorts of question–answer pairs function nondually in certain ways, but not all of them can function nondually and not in all ways. Call this the thesis of the qualified nonduality of question and answer. It is an implication of the thesis of the flavors of wonderment.

It would be unwise to proclaim that there is no such thing as nondual knowledge or experience or practice. However it would also be unwise to proclaim that all genuine knowledge or experience or practice must be nondual. That is because the deep structures of knowledge and experience and practice are question-answer structures. If all questioning were nondual, we would have nowhere to go and nothing more to know; if no questioning were nondual, there would be no contemplative wonderment. And if there were no contemplative wonderment, there would be no way of wise questioning.

Someone interested only in the zetetic search mode, who has no taste for aporetics or contemplative wonderment, might regard those others flavors as worthless or even dangerous. A conceptual puzzler who sees conceptual issues in the most well-confirmed empirical accounts, and who harbors suspicions about theoretical posits, might be tempted to downgrade zetetic inquiry or to regard it as merely provisional. A pure contemplative who regards arts and sciences alike as trifling with the dimensions of illusion may have little patience with them. But it is a mistake to disparage ways of wondering different from one's own. Attitudes that shut down whole classes of question cannot be wise. It is wise to acknowledge at least four flavors of wonderment and wise to recognize that behind all legitimate answers lie the distinctive ways of inquest that move and mold them.

With this in view, I can state my thesis more exactly. It is that there is an inquisitive "way" that (i) is open to all sorts of truths because it has a taste for every flavor of wonderment, that (ii) is able to experience and think in depth as well as in breadth because it recognizes the bottomless questions that lurk in the heart of every question, and that (iii) prioritizes questions in the thaumasic flavor.[13] The *via* (iv) can be lived fully as a way of life since all attentive thought and practice are well regarded as inquisitive, since bottomless questions can be realized in every question, and since, therefore, the thaumasic flavor can be realized in every department of life.[14] In this way the *via* harmonizes theory and practice.

A question is a wise question so far as it is, as a question, a proper part of the *via*: it either expresses a bottomless question directly or indirectly through questions in other flavors. The constant query is *"How do I make this question a wise question?"* That is to ask *"How can I make this inquiry to be part of the via interrogativa?"* Living the *via* we are taught by every question how to ask wise questions. Every question can then become the vehicle for a practice that focuses questioning and brings wise questions into the weave of a life. In a slogan: *"In every question, the question of wisdom!"*

There is a large-scale structure to the *via* that is precisely parallel to the structure of primary wisdom according to which the most basic and important truths are seen in all truths and all truths are seen to imply the most basic ones. Religious wisdom traditions have this structure, although what is held most basic is held by faith. Reason-based or experience-based wisdom traditions have this structure, although what is taken to be most basic is held to be known with adequate argument or evidence. The structure of the *via* is congruent, although it is a structure of questions in which wise questions are wondered in every question and every question is found to imply the deepest questions. It is this common large-scale structure which makes the *via* a way of wisdom.

Just as there are religious or rational wisdom traditions that are like the way of wise questioning, there are questions within those traditions that are similar to wise questions. Zen koans might be considered wise questions, so far as they are designed to promote *samātha* and insight, but not many are wise in the sense employed here since most are instrumental and are not internally related to what they promote. Questions concerned directly with *sūnyatā* or what appears as self or how compassion is the felt aspect of the world's unrestricted intercalation are the more direct parallels to wise questions in the *via*. The deep questions of the Daoists and Vedantins are "wise questions" in the intended sense only so far as they directly concern ultimate realities (as these are conceived and experienced in the home traditions) *and* human existence, *and* only so far as the questions can be lived. The question of the *dao* itself as at once nature's way, and a possible human way, fills the bill as does the question of Brahman–Atman coincidence. The question of *cheng* (integrity as "being real") in Neoconfucian tradition is a paradigmatic case of a wise question, so long as it is sustained as a question. The same is true for the good and teleology and *nous* in Platonic–Aristotelian tradition.

Still, although all of the great traditions know such queries, they do not know them as wise questions. All run briskly to their favored answers; none focuses adequately the pondering of the questions in wonderment for its own sake; none has ventured a way of wisdom that is sourced in contemplative inquest; none finds adequate clues to ultimate answers in its ways of questioning. Few fully accept all the flavors. Because they do not adequately focus the dependence of their answers on their questions, and because they do not attend to the qualifications of their answers, they too often fail to appreciate their own limits, or how the questions remain, resonating in the bass of their favored answers. It is a particular view of *cheng* in which wisdom is supposed to consist, or a definite view of the *dao*, or a specific position taken on two-truth theory, rather than the question of the *dao* or of *cheng* or of *sūnyatā* as a question which can be wise-making simply as a question. Hence the matter of wise questions is never adequately framed and the *via* as such does not emerge.

It is unwise to shut down any of the flavors of wonderment and wise to touch the question of wisdom in every question. This recognition leads directly to the *via interrogativa* as an ancillary wisdom since it turns on openness to all truths and above all to primary truths. In contemplative wonderment, with its ability to savor in every question those ubiquitous questions about ultimate things out of which all more manageable queries flow, the *via* finds its orientation and its integration. However it is untrue to the *via* to take this as a cushy conclusion. The arising of a question in the contemplative flavor is the *problem*; if the absolution of the question occurs, that counts as an answer, but whether this has occurred is not always clear. This ought to make one question whether there is legitimately such a thing at all.

It is fatal to the *via interrogativa* to speak blithely of flavors as if easy to accept them all as legitimate, fatal to speak hastily of openness to all truth as if it were obvious that acceptance of all types of question and all flavors of wonderment were the royal road to this openness, fatal to accept insouciantly the claims of thaumasic wonderment. For the pivotal moment in the *via* consists in the flavors' questioning each other to the utmost possible extent. Without this interrogation, it is not an interrogative way. The fullest flowering of the *via* occurs in the fiercest force of this cross-examination.

While every flavor offers ways of questioning the others, the grilling is most intense at the transition to contemplative wonderment. This is neither a languid pondering of big vagaries nor a slack-jawed gazing at mysteries in which burning issues become anaemic ghosts of themselves in a sort of spiritualized fog. With contemplative wonderment the problem is to find a bottomless question that functions in a definite sort of way so that it is in the apt sense an answer. This is not the sort of answer that the other flavors can recognize. Nor can they recognize this sort of question! They must fail to recognize it, at least without domesticating it into their own ways and means, which inevitably truncates the question. Here the question of the question is most intense.

There is a divide here, an interrogative divide. At this threshold, we take the three flavors on one side and the contemplative flavor on the other and observe how thoroughly each side threatens to cast the other into abeyance.

Non-contemplative inquirers should indeed wonder about the legitimacy of a mode of inquiry that is supposed to be genuinely contemplative and genuinely interrogative. On the other side of the divide, contemplative questioners should wonder about the others. Thaumasic inquest casts its strong scruples upon their nature and status, even if it does not doubt their particular answers. They may not be as they seem! It is not clear at this juncture which side better frames the situation, which is more ontological, which is more epistemic, which is more subjective, which is more objective. For example, if we take zetetic wonderment as the source of all legitimate inquiry into nature, then contemplative wonderment seems maximally subjective, if it is legitimate at all. However, as experience and history show, the thaumasic side can appear as the aspect of reality, leaving the others to sift through mere appearances, or to be left with some sort of derivative status they are incapable of appreciating. Aiming to assert its own privilege, each side says of the other that it does not know what it is doing or what it is.

This is the point of greatest interrogative intensity[15] in the ways wondering in which everything is most up for grabs. Classic ontological and epistemic worries are so intense here that there is a sort of fluctuation. Walking the interrogative divide, at the point of greatest intensity, there is a sort of ontological–epistemic flux, in which the kinds of questioning can be questioned most radically. Here we can ask whether there might be limits or dependencies that each flavor is unable to recognize or even adequately interrogate when left to its own devices. The demand is to sustain the prodigious cross-examination that occurs when all the flavors are sustained, even while what is questioned is the nature and limits of those same flavors.

The interrogative divide is not a science–philosophy split, or an ordinary knowledge–mystical knowledge gap, or an empirical–transcendental division. It requires utterly open-minded questioning in which no secret convictions prevail, otherwise the divide will seem merely to prefigure one's favored primitive ontological difference.[16] At the interrogative divide, the legitimacy of the ways of wondering must be subject to withering interrogation, full force, purging all questions so far as that is possible for the questioner.

There are analogies of this divide in many established wisdom traditions, such as two-truth theory, *kataphatic* versus apophatic theology, the nameable *miao dao* and unnameable *xuan dao*, Parmenidean *aletheia* and *doxa*, and so on. In relation to classical two-truth theory, versions of which are native to Buddhism and, later, Vedanta, thaumasic wonderment plays the role of absolute truth, in contrast to the other flavors, which play the role of relative truth. Even absurdism affords an analogy.[17] However these analogies are not exact. The *via interrogativa* is not a *via negativa*; to question is not necessarily to negate. The flavors of wonderment do not reduce to two sorts of truth[18] even though there is a divide of greatest erotetic potency. The point is to question our questions by unshackling the ways of wondering to question each other, and that is most vivid and most thoroughgoing when we walk the interrogative divide with the widest variety of world traditions in mind. These traditional options—which rarely form neat antitheses—are then used to burn away everything but the raw questions in their most primitive forms.

At this point we are, if honest, left with an experience of total resource-lessness. Curiously, this experience feeds contemplative inquest. Without this, it is bogus. For if we slide back into theory, it would not be *contemplative* inquest; if we ease forward into pure luminosity, affirming a silent simplicity beyond beings and emptiness, it would not be contemplative *inquiry*. Not something to eliminate, nor something merely to tolerate, this absolute resourcelessness is essential. Without it the *via* is in vain.

Beyond its mental status, the being of a question may be taken to be the being of possibility, or of discrete *possibilia*: candidate answers are possible situations one of which matches the actual situation. Hence if there are questions there must be possibilities distinct from the actual situations that define the answers. Or we may reason that the being of a question is the being of an indeterminacy that appears when we are unsure: in this case, we infer that actual uncertainty implies real indeterminacy with genuine vagueness. At the interrogative divide, the divide itself explains the being of the question. If there is contemplative inquest, there is an interrogative divide. If there is no divide, there is no contemplative wonderment. It is false that there is no contemplative wonderment, however; thus there is a divide in fact. What does that imply? If there is an interrogative divide, there is a question of unqualified reality as well as a question of qualified realities. And if there is a question, there may be an answer. If a thaumasic question would be just as much an answer, then there may be an unqualified reality. If contemplative wonderment is actual, then there is actually an unqualified reality as well as qualified realities. Remembering that in thaumasic inquiry the problem is to find such a question, it now seems that the question found would imply the existence of an interrogative divide, which in turn implies the existence of unqualified as well as qualified reality. And given the thesis that all operationally restricted questions are specifications of operatively unrestricted ones, it follows that the existence of any question whatsoever implies the existence of unqualified as well as qualified reality.

This line of inference is entirely valid, but eminently arguable. At this point, we need a positive account that sets out the conditions and preconditions of the question, an account that draws upon, and draws out, the implications of the *via interrogativa*.

The positive account most pertinent to the *via* is provided by Neosocratic metaphysics (DeMarco 1991, 1993). This chapter is not the place to elaborate the positive account, but it is good to say a few words about it, lest the *via* seem at odds with constructive theorizing. Far from scorning it, the *via* broadens and deepens when it uses the best constructive theorizing one can manage, but then questions it radically. That regenerates the *via*. The best theory will not only aim to give account of the *via*—of the various question-forms and the flavors of wonderment and their ways—but will tap it for clues to a better view of the conditions of all questioning and all answering.

To conclude, I offer a brief résumé of some features of this account.

In Neosocratic thought, the philosophical activity that provides positive philosophical answers to distinctively philosophical questions consists in articulating *qualifications*. Qualifications in this sense are the acts of discernment and clarification needed in every field of inquiry: identifying pertinent units, relating means and ends, distinguishing aspects, sorting out contexts, and so on. Philosophy makes a specialty of these acts of qualification and uses them in peculiarly unalloyed forms. If a question cannot be answered sheerly by making qualifications, it is not a distinctively philosophical question (see DeMarco 1991, 2004b).[19] Philosophy is the use of and reflection on the forms and acts of qualification.[20]

Philosophical thinking promotes solutions, resolutions, dissolutions, as the case may call. Philosophical absolution requires tracking ontological conditions in our means of qualification. Hence, in Neosocratic thought, the forms of qualification are ascribed their own metaphysical standing: truthful thinking employs versions of the same formative acts that go to compose that about which we think. The rough idea is that there are "elementary acts of nature" such as internalizing and externalizing, subordinating and coordinating, segmenting and sequencing, gathering and scattering, nesting and embedding—and others—which function as formatives in our thinking and in nature at large. The ontologically primitive versions of these activities are the forms of qualification. These "forms"—the *li* of Neosocratic thought—are the metaphysical condition that things have features, are capable of relations, enter into transactions, take root in situations, and so on. The forms of qualification, in turn, are said to be dimensions of a single primordial *act of qualification*. This is the taproot of mind and nature. It is that by which natural phenomena acquire their own qualifications and hence their own significance, and that by which we reconstruct the qualifications of what we signify. Posing apt questions requires making apt qualifications that adjust thought and language and allow thought to track what is thought and language to articulate what is articulable. It is because there are conditions common to knower and known—in the forms of qualification and ultimately the act of qualification—that questioning is pertinent to the questioned and questions have answers. If questions have answers at all, ultimate questions admit of absolution in these common qualifications that are the ontological prerequisites of all questioning and answering.

In this theory, natural wholes and other real singularities function as "qualifiers." To be is to be a qualifier. To be a qualifier is to be qualified for signification in multiple, limited ways defined by the forms of qualification. These forms are not beings but conditions of being by which the known has relative boundaries, admits of features and functions, occurs in transformative processes of selection and exchange, takes place in situations. Qualifiers are the real articles of nature in which the forms of activity become self-active according to the dimensions of qualification. Accordingly, natural individuals *are* perspectives (as Leibniz and Whitehead and others say), *are* contexts (complexes that themselves are contexts, as Buchler says, textualizations of context, as Gadamer says); they are purposive functions (in the broadest sense of purpose inclusive of all attractor-types [DeMarco 2008]). This is what it is to be a self-so-ing, self-actualizing singularity: a qualifier making its way through tissues of qualifications by qualifying and being qualified in its own unique way.

In Neosocratic thought, all questioners are qualifiers, though not all qualifiers are questioners. All qualifiers are aspects of a world; questioners are not merely aspects but aspectualizers capable of framing different perspectives and admitting a range of interpretations; they are contextualizers that actively constitute various orders of meaning. Questioning requires shifts in aspect and changes in context and renegotiation of the relative interiors and exteriors of things and events. A qualifier incapable of framing alternatives in this way could not be a questioner. A questioner is an active source of aspection, situation, bounding, and so on, according to structures due to some selection of the forms of qualification that are accessible. This changes the issue, the focus, frame, and formant of the question. A questioner is not merely a defined point of view on everything else, or a settled context for all events, or a purpose to which all else in the universe seems relative, but is an agent of aspection and situation, structuring and redelimiting. Any qualifier that is essentially and not incidentally a questioner is essentially and not incidentally an agent of qualification, responsively and flexibly within the verges of its singular way. At the limit, a radical questioner would become pure qualification, issuing in the utmost flexibility of mind and practice possible within local conditions.[21]

This is simply another implication, set out in the vocabulary of Neosocratic thought, of the thesis that the existence of wise questions implies the reality of unqualified as well as qualified existence. The fuller account hangs on the proposition that questions have ontological import. They must, for, to the extent that answers have ontological import, the corresponding questions must have ontological import. But must a question have ontological import as a question?

There is a strong and a weak version of the thesis that questions as questions have ontological import. The weak version requires only that we be able to account for beings' being questionable. They are questionable for us because the primitive formative acts function in different ways in different contexts, and so the ways they function in our human mental constructions readily depart from the ways they function in nature's own constructions. Hence our constructions and nature's constructions routinely diverge. Beings are, in themselves and as such, questionable because the common qualifications are questionable and qualifiers are composed through qualifying acts. To be is to be a "qualifier," to be a qualifier is to be qualified, and to be qualified is to be questionable. Therefore to be is to be questionable.

The stronger version of the thesis requires that beings *be* as questions. In the Neosocratic account, that is argued by pairing the forms of questioning and the forms of qualification and recognizing that these are two sides of the same primitive conditions, distinguished modally. In the strong thesis, not only are beings questionable as beings (since to be is to be qualified and to be qualified is to be questionable), but beings are *as beings* questions. They exist as questions because the forms of qualification that qualify items and events for being and for signification are at the same time forms of question. This implies that certain ontological structures are interrogative structures. To be is to be a qualifier that is qualified and qualifying, and to be a qualifier is to be a question. Qualifiers *exist* as questions.

Qualifiers exist as questions if there is an interrogative divide, and there is a divide just in case the flavors of wonderment have ontological import. In the logic of Neosocratic metaphysics, if there is an absolution of the question by which the most primitive questions are implicit in every question, there must be an absolution of that which is qualified for questioning, and this implies that there is a condition of the qualifications of the qualified. This condition of the qualifications of that which is qualified, that is the ground of the forms of quali-fication, would be an unqualified reality beyond all singular qualifiers—beyond their being and their emptiness. Therefore an unqualified reality is implied in the absolution of the question just as much as in the qualifications by which we have positive limited answers. These are two sides of the same coin, accessible at the extremity of inquiry at the interrogative divide.

That is an inference which takes a questioner from the one side of the interrogative divide to the other. If sound, the inference implies the falsity of unrestricted ontological relativity. We must also proceed in the other direction, beginning with an experience of an unqualified reality,[22] or at least with a claim to such an experience, which claim raises the question. We can then infer that if there is unqualified reality *and if it is questionable*, then there must be qualified reality. If sound the inference implies the falsity of unrestricted ontological absolutism. Since unqualified reality is not questionable in itself but only relatively, if it is questionable there must be some relative existence in relation to which it becomes questionable. If there is unqualified reality, it is not "in itself" a question. It cannot be composed as a question since it is not composed at all. Rather, it is questionable in relation to qualified realities which have relative being and relative emptiness.[23]

Such is the logic of the interrogative divide: relative reality is absolutely a question and absolute reality is relatively a question.

At the interrogative divide, every means of questioning is thrown most radically into question. At this point, one is most forcefully a question to oneself. For a questioner to question most radically is to interrogate reality itself and the reality of self as two margins of a wise question. As one becomes a radical questioner, one becomes a question at the limit and realizes what it is to be a questioner and realizes that the divide is the condition of her existence.[24] Just as a contemplative question in the thaumasic flavor ceases to be contemplative if it falls to one side of the divide and ceases to be a question if it falls to the other, so too the radical questioner lives only at the limit. She is then positioned to ask the wise question: *Quaero ergo intersum?*[25]

Contemplative wonderment, above all others, hangs on the questioner. Thaumasic inquest requires a transmutation of the question that is at the same time a profound transfiguration of the questioner. If the question arises at all, the questioner has a singular opportunity to grasp the questionability of her being and realize her being as a question in such a way that the interrogative structures that define her as a questioner show themselves to be ontological and existential structures. Such a question would be, again, an answer. The radical questioner then blooms in the interrogative divide, living questioning as a total mode of existence, open to the interrogatives of every engagement.

By opening her to all kinds of questions, the *via* opens a questioner to all flavors of wonderment; by opening her to the flavors, she is opened to all kinds of truths. For that reason, it is a way of wisdom in the ancillary sense of wisdom. The *via* ties questions as questions to the most fundamental questions (or, more precisely, to the *question* of "fundamental questions"), leading them to occupy a role in inquiry and in life that is typically reserved for the convictions of philosophical grand theory or the articles of religious faith. However, the *via* also is quite possibly a way of wisdom in the primary sense, because there is good reason to infer that interrogative structures have ontological import. Neosocratic theory articulates this import in the metaphysics of qualification, which is at the same time a metaphysics of the conditions of questioning and the questioned.

We need wise questions—not because there is no knowledge without a sage foundation, nor because nothing can count as a legitimate inquiry until we see it as part of a query into being, but because in the light of wise questions all other questions take on an additional orientation, status, and significance.[26] A wise questioner drinks in the thaumasic savor in every flavor. A wise question keeps us on the *via* and signposts the great transition in which the forms of questioning and qualification coincide. A wise questioner walks the limit, working to promote a taste for every flavor of wonderment in herself and in others, living to advance the question of wisdom in every question.

Notes

1   The general formula for zetesis is: $\{(Q_1 \to [A_a \vee A_b \vee \ldots \vee A_n] \to A_1) \gg (Q_2 \to [A_a \vee A_b \vee \ldots \vee A_n] \to A_2) \gg (Q_n \to [\ldots] \to A_n), \gg (\ldots)\}$, where '$\to$' is a placeholder for the pertinent forms of inference, and Q_1 and Q_2 are logically separate issues linked in an historical series in which one answer suggests in context a further question abductively ('$\gg$') but may have suggested a different one in some other context. Different symbolizations might suggest different directions for research or highlight different aspects of the research.

The general formula for aporetic inquiry is: $\mid \{[(Q_1{}^i \to A_1{}^i), (Q_1{}^j \to A_1{}^j), (Q_1{}^k \to A_1{}^k), (\ldots), (Q_1{}^n \to A_1{}^n)], [\{(Q_2{}^i \to A_2{}^i), (Q_2{}^j \to A_2{}^j), (Q_2{}^k \to A_2{}^k), (\ldots), (Q_2{}^n \to A_2{}^n)], [(Q_3{}^i \to A_3{}^i), (Q_3{}^j \to A_3{}^j), (Q_3{}^k \to A_3{}^k), (\ldots), (Q_3{}^n \to A_3{}^n)]\} \mid \to \mid [Q_N{}^i \to (Q_N{}^j, Q_N{}^k, \ldots Q_N{}^n)] \to [Q_N{}^n \to (A_N{}^i, A_N{}^j, \ldots A_N{}^n)] \mid$. Informally: if Q is an aporetic question, there will be different coherent answers because there will be different construals of the question to which those answers are apt. A weak version requires comparability of the questions across cultural worlds; the strong version requires that we be able to say—through partial reference or multiple reference, for instance—that different questions internal to those cultural worlds are versions of the same question. In the schema, the numerical identities of Qs and As are subscripted, the versions are superscripted.

Ephectic inquiry has the form: $|Q_1| \equiv \{ \mid [(\neg Q_1) \lor (\dagger Q_1)] \;\&\; [(Q_2 \to A_2) \to (\mid Q_1 \mid)] \mid \lor \mid [(Q_1 \to A_1) \to (\mid Q_1 \mid)] \mid \}$. That is, neutralization of the question ('|') either amounts to negation or undermining ('†') of the question, which lets a different line of questioning be generated, or to holding the original question in suspense such that only if it is so held may the originally intended line of inquiry be pursued.

Contemplative inquiry has the form: $\{Q_T^i \to \mid [(Q_Z^i, \ldots Q_Z^n), (Q_A^i, \ldots Q_A^n), (Q_E^i, \ldots Q_E^n)] \to Q_T^n \mid \to \mid Q_T^i \equiv A_T^i \mid \}$. That is, a thaumasic question is such that if a series of zetetic and aporetic and ephectic questions obtains only if there is such a question, then that question is equivalent to an answer, in the ways specified in the chapter. The schema presumes a semantic relationship between the Z and A and E questions such that they can track the T question, even if the purveyors of the non-T questions reject it as unverifiable or irrelevant or what have you.

2 All should be set up so that they are *critiqueable*—a more flexible and inclusive criterion than verifiability or falsifiability—which are numbered among its species. All zetetic questions should, ideally, be formulated so as to promote solutions, and all solutions should, ideally, be formulated so as to promote further zetetic questions. Were the solutions not relevantly detachable from their questions, such quasi-linear progress would not be possible.

3 *Zetesis* in this sense is also familiar from ordinary perceptual experience, whenever we are not sure what is occurring or going to occur. The general form of perceptual zetesis is "What is happening?" or "What is going on?" (More specifically, it is "What do I see?" or "What do I smell?" or "What does my proprioception tell me about the environment?" etc.) General perceptual questions are typically more tightly framed to some more specific set of expectations according to the questions pertinent to a situation. Driving on the highway, we are focused on cars and drivers, but also more peripherally on weather conditions, possible pedestrians or wildlife, road surface, and much else. In each case, the question that is in one moment answered must be asked anew in the next moment. In sport we are focused on bodies and movements but also on style of action and reaction, local conditions that might affect footing, etc. Here again, every perceptually pertinent question must be renewed continuously, even when each question at each moment can be regarded as adequately answered. The propositional detachment of a solution to a problem is always possible in such cases, but is secondary to the experiential and practical registration of questions and answers. That perceptual experience is well regarded as a continuous series of

questionings is a claim that is important to the idea that questioning can be lived. I say a more about this in "The Unexpected Utility of Neosocratic Metaphysics" (DeMarco 2004a).

4   All the dominant erotetic logics are formalizations of idealizations of the zetetic mode. (See e.g. Hintikka, for whom a game-theoretic account of "dialogues" between a questioner and an "Oracle" formalizes our questioning processes and joins logic to a semantics of questioning; Wisniewski, for whom erotetic logics are theories of erotetic arguments, et al.) These typically suppose sets of answers given disjunctively and narrow these to a unique answer (or in the more interesting cases, to uniquely best questions) by specifying presuppositions or appending additional restricting questions.

These logical formalizations of zetetic inquiry are propositional and nearly always bivalent. The minimal one-question is: "Is P true or false?" This is standardly taken to be equivalent to "Is P or $\neg P$ true?" The minimal two-question is: "Is P or Q true?" which ramifies into larger disjuncts ("Is (P v Q v R v ... v N) true?"). In these accounts the *very meaning* of a question is a set of answers, or fully determinate answer-candidates, parsed in some way. The meaning of a question is (i) the set of possible answers, (ii) the set of empirically equivalent true answers, (iii) the set of verifiable answers, (iv) the set of relevant answers, etc., such that, if there is no such set of answers or possible answers, there is in fact no meaningful question there to be asked. These restrictions help to define useful objects of study, but should not be taken to suffice as complete accounts of the zetetic mode.

5   Aporetic questioning is less linear in structure and more circular, and the answers—the resolutions—are less detachable from their motivating questions. Resolutions lead to new questions, as do questionings in the zetetic flavor, but with aporetic inquiry the motivating questions never seem to go away entirely. Instead we seem to circle around to them again and again from different angles, as questions about alternate perspectives and frameworks come to hang on different ways of framing questions and optional norms and standards. The different perspectives and frameworks clarify the aporetic situation and the different norms and standards clarify the perspectives and frameworks. It is not that aporetic inquiry never makes any progress; it is that the same thing does not count as an "advance" here.

6   If we ask what construal ought to be given for some particular matter of fact, once the fact of the matter is sufficiently settled, that question is part of an aporetic inquiry into the result of a zetetic one; if we ask which interpretation, as a matter of fact, was posited by some individual or community of inquiry at some time in some place, we are asking a zetetic question about the outcome of an aporetic inquiry.

7   Candrakirti's thesis, affirmed by Tsongkhapa and others, that the kinds of
     assertion in the tetralemma mark stages of increasing adequacy, though extremely
     helpful in the context of Buddhist traditions, is regarded here as a restricted thesis.
     It is not true in general that the mode of joint denial is better for all purposes or
     even better as regards the specific purpose of knowledge of the real. To be sure,
     these authors expertly use the ephectic flavor to show how everything has the tang
     of emptiness and they use their means skilfully in relation to the purposes of their
     tradition. I talk about emptiness in relation to logical form in "A Zero Method for
     the Ultimate Why-Question" (DeMarco 2006), and "Form, Field, and the Emptiest
     Possible Nothingness" (DeMarco 2005).

8   Martin Schönfeld remarked, on reading a draft of this chapter, that the second
     and third flavors are "part of the problem." He seems convinced that we would
     do better without them both. All the flavors hazard philosophical temptations,
     however. The most tempting is to take some number less than four as sufficient.
     For example, Schonfeld argues that we do not need an "environmental ethic"
     because the *facts* of our situation speak for themselves and will call us to do
     what we must do, without having to detour into messy questions about values
     and priorities, norms and standards. This position consistently privileges zetetic
     inquiry and aims—unsuccessfully I believe—to make it suffice for all inquiry.

9   "Absolution," a word that is etymologically correct for the semantic purpose, risks
     religious connotations that are out of place here. In Neosocratic thought, acts
     of philosophical thinking provide answers through conveying "qualifications."
     These qualifications are said to *intimate* pervasive forms of qualification evident
     in the natural world at large. Intimation is what Platonic participation becomes in
     Neosocratic metaphysics, and hence the recognition of intimation is something
     like *truth by participation*, an asymmetric sort of truth-by-identification.
     Absolution is intimation.

10   It is quite often a *holoquestion*, that is, an unrestricted version of a common
     question form, such as "Why?" or "How?" or "What is it?" addressed without
     further qualification to the whole of things. A grieving mother's "Why?"
     originating in the particular source of her grief, but flung out to the universe
     at large, either is such a holoquestion or is one incipiently. All holoquestions
     in this sense are bottomless questions, though not all bottomless questions are
     holoquestions. The central cases of wise questions are bottomless holoquestions,
     though questions that signpost these are also wise in a secondary sense.

11   See note 3 above.

12   A better understanding of this point is afforded by the Neosocratic theory of
     ontological reflexivity, in which the locus at which forms of activity become
     self-active defines the site of a singular qualifier. In the *via*, qualifications function
     as primary ways questioners modify themselves so that they are better able to ask

wiser questions. They are then better able to access the qualifications that qualify things for questioning and better able to appreciate the bond between questioning and qualification in themselves and in the world.

13 This prioritization is conditional, required of the *via* and not required of or recommended for inquiries in the other flavors.

14 This is quite a different phenomenon from dwelling constantly through one's days on a particular practical problem or an issue in chemistry or mathematics. These questions permeate everything, which is why they are so obsessive, and so potentially pathological.

15 The divide is not situated at the line between zetetic wonderment and the others because it is thaumasic wonderment that is most moot yet presents the greatest challenge to the self-understandings of the other flavors. Each can question the others in light of its own ways and means, but the primary and most powerful divide is that between the thaumasic flavor and the others.

16 In that case, the interrogative divide will look like the division between the Two Truths, or between the unnameable and nameable *Dao*, or between Parmenidean *aletheia* and *doxa*, or *nous* contemplating the *eidē* and the world as a tissue of relativities, or Heidegger's "hiding singular" that "gives" the revealing transformations in frameworks of disclosure, etc., etc. In the *via* we consider the pattern of the questioning and the form of the wondering as prior to any such answers. Only then do we proceed to probe the activity and the pattern for clues to a more satisfactory characterization of the divide and what it presupposes.

17 To assert the meaninglessness of the universe is hasty. This is the absurdist error. Had Camus defined authentic existence as sustaining the radical *question* of the meaningfulness of existence, rather than as the "absurd" understood as the clash between a universe that is and must be meaningless and the human rage for meaning and order and beauty, his view would have been close to the *via* with its interrogative divide. In fact, very rarely, Camus does admit that the universe may be meaningful, though if so he cannot or does not know it, but these occasions are few and far between ("I don't know whether this world has a meaning that transcends it. But I know that I do not know that meaning and that it is impossible for me just now to know it" (Camus 2008: 51.) His uncharacteristic claim (see Camus 2008: 51 n.6) that Vedanta provides an alternative route to the absurd struggle by rejecting the world (hence inverting his absurdism) is also an opening for the *via*.

18 In "Platonism in the Means of Construction" (DeMarco 1998), I endorse a version of the classical view that truth is adequation, and recommend a distinction between four grades of adequation: coincidence (identity or nonduality), correspondence (with allowances for alternate formulations), correlation (via relevant similarity), and dynamic covariation (a "tracking" view). This makes for

four distinctive kinds of truth, none of which covers all cases. A strong distinction between the flavors of wonderment would seem to imply a kindred difference in types of truth. In both, a systematic pluralism is recommended along with a criticism of those endless debates in which one type or flavor is held to suffice for all cases.

19 See also my *Philosophical Qualifications*, in preparation.

20 This requires a peculiar construal of categories and concepts in which the processes of category-formation and concept-smithing are variable and yet have ontological import, at least in their most primitive forms. See DeMarco 2009: 9–29; 2004b; 1991: chs 4 and 6.

21 If there are qualifiers, there are qualifications; if there are qualifications, there are forms of qualification. If there are forms of qualification, there is a common condition in qualification *as such* (where the act of qualification is the common condition of transformation and formation, variation and invariation). If there are ways of knowing that do not modify what they know in the act of knowing it, qualification must not be synonymous with transformation. If questioning need not transform the questions, there must be—again—qualification without transformation. Therefore some acts of qualification are changeless forms of activity. (I elaborate this argument in DeMarco 1999.)

22 Candidate accounts include Parmenidean *Eon*, Aristotelian *nous*, Brahman as identical with *nirvikalpa samādhi*, *sūnyāta* as identical with the skylike mind in which all codependencies rest, and *nirvana* when that is understood as a liberated and liberating unconditioned condition. In Neosocratic thought it is *the unqualifiable* that issues in multiple forms of qualification in order that it may serve as the condition of the qualifications of the qualifiers. Once there are multiple forms of qualification, there is the possibility of multiple, multiply qualified, beings. The unqualifiable issues in multiple forms, the conditions of a multiplicity of real relative singularities, so that it can qualify as the condition of the qualifications that let them qualify for being and for signification. Though Neosocratic metaphysics implies a contextualist radicalism about variable, interdependent beings, it implies a preservationist conservatism about being, since on issuing the forms of qualification through the onefold act of qualification, the unqualifiable remains unqualified. That is, it does not become qualified in its being when it becomes qualified for signification.

23 The philosophy of qualification shows how we can speak truthfully of being and of emptiness, though the qualifications shift. The real article that in its unique and self-referential singularity is rightly signified as "qualified being" is also in its constitutive dependencies rightly signified as "qualified emptiness". These quite different qualifications are underwritten by the fact that the real articles are qualifiers of which we may speak truthfully—with qualification—in very different ways.

24   To understand how the singular questioner "is" a single question in her reality
      as a qualifier, start with the thesis that behind every answer is a question and
      inside every question is an ultimate question. Since questioning is at the base of
      all her definitive activities—this presumes the vigilance thesis according to which
      perceptions and practices are answers to questions of attention and engagement—
      the perceiver and practitioner is first and foremost a questioner. Now take the
      unique questioner, summing the whole arc of her life as a fullness of *actual and
      possible questions* in this boosted sense. Defined by the actual and possible questions
      by which she engages everything, then, so far as this has a singular integrity, we
      may say for short that the individual is a question. The questioner then is this arc, a
      centered configuration of interrogative engagements. Call this a "question star" or
      interrogative asterisk. The individual is this asterisk, radiating questions, throwing
      all about her into question, defined by the interrogative difference she makes.

      It would be more common to approach this from the side of answers, but the
      result is the same. Take the individual as the bundle of the answers she gives in the
      course of her life. Start with mental functions as answers to problems of thought,
      coordination, movement, perception, etc., then add various biological functions
      and physical states as answers to their own brands of problem (as above). All
      the properties of the individual are then framed as answers and the individual
      is either an answer-bundle or (more substantially) a source of answers. That is
      the individual as a bundle of facts or a factive fact-maker. But every answer is an
      answer to a question that is in several senses prior to it. Hence the individual is in
      every one of those same senses a questioner *as* an individual. Adding her unique
      temporal envelope of possibilities to the actualities of her historical time-line, she
      is again a question star.

      The questioner as an ontological asterisk has an inclusive and well-integrated
      unity just in case the questions do. Hence the unity of the person is the unity
      of her questions. One way the questions have inclusive and well-integrated
      unity—perhaps the only way, given our limitations; perhaps the best way, given
      its honesty—is when the life is committed to the *via interrogativa*, in which all
      questions are oriented to the singular question of wisdom.

25   That is, "I question, therefore I participate [in qualified and unqualified reality]?"
      This is no Thichian neologism, just workaday Latin. This then turns to the
      question: Is it true that radical questioning *intimates* the conditions of what it
      queries, simply as questioning?

26   It is said that a wise person always knows what to think and what to do and is in
      that sense never surprised; how then can a wise questioner be said to be wise? It
      is because though she is always surprised by particulars she is never at a loss for a
      wise question! Every event becomes for her an occasion for questioning and every
      question an opening for a wise question.

Works cited

Camus, A. (2008), "Absurd Freedom," in J. O'Brien (trans.), *The Myth of Sisyphus and Other Essays*, New York: Vintage International.

DeMarco, C. W. (1991), "Wittgenstein and Philosophical Signification," PhD thesis, Vanderbilt University, Nashville, TN, 1991.

DeMarco, C. W. (1993), "Philosophical Semiotic," presented at the *Society for the Advancement of American Philosophy*, Vanderbilt University, Nashville, TN.

DeMarco, C. W. (1998), "Platonism in the Means of Construction," presented at the *Meeting of the Central Division of the American Philosophical Association* and the *Meeting of the World Congress of Philosophy*, Boston, MA.

DeMarco, C. W. (1999), "Questions Between Deconstruction and Reconstruction," presented at the *Metaphysical Society of America*, Boston College, Boston, MA.

DeMarco, C. W. (2004a), "The Unexpected Utility of Neosocratic Metaphysics," presented at the *Metaphysical Society of America*, University of Georgia, Athens.

DeMarco, C. W. (2004b), "The Generation and Destruction of Categories," in M. Gorman and J. Sanford (eds), *Categories: Historical and Systematic Essays*, Catholic University of America Press, Washington, DC, 238–67.

DeMarco, C. W. (2005), "Form, Field, and the Emptiest Possible Nothingness," presented at the *International Institute for Field-Being* at the *Eastern Division Meeting of the American Philosophical Association*, New York, New York.

DeMarco, C. W. (2006), "A Zero Method for the Ultimate Why-Question," presented at the *Meeting of the Metaphysical Society of America*, The Catholic University of America, Washington, DC.

DeMarco, C. W. (2008), "The Emergence of Normativities in General Attractor Theory," presented at the *Meeting of the Metaphysical Society of America*, University of Southern Maine, Portland, ME.

DeMarco, C. W. (2009), "Righting the Names of Change," in *Journal of Chinese Philosophy* 36/1 (March): 9–29.

11

Future-Oriented Philosophy and Wisdom East and West

Martin Schönfeld

If philosophy wants to be relevant in the age of overshoot and climate change, then its leanings towards doubt and dissolution will not do anymore. These leanings are expressed in two styles of reasoning in Western philosophy, analytic dissection and postmodern deconstruction. They are embodied in stances such as Wittgenstein's withdrawal into language games, Derrida's insistence on the limits of reason and Rorty's replacement of truth with irony. There are differences among these stances, but not over the basic epistemic relation of mind to data. Dissection and deconstruction boil down to the same thing—an ultimately sceptical response to data. Call this *negative reasoning*.

The curse of the Scottish Enlightenment[1]

Leanings toward doubt and dissolution do not characterize all of Western philosophy. Most affected are the intellectual cultures of Anglophone societies; that is, the part of civilization whose characteristic version of modernity derives from the Scottish Enlightenment and its values—liberalism, individualism, and empiricism. In combination, these three values tend to reinforce one another epistemically into a skepticist mindset.

Liberalism is the celebration of *liberté* at the expense of the two other ideals of the Enlightenment intended to balance it out, *égalité* and *fraternité*. The expression of equality and solidarity are positive, economic rights (for example, the right to social security). The expressions of liberty are negative, political rights (for example, the right to freedom of thought). Negative rights protect personal prerogatives from political or legal power. Liberalism essentially suggests: *We have a right to rejection.*

Closely tied to liberalism, but not identical to it, is individualism, which endorses the value of personhood. Just as the negative rights of liberalism open up a space of freedom, the positive claims of individualism turn this space into the sanctuary for self-realization. In the interface with the outside world, the individualist's self-realization is posited on top of the claimed right to rejection. Thus the mentality of the individualist would be left unimpressed by pressures such as those arising from a scientific consensus and its consequent warnings.[2] Liberalism and individualism are cultural leanings, and as such rather diffuse, but they become concrete as effective ideological cover for capitalistic mischief. Corporate interests exploiting these leanings erode environmental legislation (in the name of "freedom") and succeed in the regulatory capture of democratic institutions (in the name of protecting the "little guy" from "big government").

The ecologically unlucky combination of liberalism and individualism becomes explosive when empiricism is added to the mix. By spreading uncertainty, obfuscating facts, and paralysing policymakers into inaction it allows corporate interests to turn regulatory capture into failing governance. Classical or naive empiricism appeals to the authority of the senses and validates claims by observation. The empiricist focuses on the concrete and the particular. That is, truth is what can be seen and pointed at. In the age of climate change and ecological overshoot, this focus darkens into biospherical blindness. The reason is that the degradation caused by climate change and ecological overshoot is systemic, and systemic issues are "everywhere and nowhere" at the same time. They tend to become conspicuous only at thresholds, as when a system is irrevocably impaired, enters failure mode, or goes terminal. Think of diabetes or hypertension: there is more to such medical disorders than meets the eye. Although these systemic conditions have discrete causes, their empirical symptoms can be elusive up to the point of no return. They are not necessarily observable. Hence diagnosis and treatment depend on quantitative data supplied by measurement.

Weather is observable as a local, short-lived phenomenon, but climate, which describes regional meteorological averages over at least thirty-year time-spans, is not. I cannot "see" climate, because it is quantitatively a dataset and qualitatively a holistic structure. I cannot point to it, since it envelops me, not only in space but also over time, in the past, at present, and in the future. Climate change consists in long-term shifts in global temperature averages that are tiny compared with the daily and seasonal temperature variations at the local level. Climate change, like climate itself, is not tangible to the senses. It is therefore elusive to the naive empiricist. As the jeers of conservative US politicians against climatologists illustrate every American winter, in particular when it is cold outside, an empiricist mindset can be genuinely puzzled by global warming (see *Huffington Post* 2015).

The same cognitive issues obscure the "ecological overshoot," which is a concept that stems from comparing two datasets. One dataset is the rate of supply by the Earth System. Another is the rate of demand by global civilization. On the supply side is the renewal rate of biotic resources, such as wood fiber, together with the assimilation rate (the absorptive capacity) of environmental services like the carbon cycle. On the demand side are the rates of resource use and service pressure. The spatial frame for the datasets is the entire planet, and their time frame is an entire year. Should human demand outpace natural supply in a given year, overshoot obtains. Demand reached 100 percent of supply in 1970 and has since then exceeded Earth's limits by a wider margin every year (Wackernagel et al. 2002: 9266–71; esp. 9266). In 2014, overshoot passed 160 percent (Global Footprint Network 2014). Civilization is going about its business as if it had at its disposal the resources and services of one-and-a-half planets. Clearly, this cannot last. Like climate change, the overshoot is an abstract measure and a holistic structure. It is not directly visible, but this does not make it any less real.

With the triple whammy of liberalism, individualism, and empiricism, climate change and overshoot hit Anglophone culture in a blind spot. They are inconvenient truths that freedom-loving individualists feel entitled to reject, and they also constitute an inferential type of knowledge, of a systemic level of reality, that is difficult for empirical mindsets to absorb. Hence disbelief is intuitive.

The international community has been witness to the geopolitical fallout. The largest cumulative per capita carbon footprint is that of the UK; the top national emitters, in annual per capita footprints, include Australia, Canada, and the US; and the failure of climate legislation, from Kyoto (1997) to Copenhagen (2009), has been the result of political pressures by the US. Seen from the position of the Scottish Enlightenment, marked by the likes of David Hume and Adam Smith, climate change must be meaningless—either it's not real, or if it is, it's surely not manmade; or if it is real and manmade, it's probably harmless and perhaps even good. Naive empiricism is negative reasoning put into anti-ecological practice.

On an intellectual level, negative reasoning in the guise inspired by the Scottish Enlightenment is *the rejection of universal information of existential import*. The overshoot once again illustrates this. Civilization has crossed already three planetary boundaries: of biodiversity loss, of the nitrogen cycle, and of the carbon cycle. These boundaries constitute biological, chemical, and climatic limits of our habitat (Folke 2013).[3] Stepping over these boundaries and proceeding to operate as if this were of no political or socio-economic consequence is precisely what has made civilization unsustainable. One particular issue is the mounting adverse impact of climate change on worldwide agricultural productivity. As global warming continues, food security will become a challenge.[4] Since overwhelming the capacities of our planetary habitat is not in our collective interest, such information is of *existential* significance. And, since we have no choice but to live on this planet, our collective dependence on the integrity of the Earth System and on the biotic productivity of its planetary surface is *absolute*. Finally, since this situation, with its existential significance and its absolute vulnerabilities, applies to every society on the planet, its relevance is, for want of a better word, *universal*.

So for all practical purposes, such information is a complex truth that has, all at the same time, an existential, an absolute, and a universal component. But according to negative reasoning, we have no access to absolute and universal truths, since they are ontologically impossible or epistemologically inaccessible. Adding an existential dimension to absolute-universal truth must be even more mystifying to conventional sensibilities. A concept such as an "existential absolute" or an "existential universal" is an oxymoron, a contradiction in terms and thus abstruse in light of standard logic. Once again disbelief comes naturally; the new information happens to be counterintuitive.

As with any pattern, there are exceptions. Environmental ethics, for instance, amounts to a critique of the implications of the Scottish Enlightenment and is quite free from the bias against complex truth as described above, but it also exists in Philosophy curricula only as an elective, not as a requirement. Progressive approaches, such as the evolutionary spirituality of Teilhard de Chardin, the Leninist critique by Slavoj Žižek, or the existentialist Marxism of Erich Fromm, register as counterculture to the Anglophone mainstream. Alien to the neoliberal West is all leftist, evolutionary, and ecological thought. So there are exceptions to the ideological normalcy of Canada, the US, the UK, and Australia, but they serve to confirm the rule. It is this normalcy, represented by the leading schools of thought in Anglophone culture—analytic philosophy, deconstructive postmodernity, and neoliberal political thought from Ayn Rand to Leo Strauss—that has been the ideological perpetrator of the ecological crisis.

The alternative spectrum of positive reasoning

Philosophy's reduction to negative reasoning has made it lose its way. To find its direction again it needs to change course. One thing it can do is to learn from the type of rationality displayed in the climate sciences. Climatology proceeds with a style of reasoning that starts with analysis and ends in synthesis. Synthesis is important in all sciences, but is disproportionately so in climatology because of the cross-disciplinary complexity of its subject-matter.

All science integrates data to gain knowledge, but climate science integrates data from other disciplines. Climatology is not just meteorology writ large (like cosmology in relation to astronomy) but also the inquiry with the broadest scientific interdisciplinarity. Unlike traditional research programs generating their own data (such as organic chemistry), climatology arrives at conclusions by integrating data from its core discipline, meteorology, as well as from fields as diverse as astrophysics, biology, chemistry, ecology, geology, glaciology, marine science, paleontology, and polar science.

And, since climatology is not concerned only with the physics of the events and how they play out in the biosphere but also with urgent questions of mitigation, vulnerabilities, and adaptation, data from even more disciplines are tied in, such as from economics, social science, public health, and engineering. This is necessary, for comprehending climate change requires an understanding across multiple tiers: how the climate system functions and what its parameters are; why and how climate is changing; what impacts the changes entail; and lastly, how to respond—how to mitigate climatic changes, and how to adapt to those changes that resist mitigation. "Connecting the dots" is a heuristic ideal in all science, but climatology is the inquiry that makes synthesis its central goal.

Scientific synthesis suggests one model of an alternative to negative reasoning. There are other models, outside science, and in philosophy itself, that illustrate what positive reasoning, intellectually, can be about. These examples are part of the history of philosophy. Two intellectual periods are particularly noteworthy: the rise of Daoism in the Zhou 周 dynasty in China and the pioneering of the Enlightenment, the Age of Reason, or *Aufklärung* in Germany. A role-model in Daoism is Laozi 老子 (c. fourth century BCE), who needs no introduction. In the German Enlightenment, two pioneers present themselves, contemporaries of Leibniz, but with far greater social and cultural impact on their generations, namely Christian Thomasius (1655–1728) and Christian Wolff (1679–1754).[5]

By normal academic standards, Laozi, Thomasius, and Wolff cut exotic figures. Although Laozi is of a towering stature, and one would be hard pressed to find any text with more English translations than the *Daodejing* 道德經, his work today is more relevant to sinologists and religious studies scholars than it is to philosophers. The same cannot be said about the other great ancient Daoist, Zhuangzi 莊子. His work is full of questions and doubts, about reason, facts, and firm limits, which resonate with the zeitgeist. His dialectical, irreverent style allows more room for debate than do Laozi's rigid and solemn exhortations. But the *Daodejing* is quite dogmatic; if anything, it silences philosophical debate.

Similarly, Thomasius and Wolff matter to Enlightenment historians, but unlike Leibniz and Kant, they are not on the radar screen of philosophy. Leibniz was not only a polymath interested in diverse and difficult topics, but also a thinker with evolving views on many subjects. He was profound but protean, and productive but puzzling. A shimmering multiplicity of ideas, he remains a moving target for interpretation, which needs clarification and stimulates debate.

Kant fuels discussions for another reason. The last page of his magnum opus, *Critique of Pure Reason*, defines his "critical path" as a dynamic in-between of two poles of reason: the skepticism of the empiricist Hume and the dogmatism of the rationalist Wolff. Between them, intellectual progression ensues.[6] Kant straddles the critical fence, time and again balancing a provocative thesis with an equally powerful antithesis, often in the same paragraph and sometimes in the same sentence. His style is a consistent qualification, a critical balancing-act, and it is this tense "in-between" which Kant identifies as the actual room for debate.

By contrast, philosophers have been at a loss to know what to make of Thomasius and Wolff. Like the naturalistic wisdom of Laozi, the empathetic commonsense of Thomasius and the trivial rationality of Wolff are versions of dogmatism. And Kant is right: together with scepticism, dogmatism is one of the poles of reason that are the boundaries of discourse. The gesture of skepticism is negation, to be summed up in the dismissive phrase, "that's what you say!" The gesture of dogmatism is affirmation, mirrored in the resigned (or reverential) phrase, "this is how it is." Neither gesture leaves any room, which is the point, for this is where debate hits the wall. So it seems paradoxical to ask from philosophy, on the one hand, to be true to its identity, which should be debate, and, on the other, to debate what silences debate.

Unless, that is, the point of silencing debate is *to ascend to a higher level of debate*. And, in the framework of progressive reasoning, this is how dogmatism is superior to skepticism. Both are limiting conditions, but dogmatism is also a stepping stone. Skepticism is regressive, pulling the interlocutors back from speculative claims and down to an earlier, lower, and more cautious tier of certainty. But dogmatism is *progressive*, firing the interlocutors on, and encouraging them to move on to the next topic, not because they do not have a point, but because, on the contrary, *the point has been made*. In spatial terms, the critical path is located on a middle ground between the two poles, but in temporal terms, and seen as a progression, the critical path goes from firm answers toward open questions and thus from dogma to doubt. Dogma is the crystallization of fluid research into fixed textbook information. A progressive inquiry adds chapters to the (technically) so-called standard model underlying scientific research. For the investigator, settled findings are rungs on a ladder to the next level. The dogmatic gesture of "this is how it is" works as a push for "getting over it"—to trust the info, deal with it, and step up. Hence the gestures of Laozi, Thomasius, and Wolff are reminders of what has been established beyond reasonable doubt—and as guides for letting go and moving on to the next level.

It is understandable that their gestures seemed to be of little use to philosophers in the twentieth century, when everything seemed possible and when there were no limits in sight. But the twenty-first century is different. Since climate change and overshoot represent a game-changer for life on this world, the very reasons that marginalized these gestures before the shift are also those that put them at the center in the unfolding shift. The three stated platforms of dogmatism—naturalistic wisdom, empathetic common sense, and trivial rationality—offer heuristic resources for a creative philosophical response to the unprecedented maladaptation of civilization to its habitat in the present age.

If philosophy integrated such moves into its arsenal, it would be better positioned to engage with the global maladaptation. With conventional means, philosophers confronted with the crisis cannot easily participate, unless they are philosophers of science studying methods of climatology, or philosophers of law, and climate ethicists, finding ways to identify and resolve climate-related torts.

By the same token, it must be noted that these two branches of philosophy, which are linear outgrowths of the current paradigm, do participate. They already engage with the crisis, and they do so well. This would seem to contradict this chapter's thesis, that the analyticity of negative reasoning prevents a proper philosophical response to the new reality. As a matter of fact, philosophers of science study the methods of climatology; climate ethicists examine the legal and moral aspects of impacts of climate change; and both of these analytic lines of inquiry are productive. So what need is there, really, for philosophy to change its ways?

The work of climatology-oriented philosophers of science and climate ethicists is valuable and innovative. The value of their research speaks for itself, but the innovative nature of this work suggests that both lines of inquiry form bridge-disciplines. Since the crisis is a paradigm shift for civilization and culture, it will be only natural for both of these branches to extend into the new paradigm. At present, though, the limitations of both fields are clear to see. Philosophers of science scrutinizing climatology work as analysts, critics, and reviewers. While such inquiry is needed, not least because of the post-normal methods that characterize climatology, it is also the work of specialists and technicians. The problem is just this: the creative work is done in climatology, not in philosophy; and philosophers of science are scrutinizing this creativity— like theater critics reviewing a staged performance.

Climate ethics is similarly situated. Like climate-related philosophy of science, it is the work of ethical specialists and legal technicians. And like current research in philosophy of science, their work contributes to analysis and review. While this is timely and important (particularly in light of the political pressures to abstain from doing such work in the first place), it is also, and equally, limited. It fails to contribute to insight about the existential *meaning* of the crisis. Matters of climate-related justice and fairness need to be determined, and legally relevant conflicts of interest need to be adjudicated, but this is only the tip of the iceberg. Since climate change is a market failure, it is more than a normative problem. It is a material problem—a *structural* problem with existential significance; and it highlights flaws in the hegemonic design of civilization. As a fundamental game-changer, the climate crisis has very broad ramifications. This is at odds with the rather narrow technical approaches of climatology-oriented philosophy of science and analytic climate ethics. The disparity of broad significance and narrow engagement demonstrates the need for alternative models of reasoning.

In the new paradigm of synthetic rationality, the philosophical response to the crisis aims for interdisciplinary consilience and intra-disciplinary creativity. Instead of criticizing climatology or sounding it out for possible failings and errors, philosophers will respect research by peers in other departments and take their convergent findings as their own factual—or dogmatic—premise. Their tasks will be figuring out what to make of this premise, how to step up to a forward-oriented level, and what to infer from this about wisdom, rationality, and meaningful existence.

The crisis, in sum, consists in the overshoot and its climatic effects. As we turn Earth into a harsher world, we make it into an enemy of civilization.

What this crisis will ultimately mean remains to be seen, but several strands of meaning are already in plain sight. The most obvious is that it is a problem not only for nonhuman life but also for humankind. The ecological crisis of the twentieth century is becoming a *human* crisis in the twenty-first century. And as that, its root cause is a market failure; its beneficiaries are corporations, banks, and the top one percent income holders. Everyone else is in harm's way: young and old, men and women, states and societies, affluent and poor nations, we and posterity. This is yet another illustration of the existential impacts of the crisis. And since the impacts know no geographic and social boundaries (excepting the globalized superrich guarded by their minions), the existential crisis is a universal problem.

Another strand of meaning is its novelty. Environmental crises that acquired existential significance occurred in various places in the past, perhaps most famously on Easter Island before modernity. *But it is unprecedented that this crisis is hitting everywhere at the same time.* This underscores the need to think outside the box. Put differently, since the crisis is the fruit of normalcy, its resolution requires a break with, or a leap beyond, what has brought it about.

Equally unprecedented is the causal dimension of the crisis, and what this reveals about structures of existence on Earth. From the dawn of civilization until today, humankind has followed a trajectory of growth, in terms of population, territories, energy use, material consumption, waste output, and emissions. Its most recent phase was marked by the "Great Acceleration," a quickening succession of growth-bursts during the twentieth century, whose effect has been the crossing of planetary boundaries. And since the consequences of boundary-crossing will only worsen the deeper the overshoot gets, the consequence of this outcome is that any further demographic and material growth is unsustainable. This is the ultimate meaning of the crisis: *we have finally reached the limits of growth.*

This has two implications, which show the leverage for philosophers intending to make a difference. One is that *the crisis is a problem of wisdom.* Only rightwing ideologues and illiterate deniers would claim that the crisis is a scientific "problem." It is not. Science knows what is happening and where the trends are going. Businesspeople might claim that the crisis is a technological problem, and that the market will fix it as soon as engineering has sufficiently advanced. This is not the case either, because the technology for decarbonizing civilization and designing closed matter-and-energy loops is at hand. It exists not only on the drawing board or merely in expensive prototypes, but already in affordable mass-produced units, whose production is easily scalable and can be ramped up further. No, the crisis is due to our growth-based economic system, to the regulatory capture of our political institutions by corporate interest, and to the cursed Scottish self-understanding of this political economy. So the crisis is located in culture. This drops it into philosophy's lap.

Chinese "wisdom-science" and German "eco-wisdom"

Well then: how can philosophy overcome negative reasoning? How can it muster enough creativity to adapt to the evolving ways of information processing? And yet, how can it do this without dissolving into a humanities version of interdisciplinarity? How can philosophy—as *philosophy* and nothing but philosophy—make an authentic contribution to the resolution of the crisis?

The questions are phrased in terms of "how" instead of "whether," because philosophy already has what it takes. Indeed, if negative reasoning is an aberration, then it should be possible, even natural, for philosophers to return to a more authentic path. The first result reveals a contrast between the epistemic state of philosophy and the heuristic alternative suggested by climatology—unfruitful analysis here, fertile synthesis there. But whether philosophy can go from here to there will be dictated by the constraints of its subject matter. This suggests, as the next step, a path from form to substance and from method to material. So we should look, in deliberately undifferentiated and sweeping terms, at the essential subject matter of philosophy and at the essential subject matter of climatology. If philosophy can "deal itself back in," then in its ability to bridge these topics.

So, what is the subject matter of philosophy? The answer is obscured by the fact that there is not one philosophy, but many. At one end is the academic philosophy described above. At the other end are philosophies that are not taught in the academy, but, instead, studied in ethnography and anthropology: the traditions of sagacity in indigenous societies, in which the philosopher is also a sage, and the sage is also a witch, and the witch is also a seer and a healer.

In between are the types of philosophy that are taught in the academy, but only as artifacts of the past. This canon contains three traditions, from China, Greece, and Germany. While the Chinese term for philosophy, *zhexue* 哲學, was coined by Western scholars (ironically, to explain Western thought to Chinese speakers), it is none the less *le mot juste* for Chinese philosophy, for it captures what Confucianism 孔孟哲學/儒家, Daoism 道教, and Chinese Buddhism 佛學 are about: "study of wisdom" or "wisdom-science" (哲學). The Greek term for philosophy is the familiar "love of wisdom" (from *philein*, love; and *sophia*, wisdom). The German term is *Philosophie*, but before this cognate was adopted about two centuries ago as the German label for the discipline, the earlier term, during the Enlightenment, was *Weltweisheit*—"wisdom of the world" or "world-wisdom."

All three terms identify the subject matter as wisdom, but relate to it in different ways. Generally, wisdom is existentially relevant information. It is information that matters to the flourishing of existence, or to mental, emotional, physical, and social wellbeing in the material world. So understood, wisdom has three characteristics. One, it is practical in the old virtue-theoretical sense, in subjecting life to an economy of existence which directs the investment of one's wits, powers, and labors towards stable, social, and long-term yields. Wisdom is thus *ethical*. Two, it is practical in another ancient sense, in gearing this existential economy to the creation of an image of life that elicits pleasure and admiration. Wisdom is thus *aesthetic*. And three, it is theoretical in the ontological sense of reflecting patterns in the ripple and flow of the currents of life; these currents are infinitely unique and yet bounded by firm constants and fixed markers—solitude and love, suffering and solidarity, sickness and health, youth and aging, birth and death. Wisdom is thus *holistic*.

The Greek term relates to wisdom through love; the Chinese term does so through study; and the German term relates to it by grounding it in the world. Love is a relation fraught with uncertainty, for the nature of love is freedom, which includes the freedom of the beloved from the lover's courtship. There is no rule that decrees that love must be requited by the beloved. Hence, relating to wisdom by *loving* it means to relate to it without assurance that one will harvest the fruits of one's labor. The intensity of a lover's devotion does not necessitate a correspondingly positive response. The modern academic variant, following the Greeks, conceives of the philosophical inquiry not so much as an investigation of wisdom but rather as an aspiration toward it, in the awareness that the topic aspired to is elusive. Conventional philosophy relates to wisdom in terms of questions. Considering this as a label for Far Western philosophy the Greek term is apt.

The match of the Greek conception to mainstream philosophy is far from perfect. Seen from a Greek vantage point, much of what counts as academic philosophy in the tradition of the Scottish Enlightenment would have been, in antiquity, the business of the sophists, the enemies and rivals of Socrates. And, seen from a modern perspective, there also seems to be little connection between the purview of academic philosophy and the authentic aspiration of the original inquiry, since wisdom is not a central topic of philosophy today. The preponderance of negative reasoning pushes wisdom into the background. Wisdom remains an undercurrent of philosophical debate, but not, unlike themes such as mind, logic, language, culture, or gender, as a topic in its own right.

The Chinese term, by contrast, evokes a notion of philosophy that is truly distinct from the contemporary aberration. To the extent that Western scholars had tried to capture their own, occidental sense of philosophy with the label *zhexue* 哲學, they failed, for "love of wisdom" would be *zheai* 哲愛, not *zhexue*. The word *xue* 學 does not map on the Greek *philein*; instead it means "to study," "to learn," and also "science." Chinese philosophy, at least in its ancient forms, is less of a *philo-sophy* and more of a *sopho-logy*—a study of wisdom. Studying is an activity, just as is loving, but there is a difference in freedom and control. While there are no certainties in studying, either, and there are no guarantees of progress in, or mastery of, its subject matter simply by the effort invested in it, the risk is none the less smaller. In contrast to love, there is a rough correspondence between learning and mastery: the more one works at something, the better one tends to "master" it. Practice, as they say, makes perfect. For the Chinese, the topic is not elusive. Chinese philosophy accordingly relates to wisdom in terms of answers.

This characteristic suggests that there is an intrinsic alternative for philosophy. Redesigning philosophy with a view to lending it future-oriented relevance does not require one to start with a blank slate: ancient Chinese philosophy, by virtue of being a wisdom-science, already suggests the feasibility of transforming negative reasoning to its positive version. How this suggestion plays out, specifically, remains to be seen, and will require a look at such gestures of positive reasoning as are part of the tradition, as in Daoism, and with Laozi 老子 in particular.

The German term, *Weltweisheit* or "world-wisdom," suggests yet another way out of the crisis of philosophy. Here, the relation between the inquiring subject and the subject matter is a non-issue. The accessibility of the topic is taken for granted. If Chinese *sopho-logy* is reminiscent of sciences such as geology, the science of stones; biology, the science of life; or cosmology, the science of the universe, the German "world-wisdom" is a label more aligned with sciences such as mathematics, astronomy, or physics—all disciplines that put *working on the subject-matter* in the foreground and simply do not worry about the epistemic liabilities of such labors. The work is its own warrant.

Yet what does happen in the German conception of philosophy, and what makes it just as significant as the Chinese variant for suggesting an alternative, is a fundamental *material* qualification of the subject matter. Wisdom is not just wisdom; it is wisdom of and for the world. In contrast to any other object, to which an inquiring subject can relate in a directional fashion, the world is an object that is literally everywhere—it is the ground underneath one's feet as well as the sky above one's head; it is as close as one's fingertips, and as far as the eye can see and even farther. Omnipresence and ubiquity of the world express themselves in the phenomenon of total surround. *Welt* is, by definition, *Umwelt*; the world is experienced as environment, as a house or *oikos* of existence. Seen in this way, world-wisdom is *eco-sophy* or simply "eco-wisdom."

The analogy between *Weltweisheit* and eco-wisdom highlights that negative reasoning in conventional philosophy also expresses itself in an aberration of topics. Areas of specialization for professionals, and curricular requirements for college majors, are topics such as mind, logic, language (in analytic philosophy); culture, gender, body (in continental philosophy); personal identity (in either); plus ethics, aesthetics, and European topics in the history of philosophy. The self-centeredness and retrospective orientation of this roster are striking. Nearly all mainstream topics today concern subjectivity instead of objectivity—how the self thinks, reasons, and talks; how it acculturates, defines its sexual persona, inhabits its embodiment, and constructs its, well, self. Philosophy today is a narcissist ego-trip, reflecting on one's own specialness.

Not so world philosophy. Topics here are matter, not just mind; material patterns, not just formal logic; processes, not just speech; nature, not just culture; humanity, not just gender; cosmos, not just body; and also, and finally, truth and universality and not just identity and difference. Furthermore, what matters in *Weltweisheit*, or eco-philosophy, is not just a wistful look at the past but a courageous look forward, envisioning the future. This is the challenge the old Enlightenment term suggests for our century: to turn philosophy inside out, in an act of *umstülpen*, and to turn its egocentrism into a cosmo-centrism.

In sum, as a merely critical or negative inquiry, as a repository of questions and misgivings, philosophy will provide little help for dealing with the challenges of the twenty-first century. What is needed, instead, is a reconceptualization of philosophy, as a wisdom-study and an eco-wisdom, and thus as a repository of answers. Three philosophical gestures present themselves, and, while they hail from vastly different times and places, they converge into a coherent alternative, which may serve as a template for constructive, future-oriented philosophizing.

Laozi presents the reader with three intellectual moves. One consists of sweeping metaphysical statements; an example would be: "Tao in the world is like a river flowing home to the sea"[7] (Feng and English 2012: §32). Another consists of equally sweeping statements, at the intersection of metaphysics and ethics, or propositions that concern the interface of humans with the world: "That which goes against the Tao comes to an early end"[8] (Feng and English 2012: §30). A final move involves statements that, in context, are ethical assertions: "Soft and weak overcome hard and strong"[9] (Feng and English 2012: §36). Unlike the words of other Daoists, such as Zhuangzi, Laozi's pronouncements are sweeping and dogmatic. The constructive pattern—the philosophical gesture—consists in the readiness to state substantive and general information, to articulate and communicate existential universals.

Thomasius pioneered the German Enlightenment with a provocative legacy. In *De Criminae Bigamiae* (1685), he argued against the condemnation of polyamorous relationships.[10] In *Rechtmäßige Erörterung der Gewissensfrage* (1690), he made the case for the legitimacy of marriages across religious boundaries.[11] In *An haeresis crimen* (1697) and *De crimine magica* (1701) he argued for three principles: the rational necessity of tolerating unorthodox readings of Scripture (since the failure of the Thirty Years War to mend the Christian schism implied a need to accept religious alterity for the sake of peace and prosperity); the unreliability and ineffectiveness of "enhanced interrogation" techniques (since people being tortured will be ready to confess to anything as long as it stops the pain, regardless of what US Republicans may believe in these matters); and that (following from the latter) there were no longer any substantive legal grounds for burning witches.[12]

The constructive pattern one finds in Thomasius consists of a moral compass. Its four corners are the absolute of humanity (over equality, liberty, solidarity, and fairness); the absolute of gender equality (over female empowerment); the freedom of religion (a freedom "to" as well as a freedom "from"); and the freedom of sexuality (moving from a paradigm of procreation to a paradigm of recreation). Similar to the style of Laozi's pronouncements, the values espoused by Thomasius are absolute. There is no wiggle-room, and there is no postmodern dissolution and relativistic softness about them. The absoluteness of this moral compass reveals it as the weapon of a warrior. As a pioneer of the new age, Thomasius was a fighter for rational, benevolent, and universal values.

Wolff added the theoretical dimension to the German Enlightenment with works such as his best-selling, trail-blazing *German Metaphysics* (1720). The full title of this work, rendered into English, is a mouthful: "Reasonable thoughts about God, the world, the human soul and all other things in general, communicated to the lovers of truth." The influential Kant scholar L. W. Beck provided the authoritative Anglophone verdict on Wolff and his oeuvre:

Christian Wolff started his career, with the encouragement from Leibniz, as a mathematician. He became professor of mathematics at Halle, but was soon teaching in all branches of philosophy. His rationalism and commitment to the spirit of the Enlightenment offended the strong Pietistic faction in the University, who secured his banishment in 1723. He took refuge in Marburg, where he taught until 1740, when Frederick the Great recalled him to his old position in Halle. For forty years, he had been "the schoolmaster of Germany", and he had his imitators almost everywhere. *Wolff is indefatigably prolix; he is extravagant with definitions; he illustrates what needs no illustration; he prefers syllogisms to enthymemes, and proves what needs no proof—but when a proof is needed, he is often embarrassingly fallacious.* Yet his pedantry has at least the merit of clarity, systematic order, and encyclopedic coverage, and his influence upon the 'professionalization' of philosophy in Germany should not be undervalued. (Beck 1969: 411)

Thus the verdict is that what Wolff talked about was of astounding triviality. Considering the bold aspiration of *Sensible Thoughts*, this scholarly judgment is not far from ridicule. An equivalent modern title would be Douglas Adams' 1982 sequel to the *Hitchhiker's Guide to the Galaxy*, the volume called *Life, the Universe, and Everything*. This was Wolff's shtick, and, seen from the negativity of reason, this can only be a joke.

But, as we have seen, outside the humanities, the negativity of reason is not unanimously shared. Synthesis of positive information is the focus of post-normal sciences such as climatology. Furthermore, in the hard natural sciences, as in physics, astronomy, or cosmology, one encounters a Wolffian aspiration to a *final theory*. This ambition is as normal in these fields today as it had been for German philosophy in Wolff's day. That philosophers today cannot take such an ambition seriously only goes to show how small our field has become—and how overdue its renewal is. One pattern in Wolff, from which philosophers can learn, is his willingness to connect the dots—instead of dismantling and severing links. The pioneer of the German Enlightenment, Wolff engaged in synthetic reasoning; he respected interdisciplinarity, and he dealt with the scientific progressions of his time. His gesture was to shoot for truth, to search for consilience, and to contribute, as a philosopher, to the eventual and sensible Theory of Everything.

Wolff's other gesture was *the courage to insist on the trivial*. It is this that Beck laments most in the passage cited. Yet this courage is perhaps the final distinction of positive reasoning. Negative reasoning belabors exceptions. But, facing the crisis, what needs to be done is to insist loudly and clearly on earthy and trivial truths. Positive reasoning insists on what *should* be obvious. Maybe profit is not as important as wellbeing? Maybe we should change the design of our economies in the overshoot, so that we can finally and safely stop growing? Maybe we should aspire to a legacy that would allow posterity to honor our memory instead of calling us the "locust generation" and spitting on our graves?

All these questions could well be prefaced, colloquially, with a "hello?" and be concluded with "duh!" Trivial queries are also hard questions; hard enough to serve as stepping stones and carry weight for cultural progress. The trivial and the obscure are two sides of the same coin of civil evolution. Philosophers orienting their work toward the future should insist on the trivial and be comfortable with defying convention, for the sake of wisdom and for the sake of innovating our discipline.

Notes

1   For pointing me to the connection between the Scottish Enlightenment and contemporary climate denial, I thank Jau-Wei Dan, Taipei City University of Education, Taiwan.

2   (http://www.climate.nasa.gov/scientific-consensus/; accessed 15 Feb 2015): 'Ninety-seven percent of climate scientists agree that climate-warming trends over the past century are very likely due to human activities, and most of the leading scientific organizations worldwide have issued public statements endorsing this position.' The *American Association for the Advancement of Science* states: 'The scientific evidence is clear: global climate change caused by human activities is occurring now, and it is a growing threat to society'; cf. AAAS Board Statement on Climate Change, 9 Dec 2006; URL http://www.aaas.org/sites/default/files/migrate/uploads/aaas_climate_statement.pdf; accessed 15 Feb 2015.

3   Cf. esp. p. 23, table 2-1.

4   As Lester R. Brown puts it: "Agriculture as it exists today developed over 11,000 years of rather remarkable climate stability. It has evolved to maximize production within that climate system. Now, suddenly, the climate is changing. With each passing year, the agricultural system is becoming more out of sync with the climate system" (Brown 2012: 83).

5   The problem with Leibniz was, in a manner of speaking, that he was ahead of his time. His oeuvre consists mainly in a vast body of correspondence with leading thinkers of his age, very little of which was shared and disseminated. It did not help matters that he had to earn his living as a provincial librarian in the employ of nobility and never managed to secure an academic appointment (in contrast

to Thomasius and Wolff). After his death (1716), and helped by the late popular success of the only book published during his lifetime, *Theodicy* (1710), admirers hunted down the scattered letters and private memoranda (the ones we are familiar with today, such as the *Monadology*) and initiated an editorial project that lasted well through the eighteenth century. Leibniz's impact was delayed, but was all the more important for the mature shape of the Enlightenment. But for its beginning, it was others—Thomasius and Wolff—who spearheaded the effort. Cf. Wilson 1995.

6 "As regards those who adopt the *scientific* method, they have the choice of proceeding either *dogmatically* or *sceptically*; but in any case they are under obligation to proceed *systematically*. I may cite ... Wolff as a representative of the former mode of procedure, and ... Hume as a representative of the latter ... The *critical* path alone is still open ... to secure for human reason complete satisfaction in regard to that with which it has all along so eagerly occupied itself, though hitherto in vain" (Kant 1929: A856/B884).

7 In the original: 譬道之在天下猶川谷之與江海.

8 不道早已.

9 柔弱勝剛強.

10 *De Criminae bigamiae/Vom Laster der zwiefachen Ehe* ["On the crime of bigamy"], orig. pub. 1685, 2nd edn Leipzig: Krebs, 1721. Cf. also Hinrich Rüping, "Theorie und Praxis bei Christian Thomasius," in Schneiders 1989: 137–47.

11 *Rechtmäßige Erörterung der Ehe- und Gewissensfrage, ob zwei fürstliche Personen im Römischen Reich, deren eine der Lutherischen, die andere der Reformierten Religion zugetan ist, einander mit guten Gewissen heiraten können?* ["Legal elucidation of the marriage- and conscience-question, whether two noble persons may marry each other in good conscience in the Roman Empire, the one of which follows the Lutheran creed, while the other follows the Reformed creed] (Halle: Salfeld, 1689). Cf. also Rolf Lieberwirth, "Christian Thomasius und die Gesetzgebung," in Schneiders 1989: 173–85.

12 *Problema juridicum an haeresis sit crimen?* [On the legal problem of whether heresy is a crime] (Halle: Salfeld, 1697); "Erörterung der juristischen Frage: ob Ketzerei ein strafbares Verbrechen sei" ["Analysis of the legal question of whether heresy is a punishable crime"], orig. pub. 1701, in *Schrifften*, Teil 1 (Halle: Salfeld, 1704): 210–307. Cf. also Günter Gawlick, "Thomasius und die Denkfreiheit," in Schneiders 1989: 256–73, and Martin Pott, "Thomasius' philosophischer Glaube," in Schneiders 1989: 224–47.

Works cited

Assadourian, E. and Prugh, T. (eds) (2013), *State of the World 2013: Is Sustainability Still Possible?* Washington, DC: Island Press.

Beck, L. W. (1969), *Early German Philosophy: Kant and his Predecessors*, Cambridge, MA: Belknap Press of Harvard University Press.

Brown, L. R. (2012), *Full Planet, Empty Plates: the New Geopolitics of Food Scarcity*, New York: Norton.

Folke, C. (2013), "Respecting Planetary Boundaries and Reconnecting to the Biosphere," in Assadourian and Prugh, 19–27.

Global Footprint Network, Earth Overshoot Day (2014), press release 19 Aug 2014, accessed 27 Feb 2015 URL http://www.footprintnetwork.org/images/article_uploads/EarthOvershootDay_2014_PR_General.pdf

Jolley, N. (ed.) (1995), *The Cambridge Companion to Leibniz*, Cambridge: Cambridge University Press.

Kant, I. (2003 [1929]), *Critique of Pure Reason*, translation by Norman Kemp Smith, orig. p. 1781/87, revised 2nd edn, New York: Palgrave Macmillan.

Lao Tsu (2012), *Tao Te Ching*, translation by Gia-Fu Feng and Jane English, 2nd and rev. edn, New York: Vintage.

"Republican Brings Snowball to Senate to Prove Climate Change is a 'Hoax,'" Huffington Post 26 Feb 2015, accessed 27 Feb 2015 URL http://www.huffingtonpost.com/2015/02/26/jim-inhofe-climate-snow_n_6763868.html?utm_hp_ref=green&ir=Green

Schneiders, W. (1989), *Christian Thomasius 1655–1728: Interpretationen zu Werk und Wirkung.* Hamburg: Meiner.

Thomasius, C. (1689), *Rechtmäßige Erörterung der Ehe- und Gewissensfrage, ob zwei fürstliche Personen im Römischen Reich, deren eine der lutherischen, die andere der reformierten Religion zugetan ist, einander mit guten Gewissen heiraten können?* Halle: Salfeld.

Thomasius, C. (1697), *Problema juridicum an haeresis sit crimen?* Halle: Salfeld.

Thomasius, C. (1704), "Erörterung der juristischen Frage: ob Ketzerei ein strafbares Verbrechen sei," orig. publ. 1701, in *Schrifften*, Halle: Salfeld, vol. 1, 210–307.

Thomasius, C. (1721), *De Criminae bigamiae* [*Vom Laster der zwiefachen Ehe*], orig. pub. 1685, 2nd edn, Leipzig: Krebs.

Wackernagel, M., Schulz, M. B., Deumling, D., et al. (2002), "Tracking the ecological overshoot of the human economy," *Proceedings of the National Academy of Science* 99: 9266–71.

Wilson, C. (1995), "The Reception of Leibniz in the Eighteenth Century," in Jolley, 442–74.

12

Conceptual Metaphors and the Goals of Philosophy

Victoria S. Harrison

Introduction

It is difficult, and perhaps impossible, to practice philosophy seriously without finding oneself drawn to thinking about metaphilosophical questions: questions such as "What does it mean to do philosophy?", "What are the goals of philosophy?", or, even more basically, "What is philosophy?" To ask these kinds of questions is to engage in what might be called the philosophy of philosophy. Interest in such metaphilosophical questions invites the investigation of a range of world philosophical traditions. The approach to metaphilosophical questions adopted here involves considering the deep conceptual structures underlying the ways in which the sense of what it is to know something is brought to conceptualization within different intellectual and cultural traditions. My hope is that this approach will open up a framework for discussion that will shed genuine light on the global philosophy of philosophy.

Let us take as our starting point the question, "What does it mean to do philosophy?" In attempting to provide an answer to this question it is easy to be distracted by the Greek origin of the word "philosophy." That term denoted something very specific in the early Western intellectual tradition—love of wisdom—and we lack clear analogues of it within other intellectual traditions, such as those of East Asia and the Indian sub-continent. None the less, the kind of intellectual activity that the early Western philosophers engaged in was surely not dependent on the use of a specific term to describe it. It would therefore seem rash to conclude that no philosophical activity was taking place in regions, and during times, when this particular word was not in use. On the other hand, it seems unnecessary to argue that "philosophers" in different parts of the world, and during different eras, were doing exactly the same thing when they practiced philosophy. Philosophy looks different in different parts of the world and in different historical periods,[1] so we should not set out on our inquiry into what it means to do philosophy with the expectation of finding lovers of wisdom in the Greek sense within Indian and Chinese traditions. I will suggest, below, that in Greek and Roman thought wisdom is typically conceived as knowledge pushed to its ideal state, and that if we want to find a notion within another cultural setting analogous to this Greco-Roman notion of wisdom we need to look, first, at how the target culture conceptualizes the pre-philosophical sense of what is to know something and, second, at how it conceives of the ideal state of knowing. This, I argue, will provide clues to the practice of philosophy in other cultural contexts.

I will argue that different conceptual metaphors underlie the practice of philosophy within different cultures and that appreciating this can illuminate different conceptions of the goal of philosophy within those cultures. In particular, these differences can be brought to light by focusing on the metaphors underlying ways of thinking about what it is to know something. In what follows, I highlight that way of conceptualizing what it is to know something that lies at the core of the Western philosophical tradition, and I suggest that, while this conception is also found in the Indian tradition, it stands in sharp contrast to the dominant conceptualization found in East Asia.

My argument draws on George Lakoff and Mark Johnson's work on conceptual metaphors (Lakoff and Johnson 1980). They have claimed that we understand something metaphorically when we understand it in terms of a structure borrowed from our understanding of something else that is more directly accessible to us. In the following section, I provide a brief account of conceptual metaphor theory.

Conceptual metaphor theory

George Lakoff and Mark Johnson argue not only that metaphors play a significant and irreplaceable role in the way we think but that huge areas of our language are structured by them. In their influential book entitled *Metaphors We Live By* (Lakoff and Johnson 1980), they undermine the widely held view that literal language is primary and that metaphorical language is dependent upon it. Indeed, they argue that what many people take to be literal language actually functions only within a context that is deeply structured by metaphor: "Our ordinary conceptual system, in terms of which we both think and act, is fundamentally metaphorical in nature," they claim (Lakoff and Johnson 1980: 3).

Lakoff and Johnson's primary interest is in our conceptual systems—in other words, in the "concepts that structure what we perceive, how we get around in the world, and how we relate to other people" (Lakoff and Johnson 1980: 3). They assume that we cannot simply look inward, and thereby study our conceptual system, but that the system can none the less be studied indirectly by means of the language we use habitually. The force of their argument largely derives from the many examples they provide in support of their case. One of the most persuasive of these is the metaphor "ARGUMENT IS WAR."[2] Lakoff and Johnson use this metaphor to clarify what they mean by the term "conceptual metaphor" ("conceptual metaphors" are sometimes known as "cognitive metaphors"). They begin by drawing our attention to a variety of expressions commonly used in English which are subsidiary to the conceptual metaphor, ARGUMENT IS WAR, and which, themselves, form part of our ordinary way of talking about arguments. Consider, for example: "Your claims are *indefensible*"; "He *attacked every weak point* in my argument"; "His criticisms were *right on target*"; "He *shot down* all of my arguments." Commenting on these commonly used ways of speaking, they claim:

> It is important to see that we don't just *talk* about arguments in terms of war. We can actually win or lose arguments. We see the person we are arguing with as an opponent. We attack his positions and we defend our own. We gain and lose ground. We plan and use strategies. If we find a position indefensible, we can abandon it and take a new line of attack. Many of the things we *do* in arguing are partially structured by the concept of war. Though there is no physical battle, there is a verbal battle, and the structure of an argument—attack, defense, counterattack, etc.—reflects this. It is in this sense that the ARGUMENT IS WAR metaphor is one that we live by in this culture; it structures the actions we perform in arguing. (Lakoff and Johnson 1980: 4)

Hence, the activity of arguing and the experience one has while arguing, are, Lakoff and Johnson aver, metaphorically structured. Without the metaphor, one cannot engage in the activity, and hence one cannot have the experience that goes with it. Because conceptual metaphors, like ARGUMENT IS WAR, have the function of structuring our thought, activity, and experience, metaphor cannot simply constitute the peripheral feature of our language use that traditional theories of metaphor have presumed. Rather, conceptual metaphors consist in structuring concepts that control whole networks of our thought and activity. Moreover, there are numerous conceptual metaphors, and together they structure most of what we think, say, and do. And only *within* such networks, Lakoff and Johnson argue, does literal language function.

Metaphors, then, can structure not only our thinking but also our activities. And Lakoff and Johnson insist that a large number of our activities are "metaphorical"; in other words, our performance of those activities is structured by metaphor. In the following section, we shall see that the practice of philosophy can be illuminated by regarding it as one of these "metaphorical" activities. I will explore the view that within Western contexts the activity of philosophy is typically structured by means of the conceptual metaphor that understands knowledge by means of sight, and that this metaphor is linked to a particular conception of the goal of philosophical activity that is in turn aligned with a particular understanding of wisdom. As we shall see, also, despite the power of this conceptual metaphor, it is not the only metaphor capable of structuring philosophical activity. Indeed, I hold that different philosophical traditions have developed and matured around particular conceptual metaphors, each giving rise to distinctive conceptions of both the practice and the goal of philosophy (see Harrison 2012: 178–83). Exploring these metaphors involves looking at different patterns of linguistic expression and using these as a window onto the basic cognitive processes grounding philosophical practices.

Conceptual metaphors and philosophy

Conceptual metaphor theory is closely associated with (some would say "based upon") a theory known as "embodied realism," the fundamental idea of which is that conceptual metaphors arise out of embodied minds. All normally functioning humans, irrespective of their culture, share basic forms of embodied experience; for example, visual experience, olfactory experience, haptic experience, auditory experience, as well as the same basic locomotive experience. Such similarities at the embodied experiential level can be expected to have an impact on abstract thought when it occurs. Conceptual metaphor theorists, such as Lakoff and Johnson, argue that primary conceptual schemas arise from these very fundamental and universal forms of embodied experience. In particular, and as we shall see later, visual experience yields a whole complex of metaphors concerning sight, while locomotive experience yields a different but related complex, focused on finding one's way.[3]

Lakoff and Johnson aver that, as a result of our common human physical constitution and the range of experiences this makes possible to us, "much of a person's conceptual system is either universal or widespread across languages and cultures" (Lakoff and Johnson 1999: 6). They go on to claim that we can understand the sense in which reason is universal if we consider it as a capacity shared by all human beings, such as the capacity for language. (Whether or not the capacity is used by any particular human is beside the point: just as some humans never develop the ability to use language, some never develop the capacity to use reason. These unfortunate exceptions do not undermine the claim that the capacity for reason or for language is universal to humans.) The capacity for reason is thought to be grounded in commonalities in the way our minds are embodied (see Lakoff and Johnson 1999: 6). More specifically: "What universal aspects of reason there are arise from the commonalities of our bodies and brains and the environments we inhabit" (Lakoff and Johnson 1999: 5).[4] Humans employ this capacity for reason in a number of ways informed by the different conceptual metaphors they use to conceptualize the abstract processes of thinking and understanding. So we can say that, while the capacity for reason is universal, reason is exemplified in practice by means of different conceptual metaphors.

Now, philosophy, in so far as it relies on our reasoning abilities, presupposes and builds upon the basic capacity for reasoning that humans share. With respect to the practice of philosophy, Lakoff and Johnson's key contention is that:

> In asking philosophical questions, we use a reason shaped by the body, a cognitive unconscious to which we have no direct access, and metaphorical thought of which we are largely unaware. The fact that abstract thought is mostly metaphorical means that answers to philosophical questions have always been, and always will be, mostly metaphorical. In itself, that is neither good nor bad. It is simply a fact about the capacities of the human mind. But it has major consequences for every aspect of philosophy. Metaphorical thought is the principal tool that makes philosophical insight possible and that constrains the forms that philosophy can take. (Lakoff and Johnson 1999: 7)

Given conceptual metaphor theory, we would expect to find that the practice of philosophy—which we know to be a complex activity—is structured by a range of (not necessarily consistent) metaphors. In this chapter, I will focus on two such metaphors: KNOWING IS SEEING and, more briefly, KNOWING THE WAY. Before considering KNOWING IS SEEING, in section 5, below, I turn to the analysis of Hellenistic and Roman philosophy provided by Pierre Hadot in *Philosophy as a Way of Life* (1995). As will be seen, Hadot's work reveals interesting connections between a conceptualization of knowledge in terms of sight and an understanding of wisdom that was widely shared by philosophers in the early Western philosophical tradition.

Wisdom and vision in early Western philosophy

Hadot provides a fascinating and much discussed account of the practice of philosophy in the Greco-Roman world. Central to Hadot's account is an emphasis on wisdom, which is regarded as the philosopher's (perhaps unattainable) goal. Here I do not aim to engage with the breadth of Hadot's comprehensive analysis of the philosophy of the Greco-Roman world; rather, I address those ideas within it that are most salient to the argument of this chapter.

Let me begin with Hadot's characterization of philosophers and their style of life. Hadot claims that, in the Greco-Roman world, to be a philosopher implied a rupture with the common conduct of life. Because of this rupture, philosophers often struck non-philosophers as bizarre and potentially dangerous characters (Hadot 1995: 56–7). A philosopher, he writes,

> is neither a sage nor a man like other men. He knows that the normal, natural state of men should be wisdom, *for wisdom is nothing more than the vision of things as they are, the vision of the cosmos as it is in the light of reason, and wisdom is also nothing more than the mode of being and living that should correspond to this vision.* But the philosopher also knows that this wisdom is an ideal state, almost inaccessible. For such a man, daily life, as it is organized and lived by other men, must necessarily appear abnormal, like a state of madness, unconsciousness, and ignorance of reality. (Hadot 1995: 58, my italics)

Philosophers could not live as ordinary people did precisely because they were philosophers. They were not people who self-identified as being in possession of wisdom; rather, they were lovers of wisdom. Hadot emphasizes that, within Greek philosophy, wisdom was typically regarded as "a state of perfection of being and knowledge that can only be divine" (Hadot 1995: 57). Given its divine character, wisdom was widely held to be unattainable by mere mortals.

As Hadot elaborates, wisdom was typically regarded as a twofold state of perfection—of being and knowledge—that the philosopher held as an ideal toward which to aspire. Yet, as he also observes, despite this widely shared view, a plurality of understandings of this state of perfection was promulgated by the numerous philosophical schools active in the Greco-Roman world. About these, Hadot writes:

Each school will elaborate its rational depiction of this state of perfection in the person of the sage, and each will make an effort to portray him. It is true that this transcendent ideal will be deemed almost inaccessible; according to some schools there never was a wise man, while others say that perhaps there were one or two of them, such as Epicurus, this god among men, and still others maintain that man can only attain this state during rare, fleeting moments. In this transcendent norm established by reason, each school will express its own vision of the world, its own style of life, and its idea of the perfect man. (Hadot 1995: 57)

Hadot adds to this rich characterization of the philosophical life that it "will be an effort to live and think according to the norm of wisdom, it will be a movement, a progression, though a never-ending one, toward this transcendent state" (Hadot 1995: 59). The link between wisdom and transcendence within Greco-Roman thought, in Hadot's analysis, coincided with the conception of God as absolute transcendence that was crystallizing at this time. It is significant that much modern Western philosophy has been structured around the ideal of knowledge as a vision that is transcendent to any particular perspective. Within current Western philosophy, people often refer, still, to the so-called "God's eye view." It is clear that this notion is closely linked to the Greco-Roman conception of wisdom elucidated by Hadot.

According to the classical conception, as wisdom is not a human state but a divine one, in his coming to an understanding of the character of wisdom the philosopher was thereby thought to come to understand something of the divine. Nevertheless, Western philosophy's traditional connection to the idea of divine transcendence alerts us to its more practical dimension. If the goal of philosophy is to help a person instantiate the transcendental ideal of wisdom, then philosophy has a fundamentally practical goal. This understanding leads naturally to the conception of philosophical activity as a practice (a *spiritual* practice, to employ Hadot's favored term). According to this conception, philosophical theorizing should not be an end in itself; it is intended to support the practical goal of instantiating the ideal of wisdom. However, as we have already seen, while this conception of the link between philosophical theorizing and philosophical practice was widely shared, difference in philosophical theory between divergent schools of thought led to different understandings of the ideal aspired to by the philosopher.

Hadot emphasizes that, despite the real differences within the theory and practice of philosophy upheld by the various philosophical schools, each of them was committed to a unity of theory and practice. On the theoretical side, the ideal state of wisdom, possessed (at least to some degree) by the sage, is characterized in terms of knowledge, and this is described in overwhelmingly visual terms. The aspiring sage seeks a *perspective*, a vision, from which to know, that is grounded in universal reason. Such a vision, moreover, will not be dependent on the individual philosopher's material state of life or historical circumstances, but will allow him or her to transcend these: "With the help of … [spiritual] exercises, we should be able to attain to wisdom; that is, to a state of complete liberation from the passions, utter lucidity, knowledge of ourselves and of the world" (Hadot 1995: 103).

The practical side of philosophy, then, was thought to consist of a way of life that supported the would-be sage in the pursuit of this, perhaps ultimately unattainable, vision.

> The philosopher lives in an intermediate state. He is not a sage, but he is not a non-sage, either. He is therefore constantly torn between the non-philosophical and the philosophical life, between the domain of the habitual and the everyday, on the one hand, and, on the other, the domain of consciousness and lucidity. To the same extent that the philosophical life is equivalent to the practice of spiritual exercises, it is also a tearing away from everyday life. It is a conversion, a total transformation of one's vision, life-style, and behaviour. (Hadot 1995: 103)

The dynamic at work here implies that philosophical theory and philosophical practice cannot legitimately be separated. Philosophical theory supports philosophical practice toward a certain goal, but it also provides the philosopher with an understanding of what the goal is that he or she must aspire to in order to progress toward it. In this classical understanding, then, wisdom cannot simply be reduced to a matter of practice; theory, also, is implicated in it.

His review of the classical material led Hadot to conclude that, in its classical form, philosophy was not primarily a theoretical activity but was "a method of training people to live and to look at the world in a new way. It is an attempt to transform mankind" (Hadot 1995: 107). If he is correct, much philosophy in the Western tradition as we find it today has departed quite dramatically from this earlier conception of what it means to practice philosophy and from what the goal of philosophy is. With certain notable exceptions, most Western philosophy from the early modern period onward has been concerned almost entirely with theory. While current philosophers may well regard themselves as practicing philosophy, there is sparse common understanding of what that practice consists of, nor is there a unified vision of what the goal of the practice is. We shall return to these observations later. By appealing to the influence of Christianity within Western culture, Hadot explains the pivotal change that occurred within the Western philosophical tradition when it switched from being primarily "theory-geared-toward-practice" toward the virtually entirely theoretical discipline familiar to us today.

Hadot notes that already in early Christian thinkers, such as Clement of Alexandria, Origen, and Augustine, Christianity is presented as a *philosophia*. Moreover, Christianity had already assimilated various practices of spiritual exercise that had previously been the preserve of philosophers. The assimilation of philosophy's traditional practices to Christianity was complete by the time of the Scholastics, and it was at this juncture, Hadot claims, that theology and philosophy parted ways. "[P]hilosophy was emptied of its spiritual exercises which, from now on, were relegated to Christian mysticism and ethics" (Hadot 1995: 107). From henceforth, philosophy would be purely theoretical, a characteristic which, Hadot argues, it has retained into the modern age.

As we have seen, according to Hadot, the philosophy of Western antiquity had a twofold aim. First it aimed to transform our vision of the world; second it aimed for a metamorphosis of our being (see Hadot 1995: 127). Hence, philosophy embraced both knowledge and a way of being in the world. Evidence for this is provided by the ease with which Christianity could be taken as philosophy—it was, in fact, principally a way of living and thus bore clear similarities to earlier philosophies associated with ways of living. As Hadot explains, in its most basic form the philosophical life was a way of living according to reason; but in antiquity there were many more or less theoretical ways of understanding what reason might be. The Christian simply understood reason within the framework provided by Christian theology. As Western philosophy transformed under the impetus of Christianity, its twofold aim was pulled apart. Philosophy became the domain of theory, of knowledge, while Christianity presented the style of life or way of being that philosophy was therefore no longer called upon to provide.

Two key ideas from this analysis are especially salient to the connection between wisdom and an understanding of knowledge in terms of the metaphor provided by vision. First, the idea that in early Western philosophy wisdom is regarded as an ideal state that is not quite of this world. Second, that an original unity between the theory and practice of philosophy was ruptured, thereby giving birth to modern Western philosophy with its almost total emphasis on theoretical knowledge.

Modern Western philosophy has remained indebted to the ideal of wisdom developed within classical thought. As we have seen, this state of wisdom is often described as transcendent and inaccessible. The sage is to some extent detached from the affairs of this world, as he is devoted to thought and, like God according to the conception that came to dominate the West, is self-sufficient. As we have also seen, wisdom is portrayed as "the vision of things as they are, the vision of the cosmos as it is in the light of reason, and wisdom is … nothing more than the mode of being and living that should correspond to this vision" (Hadot 1995: 58). Philosophy involves the transformation of one's vision (see Hadot 1995: 103). Once the split between the theory and practice of philosophy had taken place we were left with a philosophical theory which understood knowledge as correct vision irrespective of any of its practical applications. Western philosophy from that point on is typically concerned with knowledge rather than a way of being in the world. None the less, the *ideal perspective* of the sage, which had earlier been identified with universal reason, remained the philosopher's goal. The distance between post-Scholastic Western philosophy and philosophy in the classical tradition notwithstanding, the link between knowledge and sight continues to structure philosophical activity today, even though the notions of the sage and wisdom have become far less prominent than they were in the past. Even, and perhaps especially, analytic philosophy has inherited this view, with its emphasis on universality, and detachment from any particular perspective.

I cannot fully defend this claim here, but in the following section I provide some support for the view that post-Scholastic Western philosophy still presupposes a deep conceptual structure informed by the conceptual metaphor KNOWING IS SEEING—a metaphor which, as we have seen, is directly related to the conception of wisdom found within antiquity. As we shall now see, this metaphor can still serve to draw our attention to philosophy's role as a facilitator of correct vision.

KNOWING IS SEEING

Conceptual metaphor theorists regard KNOWING IS SEEING as a primary metaphor because it is based in our common human visual experience. The importance that the metaphor assumes in our understanding of what it is to know something is underwritten by the origin of the metaphor in this basic common experience of sight. In fact, the experience of learning about the world through sight is universal, and fundamental to all normally functioning human beings irrespective of their cultural background. Because of this universal dimension we would expect to find the KNOWING IS SEEING conceptual metaphor at play in all cultural traditions. With respect to the Western tradition, Lakoff and Johnson note:

> The Knowing Is Seeing metaphor defines the core of a folk theory about how the
> mind works that is so widely shared in our intellectual tradition that it virtually

defines our public understanding of intellectual operations. That this conceptual metaphor should be so pervasive makes perfectly good sense, given that vision plays such a crucial role in so much of our knowledge of our world. (Lakoff and Johnson 1999: 394)

According to conceptual metaphor theory, the structuring role of a primary metaphor in our deep cognitive processes is indicated by clusters of metaphorical expression. These are not just fixed linguistic conventions but are markers of largely unconscious conceptual structures. It should not surprise us then that, as Lakoff and Johnson point out: "Our language about mental activity is thus pervaded with expressions based on this underlying vision metaphor" (Lakoff and Johnson 1999: 394). Consider some of the linguistic markers in common use that indicate the structuring role of the KNOWING IS SEEING conceptual metaphor in the way we think and talk about knowledge in English:

- Light of reason
- Clarity (a quality of light)
- Clear ideas, clear writing
- Illuminating ideas
- Shed light on
- Enlightening, enlightenment
- View something in the light of
- Perspective, angle, viewpoint (a person is looking from somewhere)
- I see what you are saying
- Bring an idea into focus
- Theory
- Insight

These words and expressions, and many others, point to a tight conceptual connection between knowledge and vision embedded within Western and, as I will soon explain, Indian intellectual traditions. What it is to know something, within these traditions, is explained by means of an understanding of knowledge that is based on the more directly accessible experience of visual perception.

Conceptual metaphor theorists claim that, as a general principle, we understand abstract aspects of our experience by mapping them onto more concrete domains of experience. Knowing is an abstract activity and it is difficult to articulate in literal language what we are doing when we know (compare the difficulty of talking about what we are doing when we love someone). But we can map abstract activities, such as knowing or loving, onto more concrete ones. This both gives a structure to our abstract activities and provides us with ways to talk about them. When we use the KNOWING IS SEEING conceptual metaphor we unconsciously structure our mental activity as if it were the concrete activity of visual perception (recall how understanding argument according to the ARGUMENT IS WAR metaphor shapes the practice of it—what counts as success, and so on). Lakoff and Johnson conclude that:

> The Knowing Is Seeing metaphor is so firmly rooted in the role of vision in human knowing and is so central to our conception of knowledge that we are seldom aware of the way it works powerfully to structure our sense of what it is to know something. It is the commonality and experiential grounding of this ubiquitous metaphor that makes it an ideal candidate for sophisticated philosophical elaboration in a wide variety of theories of mind and knowledge. (Lakoff and Johnson 1999: 394)

The mapping of the abstract domain of knowing onto the more concrete domain of seeing within a sophisticated philosophical system can be seen especially clearly in Descartes's epistemology (see Descartes 1970). In analysing the deep structure of Descartes's way of thinking about knowledge, Lakoff and Johnson map items within the domain of knowledge onto items within the visual domain (Lakoff and Johnson 1999: 393–4):

Visual Domain	*Knowledge Domain*
Object Seen	Idea
Seeing An Object Clearly	Knowing An Idea
Person Who Sees	Person Who Knows
Light	"Light" Of Reason
Visual Focusing	Mental Attention
Visual Acuity	Intellectual Acuity
Physical Viewpoint	Mental Viewpoint
Visual Obstruction	Impediment To Knowing

As explained above, KNOWING IS SEEING is a primary metaphor in that it is based in our common human visual experience. It can be elaborated in a rich variety of ways into complex philosophical systems, of which Descartes's is just one, particularly clear, example.

Lakoff and Johnson's discussion is focused, as we have seen, on Western philosophy. However, as we shall now see, the KNOWING IS SEEING conceptual metaphor was also important within the Hindu, Buddhist, and Jain philosophies that developed in India (see McMahan 2002). This is the conceptual explanation for the close affinity often remarked on between Indian and Western philosophies: both philosophical families are structured around the conceptual metaphor of KNOWING IS SEEING.

In Sanskrit the word *darśana*—the term usually translated into English as "school," as in "philosophical school"—is derived from the verbal root "to see." The philosophical model within traditional Indian philosophical cultures was the ancient seer, whose vision was reflected in the Vedic literature. In this intellectual context, philosophy was practiced in order to clear away the obstacles to a true vision of the genuine reality lying behind the way things appear to us. Given that the philosopher's goal was to arrive at the correct perspective (*darśana*) from which things could be seen as they really are, philosophical disagreement in Indian traditions focused on the issue of which perspective was the most revealing. Testing these rival perspectives in the open context of public debate was thus central to the practice of philosophy in classical India (see Ganeri 2001). The logical culmination of this trend was the Jains' development of a method which was able to incorporate apparently rival perspectives within a larger vision.

In Sanskrit the term for knowledge, *vidya*, means both to know and to see. Likewise, not to know, *avidya*, amounts to not being able to see. These words are connected, through a common Indo-European root *weid* ("to see, to know truly"), to the Latin *videre*. The English words "vision" and "wisdom" are also derived from *weid* (see McMahan 2002: 57). This basic conceptual affinity between knowing and seeing also ramifies into the way truth is often discussed in terms of covering or uncovering aspect of reality (depending on whether the truth being referred to is ultimate, which uncovers, or conventional, which covers). Moreover, many Indian philosophical traditions regard ignorance as the fundamental philosophical problem, and ignorance is frequently characterized in terms of illusion. Our mental illusions are thus understood in terms of more concrete physical illusions.

While Indian and Western philosophies are structured around a shared primary metaphor, that of KNOWING IS SEEING, they none the less often seem very different in practice. To explain this, we can appeal to wider cultural differences, as well as to Hadot's analysis of the bifurcation which took place within Western philosophy when, under the influence of Christianity, it lost its practical dimension and was left with only the domain of theory. We can conjecture that, if this had not occurred, Western philosophies would have resembled more closely traditional Indian philosophies—many of which still consist of fusions of theory and practice—than is the case in the modern era.

I mentioned above that, because the KNOWING IS SEEING conceptual metaphor arises from universal human experience, we would expect to find it at play in all major intellectual traditions. It should then not surprise us that this metaphor is present also within Chinese conceptualizations of knowledge (Ghiglione 2010). Let me draw attention to a few obvious linguistic indicators of the presence of this metaphor within Chinese conceptual systems. The following very common Chinese characters and character combinations reveal a conceptual connection between light, vision, and understanding:

日	*rì*	sun
月	*yuè*	moon
白	*bái*	white
明白	*míngbai*	(1) clear, obvious, plain (2) understand, realize, know
明亮	*míngliàng*	(1) bright, well-lit, shining (2) clear (of understanding)

However, as I suggest below, within East Asian thought KNOWING IS SEEING plays a secondary role to a different primary structuring metaphor; one which generates a distinctive conception of the goal of philosophy discernible within classical Chinese traditions.

KNOWING THE WAY

Whereas the conceptual affinities between Western and Indian philosophies are often remarked upon, the differences between Western and Chinese philosophies are often thought to be more striking than the affinities. One explanation for this might be that in classical China the practice of philosophy was not structured by the KNOWING IS SEEING conceptual metaphor, but instead developed out of a different, culturally embedded and widely accepted, understanding of what it is to know something. We would expect this understanding to be expressed by a dominant conceptual metaphor that, like KNOWING IS SEEING, is grounded in common human experience. A clue to what this metaphor might be is found in another extremely high-frequency Chinese character combination:

知道	*zhīdao*	know

Zhī 知 by itself can mean "know," but it is most frequently used in combination with *dao* 道—way, path, method (or, if used as a verb, speak, say, tell). The absence of *rì* 日 from this character combination clearly suggests that the kind of knowledge at issue here is not principally a matter of abstract discernment. There is no implicit appeal to the connection between knowledge, light, and vision; instead, we are pointed in the direction of a different way of knowing.

Given conceptual metaphor theory, we would expect to find that in China—as in India and the West—the sense of what it is to know something will have been brought to conceptualization metaphorically. It will have informed folk theories about knowledge, as well as various more sophisticated philosophical theories. Whatever the character of the dominant conceptual metaphor for knowledge deployed within Chinese culture, we would expect it to structure a way of thinking about knowledge, and by extension a way of practicing philosophy, that is widely shared by those within this culture.

Drawing on the work of David Hall and Roger Ames (1998), Edward Slingerland, who himself has applied conceptual metaphor theory to Chinese thought (see Slingerland 2004 and 2006), contrasts two models of knowledge, one typically Western (relying on the KNOWING IS SEEING metaphor) and the other typically Chinese:

> Thus, in place of the representational model of knowledge exemplified by the "gaze" of the subject acquiring theoretical knowledge of an eternal order behind the phenomenal world, the Chinese instead emphasize the sort of knowledge appropriate to a subject already engaged in the world through the medium of "the act". This is the import of David Hall and Roger Ames's well-known contention that thinking (*si* 思) in the *Analects* is "not to be understood as a process of abstract reasoning, but is fundamentally *performative* in that it is an activity whose immediate consequence is the achievement of a practical result". (Slingerland 2006: 4)

Slingerland sought to identify a primary conceptual metaphor that functions within the Chinese context in the same comprehensive way that the KNOWING IS SEEING metaphor functions within Western (and, I would add, Indian) culture (Slingerland 2006: 5). In elaborating what he takes to be the typically Chinese way of conceptualizing what it is to know something, Slingerland focuses on the conceptual metaphor KNOWING IS ACTING. This leads him to examine the notion of perfected action, which, he argues, in the context of Chinese intellectual traditions should be understood as effortless action, in other words, as *wu wei*.

I agree with Slingerland's general approach, yet it none the less strikes me that we should be able to identify within Chinese traditions an even more basic metaphor than KNOWING IS ACTING by which to understand knowing. Acting is not as closely linked to our basic sensory experience as seeing (or hearing, which has also been exploited metaphorically in a variety of cultural contexts), and this indicates that there may be another primary metaphor that is cognitively prior to KNOWING IS ACTING. I suggest that we look for a metaphor, and recall that this is not primarily a linguistic question, that is grounded directly in the universal experience of locomotion. Given the dominance of the notion of *dao* 道 in East Asian intellectual traditions, it would seem natural to suggest that the conceptual metaphor we seek is KNOWING THE WAY.

If what it is to know something be conceptualized predominantly by means of a metaphor that maps knowing onto the more basic human experience of moving, of finding one's way, then the ideal state of knowing might aptly be characterized, using Slingerland's term, as "perfected action." As Slingerland remarks, for the early Chinese thinkers:

> the culmination of knowledge is understood not in terms of a grasp of abstract principles but rather as an ability to move through the world and human society in a manner that is completely spontaneous and yet still fully in harmony with the normative order of the natural and human worlds—the Dao 道 or "Way".
> (Slingerland 2006: 4)

In spite of the variety of philosophies that flourished within early China, it is possible to claim that early Chinese philosophers sought a way of living within this world rather than seeking knowledge of a supposed deeper impersonal reality behind the world of our experience. The philosophical model was the Sage-King, a person who combined personal virtue and the ability to rule well. Despite the Confucian emphasis on book-learning, and with the exception of thinkers associated with the School of Names, the philosophers of classical China were united in following the Way (although, as we have seen to be the case with early Western philosophical accounts of wisdom, different schools of thought came to develop their own theoretical characterizations of the Way). This ubiquitous emphasis within Chinese intellectual culture on following the Way, aligned, as I have argued, with a tendency to conceptualize knowledge in terms of locomotion, implies an understanding of successful philosophical practice in terms of perfected movement.

In conclusion: I have argued that the goal of early Western philosophy was wisdom, regarded as an ideal state of knowledge that was conceived in primarily visual terms as the God's eye view, and I have conjectured that the goal of early Chinese philosophy, which we can regard as an analogue for wisdom, will be found to be dissimilar to this in so far as it is based on a locomotive rather than an ocular metaphor. I have claimed that, in early Chinese traditions, knowledge is predominantly thought of in terms of the ability to find one's way effectively in the natural and social worlds, and that the ideal of knowledge so conceived can be characterized as perfected action. Of course, perfected action may not seem much like wisdom in the Greek or Roman sense—but that is exactly what we would expect given the approach outlined here.[5]

Notes

1   We can see this in our own day if we consider the different styles of philosophy that are often casually referred to as analytic and Continental. On these two philosophical styles see Chase and Reynolds 2011.

2   I follow Lakoff and Johnson's convention of using capital letters to indicate that a conceptual metaphor is being referred to. This is useful because not all conceptual metaphors are metaphors in the linguistic sense, that is, they do not all explicitly refer to one thing in terms of something else.

3   As Edward Slingerland notes, new technologies that change our experience can give rise to new metaphors, but, despite vast technological change throughout recorded history, visual and locomotive experience remains universal (2004).

4   They further claim that "the existence of these universals does not imply that reason transcends the body. Moreover, since conceptual systems vary significantly, reason is not entirely universal" (Lakoff and Johnson 1999: 5). In this chapter, however, as my interest is in their claim about the universality of reason, I do not discuss further the ways in which they qualify their claims about this.

5   A portion of the material in the chapter has been published in Harrison 2015.

Works cited

Chase, J. and Reynolds, J. (2011), *Analytic versus Continental: Arguments on the Methods and Value of Philosophy*, Durham, NC: Acumen.

Descartes, R. (1970), *The Philosophical Works of Descartes*, E. S. Haldane and R. R. T. Ross (eds), 2 vols, Cambridge: Cambridge University Press.

Ganeri, J. (2001), *Philosophy in Classical India: The Proper Work of Reason*, London: Routledge.

Ghiglione, A. (2010), *La vision dans l'imaginaire et dans le philosophie de la Chine antique*, Paris: You Feng.

Hadot, P. (1995), *Philosophy as a Way of Life: Spiritual Exercises from Socrates to Foucault*, A. I. Davidson (ed.), M. Chase (trans.), Oxford: Blackwell.

Hall, D. L. and Ames, R. T. (1998), *Thinking from the Han: Self, Truth, and Transcendence in Chinese and Western Culture*, New York: State University of New York Press.

Harrison, V. S. (2012), *Eastern Philosophy: The Basics*, London and New York: Routledge.

Harrison, V. S. (2015), "Seeing the Dao: Conceptual Metaphors and the Philosophy of Religion," *Religious Studies*, 51 (3): 307–22.

Lakoff, G. and Johnson, M. (1980), *Metaphors We Live By*, Chicago: The University of Chicago Press.

Lakoff, G. and Johnson, M. (1999), *Philosophy in the Flesh: The Embodied Mind and its Challenge to Western Thought*, New York: Basic Books.

McMahan, D. L. (2002), *Empty Vision: Metaphor and Visionary Imagery in Mahāyāna Buddhism*, London: Routledge/Curzon.

Slingerland, E. (2004), "Conceptual Metaphor Theory as a Methodology for Comparative Religion," *Journal of the American Academy of Religion*, 72(1): 1–31.

Slingerland, E. (2006), *Effortless Action: Wu-Wei as Conceptual Metaphor and Spiritual Ideal in Early China*, Oxford: Oxford University Press.

Index

CPSIA information can be obtained
at www.ICGtesting.com
Printed in the USA
LVOW10s1432200118
563176LV00033B/393/P

7571414

9 781350 045507